Training the Nihilists

EDUCATION AND RADICALISM
IN TSARIST RUSSIA

By the Same Author

The New Jacobins: The French Communist Party and the Popular Front, 1934–1938

(Editor) *The Soviet Experience: Success or Failure?*

Training the Nihilists

EDUCATION AND RADICALISM
IN TSARIST RUSSIA

DANIEL R. BROWER

Cornell University Press | ITHACA AND LONDON

First published 1975 by Cornell University Press.
Published in the United Kingdom by Cornell University Press Ltd.,
2-4 Brook Street, London W1Y 1AA.

International Standard Book Number 0-8014-0874-1
Library of Congress Catalog Card Number 74-25371
Printed in the United States of America

à F. K. B.
contestataire chronique

Preface

In the mid-nineteenth century, Russian schools began to play a key role in training young "nihilists," that is, radical youth. The evolution of this peculiar relationship between education and radicalism forms the theme of my book. It examines Russian education—the term is used loosely to include the entire system of socialization and learning in the advanced and secondary schools—in order to explain the factors producing the young rebels: Where did they come from? How did it happen that year after year the schools turned out a steady stream of recruits for the revolutionary movement?

The evidence and conclusions in answer to these questions are presented in analytical, rather than chronological order. I treat the period of the 1840's to the 1870's as a whole, during which time the important innovations in radical recruitment took place. The radicals began their lives among Russia's upper and middle classes, where they received their first instruction in moral behavior and social relations. Later, formal education assumed these responsibilities; young people deviated toward radical revolt in their years of schooling through a unique adaptation of the process of learning. The argument is summed up schematically in a flow chart in the concluding chapter.

My work began as a study of the Russian intelligentsia. Some readers may still see it as such, although I have chosen to avoid use of the word completely, for reasons made clear in Chapter 1. The impact of education on recruitment into the radical movement raises complex issues having nothing to do with the old debate concerning the intelligentsia. I have tried to solve the problem of terminology by using the simplest labels for groups defined by easily identifiable traits. What the argument loses in sophistication it gains, I hope, in clarity.

During the years of preparing this book I have accumulated a large number of professional and academic debts. The research began in the academic year 1965–1966 in Leningrad and Moscow. I was at the time a member of the Soviet-American cultural exchange sponsored by the Inter-University Committee on Travel Grants. That year away from teaching was made possible by a fellowship from the Great Lakes Colleges Association. The first results of my research appeared in an article published in the *Slavic Review* ("The Problem of the Russian Intelligentsia," XXVI [September 1967], 638–47). Portions of this article reappear, with the permission of the editor of the journal, in Chapter 1.

A second period of research in the archives of Moscow and Leningrad came in 1970–1971, under the auspices of the International Research and Exchanges Board. Then, as during the earlier Soviet trip, I was particularly grateful for the assistance of the archivists of the State Historical Archives in Leningrad. Their patience and cooperation in ferreting out archival material made my research in their institution both rewarding and enjoyable. My research and writing that year were facilitated by a grant from the Mabelle McCleod Lewis Memorial Fund, which also contributed financial assistance for a period of writing in 1972. The University of California, Davis, has given me several grants, including a Humanities Fellowship, for completion of this study. Finally, I owe an enormous personal debt to my wife, who has had to live with this work from its inception, through periods of temporary widowhood during my stays in the Soviet Union, until its long-awaited completion. During this time, she showed patience far beyond the call of duty or love.

DANIEL R. BROWER

Davis, California

Contents

Tables and Charts

Note on Transliteration and Abbreviations

The Library of Congress system of transliteration has been followed here with a few minor exceptions. I have taken some liberties with Russian given names, but have generally adhered scrupulously to the Russian spelling of surnames (the "-ii" ending is shortened to "-i"). The following abbreviations appear in the footnotes.

Archives

TsGAOR: Tsentral'nyi gosudarstvennyi arkhiv Oktiabr'skoi revoliutsii (Central State Archives of the October Revolution)
TsGIAL: Tsentral'nyi gosudarstvennyi istoricheskii arkhiv Leningrada (Central State Historical Archives in Leningrad)

Archival references

ch.: *chast'* (part)
d.: *delo* (item)
f.: *fond* (record group)
l.: *list* (page)
ll.: *listy* (pages)
o.: *opis'* (inventory)
tr. eks.: *tretaia ekspeditsiia* (third bureau)

Multivolume collected works of individual authors

PSS: *Polnoe sobranie sochineniia* (complete collected works)

Publications by Central Statistical Committee

MVD-TsSK: Ministerstvo vnutrennykh del, Tsentral'nyi statisticheskii komitet (Ministry of the Interior, Central Statistical Committee)

Training the Nihilists

EDUCATION AND RADICALISM
IN TSARIST RUSSIA

There are periods in the life of human society when revolution becomes an imperative necessity. . . . What formerly seemed just is now felt to be a crying injustice. The morality of yesterday is today recognized as revolting immorality. The conflict between new ideas and old traditions flames up in every class of society, in every possible environment, in the very bosom of the family. The son struggles against his father, he finds revolting what his father has all his life found natural; the daughter rebels against the principles which her mother has handed down to her as the result of long experience. . . . Those who long for the triumph of justice . . . perceive the necessity of a revolutionary whirlwind which will sweep away all this rottenness.

—Peter Kropotkin (1880)

1 | The Radical Community

By the 1860's subversive groups of dissident students and intellectuals were active in Russia. A few journals had already begun publishing articles by young writers challenging, though in veiled terms, the fundamental institutions of Russian society. No one could mistake the message of Dimitri Pisarev, presenting in 1861 the "ultimatum of our camp: what can be smashed should be; what stands up under the blows is acceptable, and what flies into a thousand pieces is trash."[1] Appeals for the overthrow of the autocracy and for social revolution were circulating in the major cities of the country. Students were organizing protest demonstrations and strikes. Student agitators and radicals differed on objectives but shared a readiness to disrupt public life. During the disturbances of 1869, the radical Sergei Nechaev sought to recruit student youth for his revolutionary organization. Later that year he wrote a lurid description of the "doomed men" he sought. He wanted them to have "broken all ties with the social order and with all educated society, with all laws, manners, accepted customs and morality of this society."[2] He never found such supermen in Russia, but they were not entirely a figment of his imagination. The authorities knew he was talking about the nihilists.

Many of these rebels translated their political convictions into standards of personal dress and behavior. In those years, dress was a mark of status in Russian society. Fashion dictated that men of the upper classes wear in public a starched collar, tie, narrow boots, gloves, and frock-coat. Women were expected to wear multicolored

---

1. Dimitri Pisarev, *Izbrannye sochineniia* [Selected essays], I (Moscow, 1934), 66.
2. Cited in V. Bazilevski, ed., *Gosudarstvennie prestupniki* [State criminals], I (Paris, 1903), 183–84.

dresses with frills, ribbons, and lace, to add hoop skirts for special occasions, and to arrange their long hair elaborately. But these radicals flaunted their personal emancipation publicly. The young women made a sensation by cutting their hair very short, wearing plain, black dresses and men's boots, hiding their eyes behind dark glasses, and frequently smoking cigarettes. The head of the Third Section, the tsar's secret police, felt scorn, mixed perhaps with an element of fear, in considering these "emancipated women," whom he described in an 1869 report going about in public with "short hair, bluetinted glasses, sloppy dress, uncombed and unwashed," and living "in the company of a similarly repulsive individual of the male sex, or with several of them."[3]

The appearance of the young men was just as convincing a demonstration of revolt. They wore working-class clothes—red shirt or greasy coveralls—together with long hair and the usual dark glasses. Dressed in this manner, radicals could not be mistaken for proper bureaucrats, noblemen, or merchants, nor did they much resemble real workers, who usually abandoned their dirty clothes when they left the factory in favor of clean, "bourgeois" dress. The radicals chose their attire to differentiate themselves from their social peers. The unique social position of the radical community created the desire for unique appearance.

The government had good reason to view this group with great hostility, mingled with some bewilderment. Russian laws were very strict toward intellectual dissent against church and state. The Decembrist uprising had confronted the regime with a serious challenge. The leaders of this insurrection had demanded a constitutional regime. But the quickly repressed plot had no direct repercussions on the political behavior of the officer corps or on any other identifiable group in society. Alexander II, Nicholas I's son and successor to the throne in 1855, began a program of sweeping reforms. But the Third Section retained its powers of arbitrary arrest, interrogation, and exile in order to repress any oppositional activity. Political dissent, dangerous even in private, was a crime in public.

How was it possible for Russian society to spawn such undesirable individuals? The question preoccupied the head of the secret police,

3. "Revoliutsionnoe i studencheskoe dvizhenie 1869 goda" [The revolutionary and student movements of 1869], *Katorga i ssylka,* No. 10 (1924), 199.

who mentioned it frequently in his reports to the tsar in the 1860's. In 1869 he seized upon the title of a book published shortly before by a radical journalist (and former officer), Nikolai Sokolov. Called *Otshchepentsy* (The Rebels), the work actually focused on the tradition of religious dissent in the Christian churches, seeking to associate political opposition with the religious brotherhoods of earlier times. The Third Section chief ignored the religious implications and found the radicals actually rebels against society. They considered the "division of society into classes" to be a "crime against humanity" and had therefore renounced all loyalty to the moral code and style of life of the classes to which they properly belonged. Referring to the French estate system of the *ancien régime,* he concluded that they had become a "fourth estate."[4] Though couched in quaint terms, this idea suggested clearly that the radicals were a new social phenomenon, a situation which made their political attitudes particularly dangerous. Opposition to the autocracy was not the invention of an isolated collection of individuals. By the 1860's it had established firm roots somewhere in the structure of Russian society. Unless the roots could be torn up, the movement would continue to exist.

Despite constant surveillance and frequent arrests, the government failed in its efforts. The earliest repression on a large scale of dissident intellectuals occurred in 1849, when mass arrests seemingly destroyed all oppositional groups. But the radical movement reappeared in the late 1850's, far more resistant to persecution. By the 1870's it included several thousand young people. Though its size fluctuated with the passing years, it could always recruit new volunteers. This process functioned independently of governmental policies toward dissenters. Periods of repression alternated with relative conciliation, but had little effect.

What historical forces created this process of recruitment, and what were its institutional characteristics? These two questions constitute my central theme. The book describes the social environment in which the radicals of the mid-nineteenth century were raised. It follows them from their families into the educational system. It examines the mechanism by which formal education promoted young Russians into the upper occupational strata of society. It looks at the

4. *Ibid.,* p. 120.

development of the student community, key to radical recruitment. It argues that within this group were generated the special institutions, ideals, and models of behavior that functioned as a "school of dissent" capable of disrupting the orderly process of education. In this special sense, it presents a picture of the training of the nihilists.

Because I am seeking to present a collective portrait of the young radicals, my discussion relies on considerable generalization. It presents an interpretation of a complex social phenomenon involving thousands of individuals. Variations in personal experience are neglected in order to focus on the dominant forces which shaped the school of dissent. Not all members of the movement were students. A few workers and peasants responded in the 1870's to the activists' propaganda. Men and women over the age of twenty-five who had held regular employment or—particularly the women—who never had received advanced education appeared among the radicals. Many of them as individuals took part in the activities of the groups of young people attracted by political dissent. But as groups they represent special cases beyond the bounds of my topic.

Though ideological questions figure prominently in most works on the Russian revolutionary movement, they will receive little attention in the chapters that follow. They appeared the major concern of radical journalists whose articles and books set the intellectual tone for the movement. One might loosely describe these men as socialists, since they placed greatest stress on the ideals of political liberty and social equality. Some of their works filtered down to the neophytes, addressing them in simple, understandable terms. Recruitment into the movement did include a peculiar form of schooling through which the socialist dream became real and attainable in the minds of some youth. This training in intellectual dissent and the institutions by which it established itself in the student community constitute in my opinion a form of education, quite outside the regular schooling of advanced educational institutions, best characterized as a school of dissent. Its appearance among Russian student youth in the mid-nineteenth century cannot be explained by the existence in Russia of a body of literature on socialism.

In fact, much of the writing of the radical journalists was far above the heads of potential recruits. They formulated complex ideological systems uniting all branches of knowledge in the service of revolution. They argued bitterly among themselves and stirred equally impassioned debates among their readers over issues of individual morality, social justice, Western political ideals, and the readiness of their country for socialism. Each in his own way explained, in the Aesopian language necessitated by official censorship, the necessary reasons why any intelligent Russian had to join the struggle against oppression. But rational analysis was not by itself adequate to generate large-scale, collective recruitment of radicals. Family, peers, church, and state all combined to discourage collective resistance and to direct that small part of the youth with access to formal schooling into some politically and socially sanctioned position in society. Some of the radicals did follow an individual, intellectual path to dissent. But the evidence suggests strongly that only the institutional force of the school of dissent made possible massive recruitment into the radical movement during the 1860's and 1870's. In fact, the process of recruitment that developed in those years was probably more influential in sustaining the movement in later decades than the ideological systems so passionately debated by the writers. Its endurance constitutes one of the unique aspects of the Russian revolutionary experience. For all these reasons, the emphasis of this book is placed largely on the social dimension of the radical movement.

New People

The formative period in the development of the school of dissent extends from the 1840's, a time of timid experimentation, to the early 1870's, when the system was remarkably effective. In these years a distinctly Russian revolutionary ideology and an array of tactical weapons with which to fight the autocracy were created. Innovation in recruitment paralleled innovation in action and organization. Directly related to these institutional developments was the growth of close social ties marking the radicals as a unique group in Russian society. Bonds of loyalty and protection and a perception of common enemies helped to maintain the internal cohesion of the group. By the 1860's a real radical community existed, defined internally by institutional and ideological bonds and externally by a strong sense of social disaffection. Social identity has a direct bearing on the process of recruitment. Only by locating the radicals in relation to other groups in Russian society can one judge the distance they had to travel as individuals from the traditions and patterns of behavior in which they had been raised.

The point of personal conflict clearest to both radicals and ob-servers was their rejection of parental authority. The theme was echoed in public and in private, in fiction and in essays. The critic Dimitri Pisarev stood out in the early 1860's as spokesman for all those young Russians who had thrown aside the "petty ideas and paralyzing prejudices" drummed into them in that "suffocating en-vironment" of their childhood.[5] Nikolai Dobroliubov's diary reveals the moral development of one of the early intellectual leaders of the radical movement. A loyal and obedient son of a priest, by the age of nineteen he had concluded that "some principles instilled in me from the first years of childhood" were "insignificant and shallow." He felt convinced that he had successfully freed himself from "everything [in my former life] which was oppressive, deceitful, and petty."[6] Ivan Turgenev fixed the image of the youth revolt in the literary imagina-tion of the country in his novel *Fathers and Sons,* published in 1862. In the controversy that flared up immediately afterward, the novelist argued that he had merely reproduced in fictional form his observa-tions of contemporary Russian life.

In its broadest sense, the conflict between the radicals and the older generation implied a cultural schism. The attitudes toward authority, religion, and social class defended by the elders appeared untenable to the young rebels, and the challenge brought frequent personal confrontations. Shortly after the novel appeared, a group of medical students in St. Petersburg met to discuss its meaning for themselves. The organizer of the discussion, Sergei Rymarenko, had been active for three years in the radical movement, and his notes, seized shortly afterward by the secret police, presented the generational conflict far more dramatically than had Turgenev. He asserted that in earlier years fathers had dismissed as "youthful outbursts" the refusal of their offspring to be molded in their "own image and likeness," but that laxity toward deviant behavior had disappeared. Now, fathers were "intolerant" and determined "to maintain absolute parental au-thority." This "parental despotism" had "forced some [youth] to flee thousands of miles without a cent." This description may have applied to Rymarenko. It certainly applied to his sister, from whom a letter was found later by the police in his papers. She had fled from home

5. Pisarev, *Izbrannye sochineniia,* I, 199.
6. Nikolai Dobroliubov, *Dnevnik* [Diary] (Moscow, 1932), p. 397.

after their father, a hereditary noble working as a petty bureaucrat, had threatened her life if she did not abandon her rebellious ways.[7]

In fact, young women in the radical movement faced personal crises more frequently than did men. Although the evidence is sparse the cases of parental conflict in the files of secret police and in contemporary memoirs leave the impression that fathers and daughters were the chief protagonists. There was good reason for such a situation. In the mid-nineteenth century, a daughter of a respectable family was closely supervised by her parents. She received training, at home or in a private school, to prepare her for future domestic duties as wife and mother. She married with parental approval. Male superiority was written into the laws. No woman could obtain an internal passport, necessary for residence in any city or for travel through the country, without the consent of her father or husband if married. Emancipation for women was bound to stir up scandal; a woman among the radicals appeared a slap in the face of good society.

By the late 1860's their presence was common. The rebellious young man (*nigilist,* in Russian) had often by his side a woman (*nigilistka*) sharing his views and style of life. She might have run away from home. Even minor disobedience was sufficient to create family strife. Those women who later wrote of their lives as radicals left the impression that they had resolutely struck out against, in the words of one, "material and intellectual enslavement,"[8] and perhaps some actually did maintain this heroic posture. The account of the flight from home in 1870 of seventeen-year-old Sofia Perovskaia, later hung for her part in the assassination of Alexander II, suggests that she felt no sentimental distress. Records of girls who did suffer are difficult to find. One intimate diary, seized during a search by the secret police in the early 1870's, gives a revealing glimpse of an eighteen-year-old student in a women's *gymnasium* (secondary school) during a prolonged struggle with her guardian aunt. She had begun to move in the circle of her provincial town's student rebels,

7. Tsentral'nyi gosudarstvennyi istoricheskii archiv v Leningrade [Central State Historical Archives in Leningrad; abbreviated TsGIAL], *fond* (f.) 1282, *opis'* (o.) 1, *delo* (d.) 71 (1862), *listy* (ll.) 199, 202–4. Some of the material appears in R. Taubin, "Revoliutsioner-demokrat S. S. Rymarenko" [The revolutionary-democrat S. S. Rymarenko], *Istoriia SSSR*, January-February 1959, pp. 136–54.

8. A. Kornilova-Moroz, "Perovskaia," *Katorga i ssylka*, No. 22 (1926), 19–21.

under the patronage of a young mathematics teacher and his common-law wife. Her aunt ordered her to end these ties. She stood by her "freedom and independence." But at one point in her diary, she asked: "Why am I so harsh with her, refusing to give in on anything? My behavior with my aunt makes me feel oppressed, as though a heavy stone were lying on my heart." She felt that "honorable people" could not possibly behave as she was,[9] yet she did not back down. Despite her anguish, she kept to this new life. Similar experiences were probably multiplied many times over. Only a powerful force could have overcome the emotional and institutional ties binding young women to their designated places in society.

For both the young men and women, the conflict with parental authority represented a personal confrontation between the old order and new ideals which could spark an interest in libertarian principles. Other times the conflict may have resulted from the commitment. One young woman, participant in youth circles in the 1860's, thought that the "tragic family crises" of those about her were more often the effect than the cause of ideological intransigence. These young people were trying to "rid themselves of all the injustice of former times" by "cutting all their ties with the past." Despite the prospect of misery and financial hardship, their "cruel forthrightness" obliged them to deny "all authority, and especially parental authority."[10] In the situation she perceived, the conflict of generations appeared an inevitable part of the radical movement.

For this very reason it cannot stand by itself as a sufficient cause for the political protest—student and nonstudent—that erupted in Russia in those years. The records left of the upbringing of radicals reveal many instances of amicable personal relations between parents and children. When hostility appeared, the behavior of the sons or daughters was predicated on their new loyalties and ideals as members of the radical community. It is impossible to separate the defiance of parents from the commitment to principles of political and social liberation. The major weakness of the arguments of Lewis Feuer, author of a massive comparative study of youth revolt, resides in this

9. Tsentral'nyi gosudarstvennyi arkhiv Oktiabr'skoi revoliutsii [Central State Archives of the October Revolution; abbreviated TsGAOR], f. 109, *tretaia ekspeditsiia* (tr. eks.), d. 78 (1871), *chast'* (ch.), 2, ll. 128–30.

10. E. Vodovozova, *Na zare zhizni* [At the dawn of life] (Moscow, 1934), II, 99–100.

confusion of cause and effect. Feuer's book *The Conflict of Generations* treats the Russian case as one important example of the disruptive consequences of the "de-authorization" of the older generation as a collective whole.[11] From this point of view, the student movement in Russia is literally a case of "sons versus fathers" since the generational conflict appears to be its origin. But if the conflict had as often followed as preceded the commitment to political revolt, the argument is reduced to an arbitrary diagnosis of a supposed social disease.[12] It seems far more reasonable to try to find the origins of this youth movement in a collective process of recruitment forceful enough to break the ties and justify the rupture with established patterns of behavior and belief taught in the family. The generational problem in mid-century Russia becomes in this light important primarily as a point of reference for the radical community, clearly at odds with the "fathers" as symbols of the life its members rejected.

The diagnosis of contemporary political authorities emphasized symptoms of a disease far more widespread than generational conflict. Abundant evidence existed of wholesale defiance of accepted social behavior. Any single act of social nonconformity was sufficient to brand a person as a radical. When one young woman went to work in a peasant village as a midwife, the local police judged significant the fact that "she does not allow the presence of icons in her room." She was dismissed from her position and put under surveillance as a potential troublemaker by reason of her "nihilistic" inclinations, [and] her lack of modesty and piety."[13] When the central authorities began in the 1860's to turn their attention to the problem, their conclusions were ominous. The head of the Third Section warned the tsar in 1867 of the increasing numbers of young men and women who showed neither "religious faith" nor "that feeling of veneration for the Monarch and the established order which children instinctively learn in their family."[14] In his eyes, such individuals were beyond the pale of society.

At times, tsarist officials seemed to view the radical community as

11. Lewis Feuer, *The Conflict of Generations: The Character and Significance of Student Movements* (New York, 1969), pp. 12–13, 89–96.

12. See Alan Spitzer, "The Historical Problem of Generations," *American Historical Review*, LXXVIII (Dec. 1973), 1364–66.

13. Quoted in E. Vilenskaia, *Revoliutsionnoe podpol'e* [The revolutionary underground] (Moscow, 1965), p. 278.

14. TsGAOR, f. 109, o. 85, d. 32 (1867), l. 14.

a sign of the decay of the entire social order. After a particularly agitated period in 1873 and 1874, the tsar formed a special committee of ministers and advisers to analyze the nature and origins of the youth revolt. Their conclusions revealed—not unexpectedly—that the rebels had no redeeming social qualities. The head of the Third Section returned to his concern over religion, lamenting that "our Orthodox priesthood has no influence." In Russian Poland, he argued, the Catholic community knew how to hold the loyalty of the young people. But the Orthodox church had failed to "establish its influence in the upbringing" of Russian youth. The minister of the interior was even more pessimistic. "Every segment" of Russian society, he concluded, lacked "that spirit of discipline without which societies cannot exist."[15] The radicals were further removed from Russian society than even the schismatic Old Believers, for nothing bound them to the land of their birth.

This situation was unique. Germany had known a radical movement among its students in the early part of the century, but its youth appeared less alienated from the country's customs and traditions than their Russian successors, according to one *émigré* radical, Sergei Kravchinski, in the 1880's. He seemed to envy the Germans. They "had not so much to destroy," he wrote, for "there was much in their past which they had reason to love and respect."[16] The Russians were not so fortunate. Like the members of the tsars' committee of 1874, he saw the radicals as social and political schismatics.

Within these narrow social boundaries, the radical community developed a unique set of ideals and style of life. A society sufficient unto itself, it protected, supported, and defended its members from the temptations and attacks of the state and hostile individuals. By the late 1860's it appeared to some of the radicals a sort of religious society similar to the crusading orders of the Middle Ages. Part of the feeling of unity came from the commitment to libertarian goals, despite frequent ideological disagreements. Much of its strength came from the ability of so many of its members to overlook their quarrels over tactics and goals in the interests of the community. Part of the cohesion was based on the institutional ties created by their experiences in circles, communes, and artels. This subject will be discussed

15. TsGIAL, f. 908, o. 1, d. 125, ll. 76–77.
16. Stepniak (pseud.), *King Stork and King Log: A Study of Modern Russia* (London, 1896), II, 100.

at length later in the book, for it figures prominently in my discussion of the innovations which made the school of dissent an effective system of recruitment. The community also was united around certain standards of behavior regulating relations among its members. For Nikolai Chaikovski, active in the movement in the early 1870's, the personal commitment to ethical behavior represented the single most important quality demanded of those who wished to enter the radical movement. As he explained to one young aspirant, the chief requirement of those seeking to flee the "routine life" was "moral purity."[17]

The new pattern of relations between men and women revealed most clearly the force of this code of ethics within the community. The pressure of circumstances required that women have equal footing in the movement alongside men. The traditional methods of legal dependence on male authority and arranged marriages gave families the power to block any move to emancipation by young women. Flight was only a temporary arrangement. Marriages undertaken solely to grant legal freedom to the women were the solution to this problem. Beyond the question of emancipation lay the issue of permanent relations between men and women. The legal system of marriage appeared to many oppressive and immoral; instead, common-law marriages became a frequent arrangement. For the radicals, legal marriage was useful only if it brought personal freedom; a common-law marriage represented the most moral, not the most immoral, bond between a man and a woman. This situation was a mirror image of the legal and socially sanctioned marriage system.

The practice of "fictitious" marriages, that is, to escape dependence on parental authority, began in the 1860's. It was not limited to radicals, for other women not directly involved in the political movement also sought the personal freedom this legal fiction allowed them. The only requirement was the participation of a sympathetic male willing to enter a legal marriage simply to grant his new wife the right to go her own way. It was in essence an act of comradeship and was repeated many times in those years. The first known case was in 1860, involving friends of the radical critic Nikolai Chernyshevski. He arranged the marriage between his doctor and the sister of a fellow writer. She moved quickly from this position into a real

17. Quoted in T. Polner, "N. V. Chaikovskii i bogochelovechestvo" [N. V. Chaikovskii and the religion of humanity], in A. Titov, ed., *N. V. Chaikovskii* (Paris, 1929), p. 98.

common-law alliance, while the doctor quietly removed himself from her life.[18] Chernyshevski later immortalized a variation on this unusual emotional triangle in his novel *What's to Be Done?* His fictionalized account of the unusual marriage arrangements contributed greatly to their spread.

Within a decade they were quite common. One young woman, although her father raised no objections at all to her free life, entered a "fictitious" marriage with a medical student so as "not to lead a bourgeois style of life at home."[19] Usually these arrangements disturbed in no way the separate lives of both parties. The records of the secret police describe the activities of the new wife of the populist Dimitri Rogachev. Married in the summer of 1873 in her provincial town, the newlyweds immediately parted ways. The young bride went to St. Petersburg to prepare for medical studies. The janitor in the building where she rented a room reported that her husband was entirely absent that fall except for two daytime visits of "several hours."[20] Instances were also reported, however, when the arrangements broke down by the simple decision of the new husband to exercise his marital rights. Only when a real community of friendship existed could this "antimarriage" be successful.

When possible, the celebration of the church wedding was reduced to a formality. The ceremony was for the radicals only a legal necessity, often a distasteful one. The result could be a caricature of wedding. The court records of one of the political trials of the 1870's describe a marriage ceremony conducted under "unusual circumstances." The bride, dressed in ordinary street clothes, had come to the church with her landlady. They required one more witness, however, so recruited a passerby. The bride and bridegroom "shocked observers" by their "complete disregard for the marriage rites." After the ceremony, each set off in his own direction. Out of the marriage the young woman obtained a "separate passport valid for all the cities of Russia" and an inheritance held by the conditions of her father's will until marriage. The money later appeared in the coffers of one of the revolutionary parties.[21]

18. T. Bogdanovich, *Liubov liudei shestidesiatykh godov* [Love among the people of the 1860's] (Leningrad, 1929), pp. 420–21.

19. Kornilova-Moroz, "Perovskaia," p. 19.

20. TsGAOR, f. 122, o. 1, d. 212, ll. 10–19.

21. *Protsess 50-ti* [The trial of the fifty] (Moscow, 1906), pp. 28–29.

But love was not excluded from the radical community. On the contrary, freedom was necessary for the spontaneous choice and expression of love among equals. The common-law marriage allowed bonds of love to develop on new grounds. The new sexual liberty was used with great moderation, if one may judge by the memoirs. In fact, one radical was expelled from his circle on grounds of "disgraceful behavior" in large part because of his "special attitude on free love."[22] The few records that mention this personal side of life in the radical community suggest that a very puritanical code of conduct was observed. One police agent reported in the late 1860's an animated conversation about women and communal living between two students, one of whom was a member of a mixed commune. The latter heatedly defended the "integrity" of the women in his group, who had "amorous relations with only one man."[23]

Life in normal society allowed greater room for the pursuit of pleasure than that of the radicals. Many potential radicals were probably repelled by the very rigors of this code of behavior. Even the most resolutely committed occasionally weakened. In his diary Nikolai Dobroliubov recorded the petty pleasures which now and then attacked his resolve. In early January 1857 he celebrated the New Year with champagne and thought how pleasant it would be to be rich. But he remembered that even his modest life was far better than that of his poor friends, for, he wrote, "I can eat meat and pastry every day, travel about in a cab, have a warm [fur] collar on my overcoat, and so on." Two days later, an evening at the theater aroused in him thoughts of dancing, "the devil knows what for. In any case, this shows that I have a tendency to reconciliation with society." But he reminded himself that "in order to accomplish anything, I must keep far away from [society] and swallow my own bile."[24] One pleasure he did not deny himself was frequent visits to a brothel. The portrait given here of the radical community cannot possibly encompass the range of behavior of all the radicals, especially the exceptional individuals like Dobroliubov. His case is revealing in

22. [N. Morozov], "Ocherk istorii kruzhka chaikovtsev" [From the history of the Chaikovtsy circle], *Revoliutsionnoe narodnichestvo* (Moscow, 1964), I, 211–12, 217; these notes were written by Morozov with the assistance of other participants in the circle (see B. Itenberg, *Dvizhenie revoliutsionnogo narodnichestva* (Moscow, 1965), pp. 21–22).

23. TsGAOR, f. 109, tr. eks., d. 51 (1870), ll. 4–5.

24. Dobroliubov, *Dnevnik*, pp. 161, 164.

a general sense. His personal weaknesses indicate the will and determination required to deprive oneself voluntarily, for the sake of personal emancipation, of the pleasures, satisfactions, and sense of security accompanying social conformity. A few individuals might find the strength to join the movement on their own; the school of dissent made it possible for many others, less endowed with these qualities, to follow the same path.

In the reign of Nicholas I, oppositional agitation seemed still in its infancy, in comparison with the revolutionary movements of Western Europe. The Decembrists left no direct descendants. A distinct radical style and set of beliefs did, however, begin to emerge in a few small groups, baptized "circles," particularly in Moscow University in the 1830's and in St. Petersburg in the 1840's. The most famous among the latter was the Petrashevtsy circle, formed in 1846 and destroyed by a wave of arrests in 1849. The trial of the arrested members was the only major political case between the Decembrist uprising and the Karakozov trial of 1866. The Petrashevtsy were by later standards very timid radicals, confining themselves to utopian dreams and bitter complaints against contemporary injustices. Still, their action was daring enough in Nicholas' time. They were essentially precursors, punished less for their deeds than for fear of them in a period when revolution was sweeping western and central Europe.

The promise became reality in the reign of Alexander II. The political climate changed very quickly following his accession to the throne in 1855. The burgeoning radical movement was only the most extreme manifestation of this mood. In those first years of the new reign, its numbers swelled dramatically and it acquired a distinct style. In the same period political agitation became a permanent part of the life of the country. In the early 1860's radical groups organized for the first time in secret societies. The most famous group was "Land and Liberty"; their principal activity was propaganda. Inhabitants of St. Petersburg and Moscow found revolutionary tracts in the streets with such titles as "To the Young Generation" and "Great Russia." The message of these pamphlets was revolution, their means persuasion. It was not a forceful combination, but the pamphlets gave real substance to radical agitation for the first time. Force was first attempted a few years later. In 1866 a former student, Dimitri Karakozov, shot at but missed Alexander II in a Petersburg park. His act seemed at the time the wild gesture of a mentally deranged individual, but political assassination later became one of the most effective weapons against the autocracy.

At the end of the 1860's the brief, meteoric career of Sergei Nechaev revealed that violence suited the tastes of at least some radicals. His own efforts to create a conspiratorial movement for the overthrow of the tsarist regime ended in melodrama. In late 1869 he engineered the murder of a member of a student circle he had organized in Moscow. By accusing this individual of being a police spy, he forced the other members to collaborate in the execution, hoping to bind together his fellow conspirators. He fled the country but was arrested and tried a few years later. His affair, like others before and after it, was grist for the mill of the Third Section. Its agents arrested many young Russians known to sympathize with the revolutionary cause. Treating all radicals as equally dangerous, they swept into their net the proponents of both violent and gradual political change. They left behind in their files mountains of documents and records of interrogation, an excellent source of information for later historians.

In reality, the radicals disagreed on fundamental questions of revolutionary tactics, the conditions suitable for the revolution, and the nature of the new order to follow. All the major schools of socialist and political libertarian thought contributed theories to radical debates. Various combinations of propaganda and violence were offered as the proper means to fight the autocratic regime. In the mid-1870's the term "populism" was used to designate the faction that believed the revolution must be the work of the people (i.e., peasants), not of a militant minority of radicals. That no single term described the political ideals of the whole movement indicates the ideological and tactical diversity of those years. By the end of the century Russian Marxists had adopted the word "populism" to refer to non-Marxist approaches to revolutionary action, including all the programs of the 1870's. Though the controversy over terminology continues, common usage has sanctioned the Marxists' practice.[25]

The agitation begun in the 1860's reached its peak in the following decade. The propagandists sought to spread the revolutionary message to the people through worker circles and the distribution of subversive literature and learning among the peasants. In the "to the people"

25. The subject of populism is examined in A. Walicki, *The Controversy over Capitalism* (Oxford, 1969).

movement of 1874 three to four thousand youth, most of them from institutions of higher education, went out into the countryside to educate and liberate the oppressed masses. It was a hopeless affair, a "children's crusade" of Russian socialism. Most of them were quickly arrested. These were largely young men and women from upper and middle-class families who had breathed the rarefied intellectual atmosphere of advanced learning. The peasants found most of them outlandish and suspicious creatures. By birth and education, they were the elite of the country. By conviction and behavior, they belonged to the radical community. Their remarkable outpouring of energy and enthusiasm was spontaneous, not a response to central commands. But their presence testified to the existence of an effective process of radical recruitment. To this extent, to explain the origins and functioning of the school of dissent is to reveal the conditions making possible this tragic crusade.

The failure of this first major political campaign led to more careful oppositional activity—thus more dangerous to the regime—later in the decade. The work of propaganda was carried on in a systematic, organized manner by the second Land and Liberty party, created in 1876. Toward the end of the decade, the emphasis shifted to violence. Terrorism became for the first time the inspiration for an organized political group, born partly of the desire for vengeance on the authorities responsible for the repression of the radicals. The official in charge of the Petersburg prisons, General Trepov, barely escaped an attack on his life in early 1878. His assailant, Vera Zasulich, sought revenge for Trepov's brutal treatment of political prisoners. Others, who saw in terror a means to hasten the revolution, in 1879 formed their own organization, the People's Will party, out of remnants of the Land and Liberty group. Their principal target was the tsar himself, whom they believed to be the force holding together the entire autocratic regime. On March 1, 1881, bombs under Alexander II's carriage on a street in St. Petersburg achieved their goal. But the death of the tsar was no more helpful to their cause than the "to the people" campaign. The government remained unshaken and set out again to eliminate this subversive force, although it again failed in its efforts. The radical community had established itself firmly in Russian society.

What forces had created such a tenacious movement? This question greatly troubled Russians at the time. The radicals' answer was disarmingly simple. Their commitment to revolutionary change was a direct result of the oppressiveness of the old order. After the assassination of Alexander II, the leaders of the People's Will party explained in an open letter to the new tsar that their extreme action was in defense of the interests of the people. Their very existence sprang, not from personal decisions, but from the collective will of the people. "The revolutionary movement does not originate in individuals," they argued. "Revolutionaries are created by circumstances: the general discontent of the people, [and] the striving of Russia for a new social system."[26] In other words, injustice inevitably called forth resistance. Their explanation was really self-justification.

Contemporaries outside the movement had difficulty describing the radicals. Like the leaders of People's Will, they tended to define this new group in moral terms, implicitly assuming that the good or evil such people accomplished served also to identify them. Even novelists were party to the debate. Bazarov, the most forceful representative of the "sons" in Turgenev's *Fathers and Sons,* was baptized a "nihilist" by an admiring companion. The novelist introduced the term in the political vocabulary of Russia. Previously, the word had referred to someone lacking solid beliefs. Bazarov appeared in this novel an iconoclast who used science and critical reason to refute the most cherished beliefs of those about him. Though Turgenev drew a subtle portrait of an emotionally complex individual, contemporaries quickly colored in dark shadings of deviant behavior and subversive ideals. After the Karakozov affair, a Petersburg University professor explained in a report to the government that nihilism was "an idea, a philosophical teaching" resembling a "religion of a special sort." It had "nothing in common with the simple Russian people," for it "belongs entirely to that milieu which is alienated from the people."[27] Thus the political dissenter was automatically classified as a social deviant.

The secret police followed through with the portrait of the nihilist as a destructive outsider. In a report in 1869, the head of the Third Section described such a person as "a combination of Western atheist, materialist, revolutionary, socialist, and communist. He is a confirmed

26. Cited in V. Burtsev, *Za sto let* [During the last 100 years] (London, 1897), p. 175.

27. P. Zaionchkovski, "Zapiska K. D. Kavelina" [Note of K. D. Kavelin], *Istoricheskii arkhiv,* V (1950), 327, 331.

enemy of political and social order."[28] "Nihilist" apparently satisfied the authorities more than "rebel" (*otshchepentsy*), used in the report as well, because of its strong pejorative connotation. The most imaginative negative portrayal of the nihilist appeared in Dostoevski's novel *The Possessed,* inspired by the Nechaev affair. Peter Verkhovenski, Dostoevski's answer to Bazarov, appears to be evil incarnate. "Nihilist" was an effective polemical weapon, for it explained and condemned such an individual's disruptive behavior while seeming merely to describe it.

On the other side, those who sought to justify or condone political dissent by the late 1860's employed a variety of terms. The word *"intelligentsiia"* quickly acquired considerable vogue. Like "nihilist" a term of foreign origin assimilated into the Russian language earlier in the century, it had originally meant intelligence and consciousness of truth. In the 1860's, it descended from philosophy into the political arena. Some Russians used it specifically to emphasize the moral obligation incumbent on men of learning to use truth to reform society. One young radical argued in 1868 that the Russian intelligentsia "reforms its life in accordance with the latest conclusions of social science and moral philosophy, repudiates routine and tradition, and relates to its environment with the soberness and courage of the thinking critic."[29] An advanced education, though, was no guarantee of dissent. Radicals or sympathetic observers frequently refined the concept by adding "radical" or "revolutionary." However qualified, "intelligentsia" seemed more a value judgment than a descriptive category.

A less pretentious title used by many radicals was "the new people." It first became popular with the publication of Chernyshevski's novel *What's to Be Done?* subtitled "Tales of the New People." Its paragon of the new man, Pavel Rakhmetev, recognized no moral code but his own and no social obligations except those which would hasten the revolution. He represented an idealized characterization of a young man, Pavel Bakhmetev, whom the author had known while a teacher in Samara. Son of a well-to-do landowning nobleman, he had given up his privileged life, had traveled through Russia for two years as a simple laborer, then had taken his family fortune to

28. "Revoliutsionnoe i studencheskoe dvizhenie," p. 119.
29. Quoted in Alan Pollard, "Consciousness and Crisis: The Self-Image of the Russian Intelligentsia, 1855–1882" (Ph.D. dissertation, University of California, Berkeley, 1968), p. 121.

start a new life abroad. He gave half of his funds to Alexander Herzen, then set out to found an agricultural commune somewhere in the New World. He was never heard from again.[30] For Chernyshevski, he represented the sort of "new person" few might equal but all should strive to emulate. Others in the radical movement preferred simply to call themselves nihilists, flaunting the term like a battle flag.

Contemporary Russians showed considerable ingenuity in finding words to describe these people. In every case, their use of language prejudged their conclusions on the nature and origin of the movement. For intelligentsia one might as well have read "enlightened cohorts of progress"; a contemporary equivalent to nihilist is "hippie," quite as pejorative a term in the minds of many middle-class Americans as the older Russian version. All these words put the radical movement in a moral context. Like medieval tales about saints and sinners and God's merciless judgment, Russians of those years made the radicals subjects for adoration or execration, not objects of dispassionate study.

"Intelligentsia" and Subculture

The stereotypes created one hundred years ago continue to color the histories of individuals and of the movement. "Intelligentsia" still enjoys great popularity, though it appears in such a multiplicity of guises as to defy accurate definition. Soviet scholars use the term to designate that socioeconomic stratum performing "intellectual labor" for society. The definition becomes ensnared in ideological preconceptions when applied to tsarist Russia. A recent Soviet study of the nineteenth-century "intelligentsia" includes eight excellent chapters on professional training and occupational groups, followed by two chapters on advanced education and the radical movement. The implication is that the real, "progressive" intelligentsia was naturally on the side of revolution.[31] Their choice ostensibly reflected the objective class contradictions of Russian society. Soviet scholars do not find the explanation for the rise of the radical movement in

30. N. Eidel'man, "Pavel Aleksandrovich Bakhmetov," *Voprosy istorii sel'skogo khoziaistva, krest'ianstva i revoliutsionnogo dvizheniia v Rossii* (Moscow, 1961), pp. 387–98.

31. V. R. Leikina-Svirskaia, *Intelligentsiia v Rossii vo vtoroi polovine XIX veka* [The intelligentsia in Russia in the second half of the nineteenth century] (Moscow, 1971).

unique social forces within Russia, but in Karl Marx. Their use of terminology is a clear judgment of the origins of the radicals.

A similar dilemma is shared by Western historians, who carry on the subjective, polemical traditions of the nineteenth-century Russian writers. The "central characteristics" of the Russian intelligentsia, according to one author, were "its open and articulate hatred of injustice, ignorance, censorship, delation and all that morally degrades and outrages the human personality."[32] Joining the ranks of the critics, on the other hand, is the historian James Billington. In his recent history of Russian culture, he identifies the intelligentsia by its "passionate personal engagement in ethical questions," by which it expressed its "alienation." The origins of this regrettable intellectual schism are attributable in his opinion to a "personal and moral [conflict] within the ruling aristocracy."[33] The problem lay thus in the ethical decay among the social elite of the country. His view is reminiscent of that expressed sixty years earlier by Peter Struve. This Russian intellectual had used his essay in the *Vekhi* collection, published in 1909, to analyze the moral corruption which infected the intelligentsia. It appeared to him to be characterized by—and to suffer from—"rebelliousness [*otshchepenstvo*], its alienation from the state," and "its absence of religious feeling."[34] His definition was actually a call to alienated Russians to draw closer to the national community. It, like Billington's, seemed to hide a feeling of regret that the intelligentsia had ever appeared.

The closer one gets to such definitions, the more mysterious appears the group so defined. In a recent essay, the historian Martin Malia abandoned completely any "recognized system of social analysis" to isolate the intelligentsia as a group within Russian society. He identified it by the attitude shared by its members of "an exceptional sense of apartness from the society in which they lived." Unfortunately, this characterization turns a supposed social group into a "bond of consciousness."[35] Lacking any recognizable traits to place it

32. Allen McConnell, "The Origins of the Russian Intelligentsia," *Slavic and East European Journal,* VIII (Spring 1964), 6.

33. James Billington, *The Icon and the Axe* (New York, 1966), pp. 233, 262–63.

34. Peter Struve, "Intelligentsiia i revoliutsiia," in *Vekhi* (Moscow, 1909), p. 160.

35. Martin Malia, "What Is the Intelligentsia?" in Richard Pipes, ed., *The Russian Intelligentsia* (New York, 1961), pp. 3, 5–7.

in context, the intelligentsia takes on the appearance of an intellectual concept or a figment of the imagination. It looks very much like those French Jansenists, described by Montesquieu in his *Persian Letters,* surrounding Louis XIV like an "innumerable number of invisible enemies" who "exist in general and are nothing in particular."[36]

The solution I have adopted consists of the complete abandonment of the "intelligentsia" as a tool for scholarly analysis. The word "radical" may seem banal, but it identifies the political outlook of the people in question as that of extreme opposition to the established order of Russia. It makes clear that this group does not include any individuals whose views were those of reformist "liberals." As a group, the radicals bear strong similarities to other extremist political movements which have appeared in recent times in developing countries. The term most frequently used in this context is "counterelite." As described by Daniel Lerner, its members stand out as "sufficiently alienated from the old elite's perspectives and practices" to constitute a distinct political entity with its own ideological outlook and style of life.[37] The radical community of nineteenth-century Russia fits very closely the picture Lerner draws. The Russian state was the first to experience this particularly dangerous manifestation of political opposition to a traditional regime.

The concept most useful for the study of radical recruitment in Russia is drawn from the terminology of contemporary sociology, which has studied youth revolt in recent years. Using the broad concept "culture" to refer to the basic similarity of outlook of members of a society, social scientists have identified patterns of deviant outlook which they define as "subcultures." One sociologist has further refined this approach to isolate the presence of social conflict as a part of the values of the subculture. He has suggested the use of the term "contraculture" to circumscribe groups whose beliefs "contain, as a primary element, a theme of conflict with the total society."[38] Popularized in a recent best-seller as "counterculture," this theoretical concept has acquired overtones of approval—or disapproval—sus-

36. Montesquieu, *Les lettres persanes* (Paris, 1929), I, 55–56 (Letter 24).

37. Daniel Lerner, *The Passing of Traditional Society* (New York, 1958), pp. 373–74.

38. Milton Yinger, "Contra-culture and Subculture," in E. E. Sampson, *Approaches, Contexts, and Problems of Social Psychology* (Englewood Cliffs, N.J., 1964), p. 468; see also Robert Berkhofer, *A Behavioral Approach to Historical Analysis* (New York, 1969), pp. 83–91.

piciously like those which surrounded "intelligentsia" in tsarist Russia. I have chosen to use the less colorful but politically neutral term "subculture." There are in fact striking parallels between the student unrest and "New Left" in the United States in the 1960's and the experience of the radical community in Russia one hundred years ago. Both groups fall under the definition of subculture, and both were intimately associated with educational institutions. But the chapters that follow do not pursue this tantalizing theme. They focus on the social context within which Russians created a unique set of institutions and models of behavior to begin drawing from the educational system a small but steady flow of recruits for the radical movement. In theory, the purging of "intelligentsia" from these pages will help to avoid any blatant preconceptions regarding the origins of radical dissent.

In specific geographical terms, this study concentrates on the situation in the capital of the empire, St. Petersburg. The city was the center of higher education in Russia. It attracted to its professional schools and university the cream of Russian educated youth, who could expect to join the elite of the country on completing their studies. It also became the center for the radical movement. Only the groups in Moscow and Kiev could rival the capital in prestige and leadership. The ties among these cities were close, for the burgeoning radical community was not restricted by regional boundaries. Hence the diffusion of innovations in recruitment and tactics operated almost without hindrance and by the early 1870's involved all urban centers with a sizable student group. It is hazardous to isolate the trends in one city, but St. Petersburg's contribution to the radical movement was great, in number of recruits, creation of the methods and institutions of recruitment, and new directions in ideology and tactics. In sum, the capital appears the best window on the development and implantation of the school of dissent.

Included in this study is biographical data on a large group of radicals who became active in the capital. They constitute a sample population for purposes of constructing the collective portrait of the training of the nihilists. The information is far from complete. My goal was to recreate as accurately as possible the actual social environment in which the future radicals were raised so as to identify the key factors in their radical schooling—and to eliminate those supposed causes invented by ideological bias. As will be apparent in Chapter 2, my material was particularly useful for the latter purpose.

Fortunately, a considerable amount of biographical information on individual radicals is available, chiefly memoirs and police files. Survivors of the radical movement began in the 1920's to compile a multivolume biographical dictionary on everyone involved in oppositional activities and made generous—and unsystematic—use of these records. Government biographical files were also useful for family records on radicals from the nobility or bureaucracy. Generally, however, information on schooling was more readily attainable than on social origins. These sources still left many individuals unaccounted for, and I could not gather enough material to make a real collective biography. The quantifiable data on education and estate background of the Petersburg radicals are presented in two tables.

Table 1 indicates the highest level of formal educational training received by the individuals in my sample. The total of 405 includes people from a variety of schools located in the capital and elsewhere. Over three-fourths had attended at least a university or professional school, the highest level of schooling in the empire. By comparison,

Table 1. Level of education of Russian radicals (in percent)

Level of education	1840–1855 (n=50)	1855–1869 (n=148)*	1870–1875 (n=202)	Total (n=400)*	All Russian students, early 1870's** (n=99,800)
Higher education					
University/lycée	62	52	12	33	7
Professional school	8	33	68	48	5
Military school	6	9	6	7	?
Other	0	1	1	1	—
Secondary education					
Gymnasium	8	1	2	2	65
Seminary	0	0	0	0	13
Military school	16	1	4	4	10
Other	0	3	7	5	—
Total	100	100	100	100	100

Sources: Deiateli russkogo revoliutsionnogo dvizheniia: Bio-bibliografiche-skii slovar' [Participants in the Russian revolutionary movement: Biobibliographical dictionary], Vols. I–III (Moscow, 1927–1934); the interrogation records of the Petrashevtsy (f. 9, d. 55) in the Central State Military-Historical Archives.
* Five other radicals were identified whose education is not known.
** These percentages include all of European Russia. They are very rough, for the enrollment statistics are both irregular and unreliable.

the total enrollment in institutions of secondary and advanced education for the early 1870's gave greatest weight to students in secondary education. The locus for the school of dissent lay in the upper levels of education, not among the half-educated. There are only seventeen women in my sample, indicative of their small part in the radical movement as a whole. Almost all had received only a secondary education. As will become obvious in Chapter 3, the secondary and higher educational institutions shared a common goal of training a small, elite group of the population. The students acquired a common intellectual outlook and a special position in society. Graduates and even those who completed only a few years of schooling could hope to find positions in the middle or upper occupational strata of society. Some students consciously refused these advantages, probably not because of the system of educational promotion itself, but because of some process which had grown (cancerlike, in the eyes of the authorities) within the student community itself.

I compiled data on individuals within a thirty-year period between the early 1840's and mid-1870's. This span of time is divided into subperiods, somewhat arbitrary but closely associated with important points of transition in the radical movement. The first extends from the 1840's to the mid-1850's and includes the first radicals, who came mainly from the Petrashevtsy circle. The second covers the period until the end of the 1860's. In terms of the standard—and incorrect—generational view of the radical movement, these were the "sons" of the "fathers" of the 1840's. The third subperiod spans the first half of the 1870's, including individuals who participated in the "to the people" movement. Their overwhelming preference for professional schooling constituted a major shift in educational experience and strikingly indicates the type of institutions within which the school of dissent proved most effective.

Among the 405 individuals whose biographies are included in my sample are some of the leading radicals of the time. They are buried by sheer weight of numbers under the larger group of the rank and file, distinguished by little else than a police file. This perspective fits the purposes of this book quite well. Much scholarly attention has been paid to the "greats" of the Russian revolutionary cause, such as Chernyshevski, Kropotkin, and Kravchinski, whose great strength of character and unswerving sense of commitment made them exceptional individuals. Their leadership was essential for the development of the radical movement. But without a mass following of more ordinary young people, they could never have been successful. The fact that the average youth joined the movement despite doubts and backsliding is testimony to the capacity of the school of dissent to penetrate the student community. His case, not that of the heroes, is the center of attention here.

The argument presented in the chapters that follow stresses the intimate ties which bound the radicals as youth to the society about them. Looking back on their upbringing, most were unwilling to see themselves as products of a particular environment. Their struggle put them at odds with the old order. If they had once been part of it, the fault was not theirs. English audiences became acquainted with this idealized vision of the Russian revolutionaries in the works of Sergei Kravchinski in his years as *émigré*. Writing in the 1880's and early 1890's under the pseudonym of Stepniak, he presented in his books *Underground Russia* and *The Career of a Nihilist* a passionate defense of the high ethical standards and dedication of his former comrades. Westerners had previously shown a strong proclivity to treat these people as fanatics and troublemakers, accepting the interpretation put on their actions by the Russian government. Kravchinski reversed the image, showing the radicals as people dedicated to the extirpation of evil from human society. If they had chosen this hard path, it was because oppression necessarily called forth resistance. They were martyrs to a holy cause.

This view is still vigorously defended in the English-language literature on the radicals. It appears in scholarly form in the major history of Russian radicalism, Franco Venturi's *Roots of Revolution*. The author depersonalizes the radicals to emphasize their achievements as opponents of the autocratic regime. The imperfections of individuals disappear behind the glorious struggle for liberty. The effect is to place their actions on the highest possible moral level, leaving completely in the dark the question of why so many young Russians chose the life of rebel. In a new introduction to the book, he has stated that "the preparation of this account aroused in me . . . admiration and enthusiasm for this generation of revolutionaries."[39] His feelings found a strong echo on this side of the Atlantic, where Alexander Gerschenkron hailed Venturi's work not only for its

---

39. Franco Venturi, *Les intellectuels, le peuple et la révolution: Histoire du populisme russe au XIX siècle,* trans. Viviani Paques (Paris, 1972), I, 22.

scrupulous concern for detail and veracity of facts but also for its particular point of view. In fact, Gerschenkron puts the populist movement squarely in the context of the "problem of liberty," as much an issue at present in the Soviet Union as during the reign of Alexander II.[40]

For obvious reasons, the tsarist authorities studied the radicals extensively. They devoted considerable energy to the collection of material on the movement and its participants. Both the Ministry of Education and the Third Section assembled large amounts of information, documents, letters, even charts, on the country's student body and radical community. They kept particularly careful watch over the groups in the capital. Police agents circulated within educational institutions. They penetrated circles, talked with members of communes, sampled the fare in student cafeterias, and attended student meetings and demonstrations. The comprehensiveness of their reports is at times astonishing. If the government was unable to make sense of the rise of radicalism in the midst of the country's educated elite, it was not for lack of information.

The concern of the tsarist regime is the boon of the historian. The archives of the Ministry of Education and Third Section, open in the past two decades to foreigners, are a mine of information. They cover in great detail the actual organization, ideological debates, and tactics of the radical movement. Interspersed among this material are observations and factual accounts with a direct bearing on the recruitment of radicals. These archival documents represent the primary firsthand source used in this book. Memoirs exist in abundance as well and have been consulted extensively. But their information, written with hindsight and a special interest in defending—or attacking—the cause, must be used with caution. Lacking the extensive survey materials of contemporary social scientists, the historian can only hope to perceive, as though at great distance, the dim outlines of that student world within which the school of dissent was beginning to prepare future generations of revolutionaries.

40. Alexander Gerschenkron, "Franco Venturi on Russian Populism," *American Historical Review*, LXXVIII (Oct. 1973), 973 n. 9, 984–85.

2 | Fathers, Sons, and Daughters

Most radicals first experienced Russian social conditions as well-fed, well-brought-up children of upper-class families. Only scattered records remain of their upbringing and of the social position of their parents, but these reveal a picture indistinguishable in most respects from that of bureaucratic or landowning noble families. A surprisingly large proportion, although a minority, were the offspring of upwardly mobile fathers. The parents' aspiration to give their children an advanced education seems a deviation from the old pattern of noble upbringing, but was a goal shared by many families whose children became loyal, disciplined subjects of the tsar. On the whole, the family origins of the radicals destined them for comfortable, orderly lives. Here the story of radical recruitment must begin.

These young Russians did not often talk of their background. Existing records usually indicate the estate, occasionally the occupation, and rarely the income levels of their fathers. One must therefore rely on inference from known characteristics of Russian classes to describe the probable surroundings in which they were brought up. This only shifts the problem from the particular to the general, for there does not yet exist a good history of Russian society in the nineteenth century. We do not know to what extent the estate pattern corresponded to other sources of status such as occupation and wealth. We have only a meager idea of the attitude of Russians toward various marks of prestige. We can just surmise the existence of differing styles of life corresponding to various social groups. Finally, we have very little information on social mobility, either for individuals or groups, which might have come with the expansion of cities, the growth of new professional occupations, the redistribution of wealth, and the slow economic growth of the country. Patterns of behavior and relations among groups clearly were more complex than the simple hierarchy of estates would suggest.

New and Old Elites

The basic framework of estate rankings remains the only possible basis for quantifiable findings on the social origins of the radicals. Table 2 presents the data collected on the Petersburg group. I made two modifications in the estate hierarchy to take into account one obvious social change. Though numerically insignificant, the bureaucracy represented an influential force in society. Through its division into upper and lower categories, one noble and the other nonnoble, its members had in effect forced the state to recognize two new social strata.

Table 2.   Social Origins of Russian Radicals, 1840–1875 (in percent)

Estate	1840–1855 ($n=50$)	1855–1869 ($n=143$)*	1870–1875 ($n=191$)*	Total ($n=384$)*	Petersburg University students, 1859–1860 ($n=1,026$)
Landowning nobility	46	41	33	38	} 58
Bureaucratic nobility	36	23	19	24	
Nonnoble bureaucracy	6	10	8	8	22
Clergy	4	10	15	11	9
Merchant	6	8	11	9	} 5
Petty bourgeoisie	2	3	6	5	
Peasantry	0	3	3	2	—
Raznochintsy	0	2	5	3	6
TOTAL	100	100	100	100	100

Sources: The same as for Table 1, plus the official yearbook of the state bureaucracy, the *Adreskalendar,* for the years 1835–1872; the official state records (*formuliarnye spiski*) of the bureaucracy (*fond* 1349), and the family records of the nobility in the Department of Heraldry of the Senate (*fond* 1343), both in the Central State Historical Archives in Leningrad. The enrollment figures for Petersburg University are from TsGIAL, f. 733, o. 95, d. 172, ll. 333–34.

* The social origins of 21 radicals are unknown, 10 in the period 1855–1869, and 11 in the period 1870–1875.

By the mid-nineteenth century, the nobility constituted landowning and bureaucratic groups. The former carried on the traditional pattern of noble life. Service to the state provided temporary occupation and the prestige of rank, while ownership of landed estates and serfs conferred a suitably ostentatious style of life and its own unique prestige. Service, mainly in the officer corps, probably lasted for only a few years before retirement to a country estate. The state had become aware in the late eighteenth century that "many nobles retire from service too early," but took no steps to return to an obligatory period of service.[1] The situation apparently suited the landed nobility quite well.

These tastes were not shared by many bureaucrats who had reached the service rank (eighth until mid-century, fourth afterward), automatically bringing membership in the noble estate and the right to own estates and serfs. In the 1840's over one-half of the officials in the upper ranks (fifth to the first) had no serfs by inheritance, purchased none while in service, and acquired none by marriage. Yet the occupation of these men placed them at the center of political power in the country. Only one-third of the higher officials possessed over one hundred male serfs and hence could be considered influential landowners.[2] The majority of the bureaucratic nobility clearly regarded the prestige and income of a governmental post sufficient for their needs.

My search for biographical information on the fathers of radicals usually uncovered their occupations. Family records invariably indicated rank, even if the individual had retired. Some gave no indication of length of service. I also consulted service files of the bureaucracy, but these were incomplete. More information was available on the nobles serving in the bureaucracy, but less for the landowning nobles. Some left service records of their short careers in the army or bureaucracy; some left genealogical records in the state archives; some left no records at all. I have included in the landowning nobility those nobles with no service record on the assumption that record keeping within this group was very imperfect. Into this category went those landowning nobles with less than fifteen years in the bureaucracy, a length of service which permitted them

1. Quoted in S. Korf, *Dvorianstvo i ego soslovnoe upravlenie* [The nobility and its estate institutions] (St. Petersburg, 1906), p. 159.

2. Walter Pintner, "Change at the Top and Bottom: The Higher Civil Service and the Provincial Outposts in Mid-Nineteenth Century Russia," unpublished manuscript, tables II and III. Pintner's sample included 348 upper-level bureaucrats. Similar data, though not as complete, can be found in Pintner, "The Social Characteristics of the Early Nineteenth-Century Russian Bureaucracy," *Slavic Review*, XXIX (Sept. 1970), 437, table 10.

to retire at about the age of thirty-five. Here also were put the few noble officers who made the army their lifetime career, the favored occupation even among those who served only a few years.

The nonnoble bureaucracy constituted a special social stratum. Their work in the state administration gave special privileges and power. Their reputation, however, was abysmal. Graft and corruption—the perquisites of power—were by common agreement their chief business. Government statistics on estates usually included them with the nobility. At other times they were grouped with the *raznochintsy*, the "men of various ranks." Their status was ambiguous, somewhere between the privileged, that is noble, estate and the middle classes.

A new but small element in Russian society were the professionals, such as doctors, lawyers, and engineers, sufficiently important to be included in the new estate of "hereditary honorary citizens." Many, however, earned noble rank in government service. I have grouped this estate with the merchantry. The few peasant families included in my sample could have been from the countryside or the cities, since no information on the occupation of peasant heads of household was available. Overall, the social background of the Petersburg radicals included every important group in Russian society.

But the distribution did not reflect that of the country. It was very heavily weighted toward the nobility, though the proportion declined somewhat between the 1840's and 1870's. A random sample of the population of St. Petersburg would have produced very different results. In those years, the petty bourgeoisie made up approximately one-fifth and the peasantry one-third of the city's inhabitants. On the other hand, the leading institutions of higher education included a high percentage of sons of the nobility. The university in the capital had a student body in 1859–1860, as indicated in the table, whose social origins bore a strong resemblance to that of the radicals. By the early 1870's, it too had experienced a rise in the proportion of nonprivileged sons at the expense of the nobility, to a greater extent than my sample of radicals. These statistics suggest that the life histories of the radicals began in a manner identical with that of students in higher education. The remainder of the chapter will explore in some detail this hypothesis.

By birth the sons of the landowning nobility felt the duties and enjoyed the privileges of the traditional political elite. Service to the state remained an active force in their lives as the source of honor and awards. Even noble families with titles dating back centuries felt the attraction of service. The mother of Mikhail Saltykov, one of the radical publicists of the 1860's, regarded the family's ancient patent as an obligation on her sons to serve to a rank which, in her words, "will reflect honor on your ancestors."[3] There appears no reason to assume that the fathers of the future radicals deviated from this pattern of behavior. Fedor Selivanov, whose son later joined the populists, was a well-to-do landowning noble. His father had left him 158 serfs, and a good marriage brought him another 150. He received no other education than tutoring at home, and at the age of sixteen entered the army. Eight years later he retired, having risen to "junior captain" (*poruchik*), lowest of the commissioned officer ranks. Though he later served in elective functions in his province, he never achieved a rank approaching his army position.[4] The standards of conduct he represented for his son certainly provided no sanction for political dissent.

The tradition of service worked both for and against the nobility. Dependence upon the state brought them standing in a poor and servile society, but it also emasculated their sense of class solidarity and social superiority. They never acquired the social cohesion, for example, of the Prussian junkers. It could have been somewhat easier for the Russian noble than for his Western counterpart to reorient his ideal of service for the good of the state to service in the interest of the people against the oppressive state. One historian has argued that this crucial transferal of ideals provided the inspiration for the radical movement. "Membership in this privileged class" became for a few nobles undesirable, and there emerged "an 'order' devoted to the overthrow of this system."[5] An intellectual crisis within the nobility would in this view explain the appearance of radicals. The argument has the virtue of underlining the similarities of basic motivation between the radical ideology and the pattern of behavior of the noble class. But it does not explain the actual process of disaffection by which young nobles abandoned their class allegiance. It provides no clue as to why the ideal of state service weakened, if it did,

3. Quoted in S. Makashin, *Saltykov-Shchedrin,* I (Moscow, 1949), 151.
4. TsGIAL, f. 1349, o. 3, d. 2010.
5. Marc Raeff, *Origins of the Russian Intelligentsia* (New York, 1967), pp. 9–10.

nor does it help to answer the crucial question of why most nobles, including the fathers of the radicals, continued the traditional style of life.

The Russian aristocracy, cream of the nobility, was poorly represented among the Petersburg radicals, contributing only a handful of their offspring. One of these was Peter Kropotkin. In the Moscow mansion where he was brought up, there were fifty servants, including four coachmen and five cooks, and a small serf orchestra. The family fortune, derived mainly from large estates, went to maintain a lavish style of life and to provide the children with a thoroughly European education. Kropotkin's upbringing marked him permanently. When at the age of thirty he joined the Chaikovtsy circle, one acquaintance judged him "scarcely Russian." He seemed "European from head to foot, in appearance and character."[6] Like Tol'stoi's hero Nekhludov in the novel *Resurrection,* he looked almost as alien to radicals brought up in average noble families as to the peasants.

Most of the Petersburg radicals from the landowning nobility were the offspring of middle and poor nobles. The style of life to which their families had been accustomed might include a town house in a provincial city and a tutor for their children. Many were facing serious financial problems. Before the emancipation of the serfs, they were assured inexpensive labor to work their land. Over three-fourths of the estate owners in 1858 possessed fewer than one hundred male serfs, a level generally considered adequate to maintain a satisfactory standard of living. At the other extreme, slightly over 3 percent owned over five hundred male serfs and could thus live on a grand scale.[7] Thus the majority of landowners did not possess the means to become wealthy. Compounding their problems was their proverbial inability to conduct their farming on a sound economic basis. By mid-century two-thirds of the serfs of landowning nobles had been mortgaged to the state. The possibility of serf emancipation immediately brought to the surface the differences of economic condition among nobles. The head of the Third Section, in a report for the tsar in 1857, estimated that the bitterest opponents of emancipation were the petty landowners and all the "half educated" nobles living permanently in the countryside. Support would come only from the landless nobility

---

6. L. Tikhomirov, *Vospominaniia* [Memoirs] (Moscow, 1927), p. 79.
7. Jerome Blum, *Lord and Peasant in Russia* (New York, 1965), p. 369.

and those serfowners who "preferred the good of all to private advantages."[8]

There is only scanty evidence to indicate the impact of and reaction to this social and economic decline among those nobles whose offspring became radicals. One case was that of Vera Zasulich. She came from an old noble family in the western province of Smolensk. The grandfather had apparently squandered the family fortune, for he left his son only five male serfs, the equivalent to a small village.[9] Though marriage brought the son another forty serfs, he was obliged to serve as an officer for the greater part of his life. His death left the family in very difficult circumstances. Vera, like her elder sister, had to find work as a governess. As she later recalled, "I was obliged to count myself, at first with [a feeling of] deep mortification, one of the poor."[10] The noble style of life represented only her lost world of comfort and protection. She was not forced to replace this void with a new life in the radical community. The society in which radicals from the landowning nobility were brought up was in transformation, the repercussions of which meant grief to at least a few of their families. But this trend had no specific, demonstrable impact on their recruitment into the radical movement.

To the extent it was possible, the provincial nobility led a carefree life. Most left the serious job of managing estates to a peasant overseer, whose chief function was to produce the income on which the nobles depended. They maintained appearances by fine clothes, hunting, and endless card playing. This was the main occupation of the father of Dimitri Pisarev. He too had served the state as a young man. Life later on his estate meant primarily a round of entertainment and the chance to display his good looks to the wives of the local nobility. A family acquaintance vividly remembered this "provincial Don Juan" as an older man, "with graying hair brushed in back, long white mustaches, an extraordinarily clear, pink complexion, always obliging and smiling, speaking with a soft, beguiling voice."[11] Within ten years of retirement, he had to sell his best estate to pay mounting debts.

8. TsGAOR, f. 109, d. 22 (1857), ll. 77–78.
9. TsGIAL, f. 1343, o. 22, d. 1150.
10. V. Zasulich, *Vospominaniia* [Memoirs] (Moscow, 1931), p. 16.
11. Quoted in A. Coquart, "Le nihiliste Pisarev," *Revue des études slaves,* XXII (1946), 132.

These men of leisure passed most of their lives in the midst of the lowest and most miserable class of Russia, the peasantry, whom until 1861 they owned as fully as any slaveowner. After the reform their absolute power disappeared but their political influence and social superiority remained. Two hundred years of serfdom had created a tradition of ruthless treatment of the peasants—to an extent the reproduction in miniature of the autocratic power of the tsar.

Foreigners visiting Russia before emancipation were aware of a profound contradiction between the relative refinement of the noble way of life and the inhumanity of the serf system. Yet most nobles considered the system a part of the natural order of things, to which one had to become accustomed. The radicals from the nobility who looked back on their childhood remembered with anguish the treatment of the serfs. Mikhail Saltykov looked on his family estate as a "tsardom of fear and physical suffering," where not one harsh detail of life "failed at one time or other to touch me painfully."[12] Yet these authors also recalled their feelings as children of the inevitability of this situation. They assimilated an opinion of the peasantry as "an inferior human species by comparison with themselves, as something like domestic animals, placed by fate under the power of the landlords."[13] When a neighbor of the Korolenko family purchased a young boy, Vladimir Korolenko, then the same age as the serf, felt no sense of outrage. The boy appeared to him merely part of a world filled with people who were young and old, healthy and sick, rich and poor. "All of this seemed to me as old as the ages, . . . simply basic facts, the end product of nature."[14] Condemnation of the injustice of peasant oppression had to come after the revolt against the system of which serfdom was a part. Most nobles never became critics of their own power, nor did their children.

By training and social position, they were expected to command and to provide leadership. Officer schools stressed particularly that the cadets should feel a sense of reverence for authority. This attitude became a mania in the reign of Nicholas I. Even the slightest infringement received a stern response. When the officer in charge of

12. M. Saltykov, *Polnoe sobranie sochineniia* [Complete works, abbrev. PSS] (Moscow, 1933–1941), VII, 147.

13. E. Vodovozova, *Na zare zhizni*, II, 98.

14. V. Korolenko, *Istoriia moego sovremennika* [The history of my contemporary] (Moscow, 1948), p. 45.

a regiment of cadets in one Petersburg military school discovered that he had been the subject of an anonymous satirical verse, he assembled his cadets to explain to them all the true significance of this act. "By insulting me," he declared, "you have insulted the batallion commander, who is higher than me; by insulting the batallion commander, you have insulted the director [of the school]; by insulting the director, you have insulted the minister and by insulting the minister, you have insulted His Highness the Emperor, who named me regimental commander." One of the cadets believed that he and his comrades "grew up in a sort of unconscious fear of power."[15] In their turn, they exercised arbitrary authority over all subordinate to them. Their experience as officers was the direct parallel to that of landowners, for in both cases they were placed in control of men of lower classes. They frequently commanded wife, children, and servants in the same manner.

Their sons by a natural process assimilated the manner and outlook of their fathers. Peter Kropotkin noted that he, "like all young people of my time" brought up in noble families, "entered life with the sincere conviction that it was necessary to command, give orders, reprimand, punish, and the like."[16] The assumption of natural leadership might, as in Kropotkin's case, disappear under the pressure of a totally new view of man and society. But the feeling of confidence and the readiness to take decisive action had deep roots in the minds of the radicals from the nobility, and their effect remained even after the values on which they were based had gone.

Perhaps this predisposition to command was one reason for the high proportion of sons of landowning nobles among the radicals, particularly in the early years. The break with society meant both social ostracism and political persecution. The decision to take this step required great resolve and strength of will. Russia was an authoritarian society in which the monopoly of power was closely guarded and infractions brutally punished. Those who by force of tradition were trained to submit would be less likely to find in themselves the necessary qualities of character than those educated to leadership. Ironically, men who were trained to preserve order and to maintain discipline

15. Nikolai Shelgunov, *Vospominaniia* [Memoirs] (Moscow, 1923), pp. 26, 248–49.

16. P. Kropotkin, *Zapiski revoliutsionnera* [Notes of a revolutionary] (Moscow, 1966), pp. 207–8.

were leading a movement to destroy that order. The government had cause to be disturbed.

Most landowning nobles received only a rudimentary education either from a primary school or at home. Among the officers on active duty in 1861, almost all of whom were from the nobility, only 45 percent had received some education above the primary level.[17] This figure is probably valid for the landowners as a whole. They hardly felt the influence of secular education, but spent years as young men in the army, which became naturally their primary source, next to the family, of values and models of behavior. Higher culture hardly penetrated their lives. The pattern of life unique to the provincial landowning nobility consisted of a search for prestige through state ranks and honors, military discipline, and imitation of Western culture. Its artificiality lessened with the passage of time, but in the reign of Nicholas I was still sufficiently obvious to provide ample material for literary ridicule. Mikhail Saltykov borrowed heavily from his own childhood experiences in his later writings. In one autobiographical work, he remembered the nobles among whom he grew up as creatures of unthinking habit. Local customs and ceremonies "not only did not interest them, but were considered base and demeaning." Religion was "a simple duty." Patriotism consisted in "the execution of orders from the government or simply from their superiors."[18]

Satisfactory in a time of stability, such attitudes were ill-adapted to a period of reform and expanding education. During the quarter century of relative immobility under Nicholas I, nobles could still believe that all was right with their world, but the reign of the "Tsar-Liberator" Alexander II, following the Russian defeat in the Crimean War, unsettled such ideas. For the convinced monarchist, such as the noble father of Lev Tikhomirov, "Nicholas' years" were the best of times. The "new period" of Alexander II, during which his son went off to the university and joined the radical movement, was "somehow in disharmony with his Russian sense of legitimacy [*pravoslavnym chuvstvom*]."[19] The children of such families were poorly prepared to understand and find a place in the new society taking shape about them and to grapple with the complex philosophical and social ques-

17. Cited in Forrest Miller, *Dimitri Miliutin and the Reform Era* (Nashville, Tenn., 1968), p. 95.
18. M. Saltykov, *PSS*, XVII, 347–51.
19. L. Tikhomirov, *Nachala i kontsy* [Beginnings and endings] (Moscow, 1890), p. 37.

tions being debated in the institutions of higher learning. They experienced personally the dichotomy between the noble way of life and the intellectual world of Western culture and education. Tikhomirov resolved the dilemma by joining the radical movement, then later renounced his wild youth and became an archconservative. In his memoirs, he sought public forgiveness for his youthful sins and by implication blamed his father for failing to harden his faith in Russia. A latent intellectual conflict existed between the stagnant cultural life of the provincial nobility and the intellectual ferment of the institutions of higher education. Advanced learning by itself represented a radical change for such young men.

The Ladder of Success

Many of the radicals were children of the Russian cities. The problems of adjustment to life were very different from those of their rural cousins. Almost half of the Petersburg radicals came from the urban noble bureaucracy, merchantry, and petty bureaucracy. The percentage was probably higher, since many from the clergy were brought up in the cities as well. These families belonged to that 10 percent of the Russian population living in an urban or semiurban environment. The cities were still an unusual feature in Russian life. Many had begun as administrative centers for the state, and they varied in size from large cities to small towns. The rise of commerce and industry gradually gave the cities solid foundations in the economic life of the country by offering new occupations to the jobless, and the promise of a better life to the impoverished.

Their appeal was strong to all rural groups. Peasants provided the major source of labor in growing cities. Even former landowning nobles began to arrive from the countryside in large numbers. In the city of Moscow, the size of the noble estate remained stationary in the first half of the nineteenth century. But between 1852 and 1882 it tripled, rising from 18,000 to 54,000, growing at a faster rate than the city as a whole. The influx of nobles was due in large part to the financial crisis of the landowners, to whom the city offered a place of refuge and work. In 1882, ten thousand nobles were working for a salary in the city of Moscow.[20]

Data from the bureaucracy provide the only direct indication of the

20. A. Nifontov, "Formirovanie klassov burzhaznogo obshchestva v russkom gorode" [The formation of classes of bourgeois society in a Russian city], *Istoricheskie zapiski*, LIV (1955), 240–44.

scale of the shift, but do not tell how many nobles moved from the countryside. A study of the origins of the mid-nineteenth-century bureaucracy found that 70 percent of a group of five hundred nobles owning no serfs were serving in the lower ranks and thus could not have earned title in service.[21] Some undoubtedly had inherited their title from fathers also in the bureaucracy. Many others, though, were probably *émigrés* from their family estates forced by financial pressures to begin a new occupation. The father of Nikolai Chaikovski was one such individual. The grandfather had been a small landowner with forty-one male serfs. His four sons could not continue to live on this inheritance. Probably for this reason, Nikolai's father was sent to an elite school for nobles and at the age of eighteen began working in the bureaucracy. Twenty years later, he had reached the middle ranks with an income adequate to support his large family,[22] but a scandal in his department forced him to resign and to take his family to his wife's small estate to scrape together a living once again as a landlord. He could afford to save his honor, though at the cost of abandoning a fairly comfortable life in a provincial city.[23]

Probably other Petersburg radicals came from families of landowning nobles who had transferred into the bureaucracy. The very sparse data I was able to collect indicates that nineteen of the seventy-one noble bureaucrats whose offspring were in the radical movement in the 1860's and 1870's were, like Chaikovski, serving at a rank below that granting entry into the nobility, hence were hereditary nobles. All that can be concluded is that some may well have been among the urban immigrants. Lacking much education, they would probably remain in the petty bureaucracy, but the impoverishment of the landowning nobility left no other choice.

If the nobleman was successful in his career as bureaucrat, he could consider that he had gained rather than lost status as the bureaucracy increased in numbers and importance in the first half of the nineteenth century. Under Alexander I it received an operational structure of ministries which lasted until the fall of the empire. Recruitment into the bureaucratic ranks became regularized, and state service came to appear a comparatively attractive lifelong career. As

---

21. Pintner, "Social Characteristics," p. 442, table 13.
22. TsGIAL, f. 1349, o. 3, d. 2423, ll. 50–51.
23. N. Chaikovski, "Otkrytoe pis'mo" [Open letter], in Titov, ed., *N. G. Chaikovskii*, pp. 275–80.

a result, the great majority of bureaucrats in the mid-nineteenth century were "men who had spent their working lives in that occupation."[24]

By 1850 the bureaucracy possessed unique status in Russian society in terms of economic interests, occupational recruitment, and political power. It encroached more and more on the functions of the landowning nobility in the area of provincial administration, especially after the administrative reforms of the 1860's. In addition, patent to the nobility was still accessible through service, though with greater difficulty after the 1840's. This made state service the easiest path to social advancement, particularly as the size of the bureaucracy was expanding gradually through the years of Nicholas I and Alexander II. The total number of bureaucrats with rank in the early nineteenth century was scarcely over 10,000. By the late 1850's it had increased to over 30,000.[25] This increased chance for promotion, hence ennoblement, was the major reason why in 1845, Nicholas raised from eighth to fifth the rank granting entry to the hereditary nobility (raised to fourth ten years later). His sentimental attachment to the traditional elite still could not prevent the bureaucracy from assuming a preponderant role in the political affairs of the country. The pressures of reform demanded loyal advisers and administrators, as became very apparent during the process of emancipation, which confirmed the displacement of the rural nobility by the upper, noble bureaucracy as the ruling elite of Russia.

The social transformation came without serious difficulty largely because the new elite had so many points in common with the old. At the very top, in such institutions as the Council of State, the two were indistinguishable. Even though personnel below this level were distinct from landowning nobility, their commitment to state service constituted an adaptation of the old noble tradition. The same titles of rank served as awards for loyal service and brought respect and admiration for their owners. In this sense, the expansion of the bureaucracy gave new life to the old system of service. The best known of the radical literary critics of the 1840's, Vissarion Belinski, remarked sarcastically that the "bureaucratic estate serves the purpose in Russia of crucible." Men from the "petty bourgeois, merchant,

---

24. Pintner, "Social Characteristics," pp. 431–32.
25. H.-J. Torke, *Das Russische Beamtentum in das Ersten Halfte das 19 Jahrhunderts* (Berlin, 1967), p. 135.

clerical, and even [landowning] noble estates" who enter its ranks "lose the crude trappings of these estates and, from father to son, are transformed into the estate of lords [*barin*]."[26] The bureaucracy was itself organized on rigid, hierarchical principles easily assimilated by an authoritarian society. Even the personal style of life of the upper bureaucracy tended in many respects to resemble that of the wealthy landowner. One book which discussed the "title of nobility," written in the time of Nicholas I, argued that "a man, having received a good education and occupying a rather important administrative position, has a need for the same type of carriage, with coachdriver and footman as the man who owns 200 or 300 serfs." His social life also included receptions at his city mansion, an adequate wardrobe, and an education for his children "becoming to the title" of nobleman.[27] In sum, he had to play the same sort of social role as the landowning aristocrat.

The status of the lower bureaucracy, particularly in the provinces, was humble by comparison with the Petersburg elite. There was little upward movement from the provinces to the capital, which attracted the well-educated and well-born young men at the very beginning of their careers. Like Akaky Akakievich in Gogol's story *The Overcoat*, humility was the chief virtue of the lower and provincial bureaucrats. That attitude carried one son of a deacon through thirty-five years in the same department of the same provincial city. After four years of primary schooling, Andrei Zlobin started at the age of sixteen as a simple clerk. By the time he reached fifty, he was head bookkeeper, had reached the ninth rank, and had a wife and a wooden house.[28] He had done well through perseverance and patience. His son, less endowed with these qualities, joined the populists.

Zlobin's career illustrates also the tendency of the bureaucracy to reproduce within its ranks the hierarchy of society. Over three-fourths of the top-level officials (ranks one to five) in the central administration were of noble origin. In the lowest ranks, almost three-fourths were nonnoble. A man of modest birth who entered state service was less likely to advance to a middle or high position than a nobleman. In the mid-nineteenth century, 85 percent of the sons of clergymen, petty bureaucrats, and junior officers were serving in the

26. V. Belinski, "Tarantas," *PSS* (Moscow, 1953–1959), IX, 98–99.
27. Quoted in E. P. Sarukhanian, *Dostoevskii v Peterburge* [Dostoevski in St. Petersburg] (Leningrad, 1970), p. 8.
28. TsGIAL, f. 1349, o. 3, d. 859 (1857).

lowest ranks (fourteenth to ninth). Among serfless nobles, 70 percent were in these ranks, but only 47 percent of the nobles with twenty or more serfs were at so humble a level.[29] Power thus was more easily available to the socially respectable than to the lowly. Sofia Perovskaia came from a powerful noble family in the state service. Her grandfather had been a governor of the province of Crimea, where he owned extensive property. Her father rose to become vice-governor, then for a brief period governor of St. Petersburg province, only to be demoted as a result of the Karakozov affair. Such men were at the summit of the social and political hierarchy of Russia. The radicals of Petersburg reproduced within their group a cross section, in terms of power and wealth, of both the landowning nobility and bureaucracy. No single influence in the background of the offspring of the influential and privileged explains their revolt. Yet this group, whose chances to succeed in Russian society were high from birth, provided the large majority of the radicals.

Education became increasingly important in the preparation for a career in the bureaucracy after the state set educational standards for appointment and promotion. According to regulations put into effect in the 1830's, a university graduate could begin service at the fourteenth or even the twelfth rank. Below were only secretarial positions, assigned to those without advanced training. A university degree also guaranteed speedier promotion than the *gymnasium* "certificate of maturity." The effect on personnel qualifications was by mid-century impressive. The single factor which distinguished the top officials from those below them was their level of education. They had the highest percentage of graduates of institutions of higher learning, mainly universities. Attainment of advanced education could help an ambitious bureaucrat regardless of his social origin, type of work, or influence.[30] Encouraged by this incentive and by the expanding possibilities for education, the new recruits possessed higher and higher levels of education as the years passed. By the close of the reign of Nicholas I, one-quarter to one-half of the junior officials in the central administration had received some higher education. "These were the young men on the way up."[31]

Except for law, medicine, and engineering, the subjects taught in

29. Pintner, "Social Characteristics," p. 437, table 9; p. 442, table 13; also, "Change at the Top and the Bottom," pp. 8–11.
30. Pintner, "Social Characteristics," pp. 441, 439, table 11.
31. Pintner, "Change at the Top and the Bottom," p. 9.

the institutions of higher learning stressed abstract intellectual skills and were of little practical use in government. The continued corruption of the bureaucracy proved that education could not create a real service ethic such as existed in Prussia. But nobles began to perceive the value of a diploma. "They saw," in the sarcastic words of the novelist Goncharov, "that people could not make their way in life—that is, acquire rank, orders of merit, and money—except through education." They cared only for its "material advantages" and dimly glimpsed the utility of "something called a diploma," granted after acquiring "not merely a knowledge of reading and writing but of other hitherto unheard-of-subjects."[32] For these very practical reasons, educational ambitions spread through the upper and middle classes.

The educational system created in the reign of Alexander I was intended to be nonclass, but throughout the years of Nicholas I, the state sought methods to restrict the lower classes to the primary level. In addition, the nobility and bureaucracy enjoyed the advantages of social position and at times wealth to ease the difficulties of a rigorous educational program. As a result, the sons of nobles remained the largest single social group in the institutions of higher learning through the 1870's. In Petersburg University, one of the most important institutions for training bureaucrats, the majority of the student body consisted of sons of the nobility and the bureaucracy. This was no democratic revolution for the social advancement of the lower classes. A Petersburg professor searching for the causes of the youth revolt in a report for the tsar in 1866 noted that "a greater desire for education naturally appears among those of poor noble or bureaucratic background than among rich young men, since education is for the former the sole means to provide for their future."[33] Despite the extreme difficulties of succeeding, an increasing number of young men were eager to try. By itself, the force of educational ambition did not lead to social and political revolt. It opened new career perspectives, and it probably provided the most important bond among the students in advanced education. Only in a negative sense did it unsettle traditions, breaking the patterns of social conformity by opening up perspectives of power and prestige.

32. I. Goncharov, *Oblomov*, trans. N. Duddington (New York, 1960), p. 135 (pt. I, ch. 9).
33. P. Zaionchkovski, "Zapiska K. D. Kavelina o nigilisme" [The note by K. D. Kavelin on nihilism], *Istoricheskii arkhiv*, V (1950), 335.

A few Russians by mid-century had actually climbed this "ladder of success." Their numbers were infinitesimal in proportion to the whole Russian population. Among a group of top-level bureaucrats serving in the central administration in the mid-century, almost one-fourth were of nonnoble origin and thus had moved far above their fathers' social position.[34] They could not have numbered in all more than several hundred men.

Outside of the bureaucracy, few professions offered a chance of rapid social advancement. The economy was growing at a slow pace, and the tone of urban life was set primarily by the activities of the petty bourgeoisie. It is particularly surprising, therefore, that a sizable number of the Petersburg radicals came from families that had overcome the obstacles to mobility.

I had great difficulty collecting information on intergenerational mobility for the families in my group. The biographical data on even the upper classes of Russia in the mid-nineteenth century are very incomplete. The sole group for which I could collect a significant amount of material was the bureaucracy. Among the fathers of radicals known to have served the state, thirty-two had advanced significantly above their family origins. The careers of some were extraordinary. Ivan Shamshin, a member of the Land and Liberty party of the early 1860's, was the grandson of a soldier. In the early nineteenth century, military service for conscripts was for twenty-five years, virtually a lifetime. The only advantage to their dismal existence was the right of their children not to be enrolled in the servile estates and occasionally to receive some education. Shamshin's father was one of these fortunate few. Having obtained schooling in a *gymnasium,* he entered state service, first as a schoolteacher, then in the regular bureaucracy. Within twenty years he had reached noble rank. By the age of fifty-five, he was a high-level councilor in the State Controller's department.[35] His son entered the Alexandrovsky Lycée, a school reserved for nobles' sons which virtually guaranteed its graduates a brilliant career in the bureaucracy.

The chances for a successful career were particularly good for the new group of professionals. Their numbers increased slowly until mid-century, and the range of occupations widened only gradually as

34. Pintner, "Social Characteristics," p. 437, table 9.
35. TsGIAL, f. 1349, o. 6, d. 314.

new demands appeared.[36] Those able to obtain the necessary training in one of these specialized fields could anticipate rapid advancement in service. One case was the father of Sergei Kravchinski. His service record noted that he was from the petty bourgeoisie, had graduated from medical school at the age of twenty, and had two decades later earned noble rank as an army surgeon.[37] The father of Mikhail Petrashevski followed a similar career. The father of Peter Tkachev made his way up from merchant background to nobility as an architect. The educational system also offered an expanding number of important posts. The most famous success story in this profession, one which goes slightly beyond the limits of my study, was that of Il'ia Ulianov. His father was a poor tailor, but he obtained a university education. He began to work as a teacher, then became a district school inspector for the newly expanded primary school system and rose sufficiently high in the bureaucratic hierarchy by the 1870's to become a nobleman. One of his sons, Alexander, was hung in 1887 for plotting against the tsar's life; the other was Vladimir Lenin.

In all, I found 44 instances of upward mobility out of the total of 115 families for whom information was available. There were only 8 cases of downward mobility. It is hazardous to generalize on the basis of data for only one-fourth of my sample, but if my material is reliable, career success had an important role in the family origins of the radicals. As indicated above, these fathers had good reason to encourage their sons to receive an advanced education. Their goal was occupational training, however, not radical revolt. Their own attitudes toward the social and political order of Russia may well have reflected very traditional values.

They could have been archconservatives, if the theories of contemporary sociologists have any validity for nineteenth-century Russian society.[38] One of the provincial governors seems to have agreed with this view. In a report submitted in the late 1850's on attitudes toward emancipation, he affirmed that the "most stubborn and harmful defenders of the old system" of serfdom were the landowners who

36. See Leikina-Svirskaia, *Intelligentsiia*, pp. 50–70, 107–147.
37. TsGIAL, f. 1343, o. 23, d. 8246.
38. See Seymour Lipset and Reinhard Bendix, *Social Mobility in Industrial Society* (Berkeley, Calif., 1964), pp. 61–68; J. Greenblum and L. Pearlin, "Vertical Mobility and Prejudice," in R. Bendix and S. Lipset, eds., *Class, Status and Power* (Glencoe, Ill., 1953), p. 491.

had acquired their wealth in state service.[39] Fedor Dostoevski could probably have spoken from personal experience of such attitudes, had he cared to describe the social and political outlook of his father. Mikhail Dostoevski, himself the son of a village priest, had made his career as a surgeon, after running away from home. He earned the title of hereditary noble and used his new privileges to purchase a small estate and serfs. As a father, he stressed religion and patriotic Russian history. As a serfowner, he exploited his arbitrary power beyond the limits of his peasants' tolerance—they murdered him. His life in later years was in some ways a caricature of that of the Russian gentry, of whom he was a new member.

His son played a similar role. In a school with nobles, he aped their ways and clothes. He wrote his father that "willy-nilly I must conform to the rules of my current circle. Why make an exception of myself? Such exceptions lead sometimes to horrible unpleasantness."[40] His attitude suggests a feeling of social insecurity as the son of a *parvenu* noble. Such a personality could easily shift from conformity to revolt. Within a few years, Dostoevski had written *Poor Folk* and had turned to utopian socialism. His case points to the possible influence of the fathers' upward social mobility on the process of alienation of the sons. There is a sufficiently large group of radicals from similar families to justify a close examination of the issue.[41] Unfortunately, there is at present no way to study a large sample of socially mobile families for comparison with fathers of radicals. Such families probably were attracted to the benefits of education, more so perhaps than any other group in Russian society. Their offspring may have been more inclined to nonconformity than those of parents whose social position was established over several generations. This predisposition was not likely to appear before entry into educational institutions. Once again, the only common factor in the background of the radicals appears to have been the incentive to schooling.

39. Quoted in D. Gutman, "Studencheskoe dvizhenie v Kazanskom universitete" [The student movement in Kazan University] (Candidate's dissertation, Kazan State University, 1955), p. 65.

40. Quoted in Sarukhanian, *Dostoevskii*, p. 24.

41. I discussed the problem of families of radicals in the 1840's and 1850's in an earlier article ("Fathers, Sons, and Grandfathers," *Journal of Social History*, II [Summer 1969], 333–55.)

The *Raznochintsy*

This factor appears most clearly in the lives of the radicals from the middle and especially lower classes. Their numbers were relatively small in the mid-nineteenth century precisely because so few young people from the nonprivileged strata of society could enter the world of advanced learning. Estates such as the petty bourgeoisie or the clergy were still closed groups in which ambition was restricted by custom and poverty. The physical perils of life hit them hardest, for death was common at an early age from accident or disease. Educational opportunities were very limited, and where they existed only provided necessary skills for work. The obstacles gradually eased after the 1850's, primarily because of the increased accessibility of schooling. This new situation is reflected in the gradual increase of middle- and lower-class youth among the Petersburg radicals (40 percent in the 1870's). But there were never enough of them in those years to give real leadership to the radical movement. The "arrival of the *raznochintsy*," so loudly proclaimed by some writers, was a myth, reflecting wishful thinking by those who saw no hope for the revolutionary cause as long as nobles dominated the movement. Peter Tkachev longed for the day when he would be supported by men from "another class of people, . . . something intermediate between the solidly secure estate and the completely insecure estate."[42] Soviet historians later adopted the idea of the rise of the *raznochintsy* to show the roots of the radical movement in the deepening class antagonisms of Russian society, but the argument fails for lack of the most rudimentary evidence.

The sons of the clergy attracted most attention as the new generation of radicals in the reign of Alexander II. Their numbers were actually small, though growing steadily from the 1840's to the 1870's. The writers Chernyshevski and Dobroliubov typify the young generation as opposed to the old. Their diaries are precious records of their upbringing, probably similar to that of most sons of priests, in families of modest means and above average culture. Dobroliubov looked back with disgust to his past as "son of a priest, brought up in the strict rules of Christian faith and morality, . . . living the first years of my life in close contact with the lower and middle classes."[43] Yet

---

42. Quoted in Pollard, "Consciousness and Crisis," p. 124.
43. Dobroliubov, *Dnevnik,* p. 104.

he once rendered grudging public homage to the "code of morality" he had received "at home and from all around me." "Be content with what you have," he heard, "and desire no more." The reward for patience and obedience was "public admiration." Men could never attain "complete happiness on earth," but should be content with life in "well-organized states, of which the finest is my native land."[44] This moral instruction seems to have possessed Dobroliubov entirely during his early youth. Only after the death of both his parents, a tragedy which touched him deeply, did he reject entirely this upbringing.

Protection and submission were two sides to the life of the secular priests. Clerical families were directly supervised by the church since the clergy formed a special estate. Bishops arranged marriages between widows or daughters of parish priests and their successors. The son of a priest had difficulty entering another estate or even obtaining a secular education. In theory, his career was service to the church. In the 1860's these restrictions were eased, making it possible for a much larger proportion than before of priests' sons to appear in the institutions of higher education in St. Petersburg.

The church was sensitive to the need to improve the quality of its clergy. It had long recognized the necessity for learning, but not until the late eighteenth century did it create an adequate primary and secondary system of church schools. By 1850 there were forty-seven seminaries, secondary schools for priests' sons providing religious training for the priesthood. Many graduates found employment outside their estate. The chances to rise above their class and leave their province by means of higher education were improved if the father was already a "learned" priest. One such was a young radical of the 1870's, Alexander Pribylev. His father had progressed as far as the Orthodox Academy of Kazan before lack of funds forced him to abandon his studies and begin work, first as a teacher in a church school, then as a priest. He pushed his son's education by tutoring, provided him with a wide choice of secular literature, then allowed him to enter the state *gymnasium* rather than the seminary.[45] The old patterns of upbringing were gradually disappearing, opening new careers and raising expectations of the previously meek clergy. When

44. N. Dobroliubov, *PSS* (Moscow, 1934), II, 232–33.
45. A. Pribylev, "Avtobiografiia," *Entsiklopedicheskii slovar' Granata* (Moscow, 1927), XL, 344–51.

Alexander Herzen saw some of their sons in Moscow University in the 1830's, he shuddered. "Brought up under the yoke of monastic despotism, oppressed by their rhetoric and theology," these "unhappy seminary students" depressed him by their "Christian humility."[46] By the 1860's, a few of them had forsaken this heritage of their fathers to participate in the radical movement.

The families of radicals from the other nonprivileged estates of Russian society left few traces of their life and traditions. The state and church kept only sporadic records of their activities. They provided a subject for others to explore, but only rarely left written accounts of their own. Most were illiterate. Even those offspring who joined the radicals were little disposed to write of their childhood and upbringing. They appeared in the movement in fairly small numbers, though a few stood out sharply by their strength of character and commitment.

The most unusual contingent of radicals from the lower classes were the Jews. They came from a religious community that still maintained its social integrity and isolation from the Gentiles. Their everyday language, Yiddish, and their language of worship, Hebrew, were both unique within Russia. Their dress, traditions, and occupations together formed a way of life distinct from any other religious or national community of the empire. The government had adopted an ambiguous attitude toward this group. Acceptance of the Jewish religion was part of the program of tolerance preached by the Enlightenment, whose principles both Catherine II and Alexander I professed to respect. But suspicion of the Jews was strong, and their rights were strictly limited. The government did not allow the Jews permanent residency outside White Russia and the Ukraine, a region designated as the Pale of Settlement. This measure restricted their geographical mobility and symbolized their social and cultural isolation in the first half of the nineteenth century. Living mainly in small settlements and towns and eking out a livelihood as small traders and artisans, most of them experienced a life of abject poverty.

It was thus remarkable to find young Jews active among and at times leading groups of Russian radicals. I found nine among the Petersburg radicals of the 1860's and 1870's. Though not numerous,

---

46. A. Gertsen, *Byloe i dumy* [My past and thoughts] (Moscow, 1962), I, 110.

they attracted special attention. The latent anti-Semitism of the Orthodox population came to the surface at the sight of young people from
this suspect religion among the nihilists. Radicalism and Jewishness
were clearly associated in the minds of the Russians when the assassination of Alexander II provoked the first massive anti-Jewish po-
groms of the nineteenth century. This reaction in fact misconstrued
the nature of the Jewish radical protest. Their dissent against the
established order in Russia came not in opposition to, but through,
Russian secular culture and against their own community's cultural
and social way of life. They had already abandoned the religious and
educational traditions which had for centuries united and protected
the Eastern European Jewish population.

Nicholas I had strongly opposed the presence of this alien population within his empire. He forcibly expelled Jews from certain border
areas around the Pale and instituted a program designed to encourage
the conversion of Jews to the Russian Orthodox faith. The Jewish
reaction was fear and hostility to any Russian educational programs.
Despite some efforts by the Ministry of Education to encourage Jews
to receive Russian schooling, the impact of the state's educational
system on them was negligible. "The whole Russian Jewish community continued to live its secluded life, and whatever influence of an
alien culture was felt came more from the Germans than from the
Russians."[47]

Almost all of the Jewish radicals came from the Yiddish-speaking
community directly through the Russian educational system and had
assimilated Russian culture. The old suspicion of subversion of the
Jewish religion by the Russian state disappeared with the "thaw"
that followed Alexander II's accession to the throne. The first Rus-
sian-language Jewish magazine appeared in 1860. Its editors proclaimed that "our native land is Russia" and "her language should be
ours." They attacked the Yiddish tongue as "a chaotic dialect unfit
to be called a language."[48] This attitude did not imply a rejection
of the Jewish faith, but was a direct challenge to the exclusiveness
and narrowness of the traditional way of life of the Russian Jewish
community. Its supporters were men like V. Aptekman, whose son
remembered that he stood out in their Ukrainian Jewish community

47. S. Pozner, *Evrei v obshchei shkole* [Jews in the public schools] (St.
Petersburg, 1914), p. 35.
48. *Ibid.*, pp. 36–37.

by his "firm renunciation of Jewish discrimination and intolerance."
He was "one of the pioneers of Russian education among Jews in
our town" and was "the first to introduce the Russian language into
our family."[49] In practical terms, an advanced Russian education
meant the possibility of escape from the abysmal poverty in which
many Jewish families lived—an extraordinary stroke of good fortune.
If a son lost this prospect it was a terrible disaster. After a Jewish
student in the Medical-Surgical Academy was expelled in 1874 for
participation in the student disturbance that year, his father sent a
letter to the minister of the interior begging for his son's readmission.
"I am a poor man," he wrote, "without any capital or property and
completely at the mercy of the future, for I depend [for my livelihood]
on my work in the offices of the sugar factory." He had worked for
forty years and had spent his "very last savings for the education of
my son, in whom I saw my sole support and hope." The young man's
expulsion from the academy confronted the family with a "pitiful
and horrible future."[50]

The expectation of rising through education spread among families
in the Russian urban classes as well. No first-hand sources exist to
confirm this impression, but the reaction of one artisan to his son's
abandonment of schooling indicated strong feelings. He had sent his
son to the Medical-Surgical Academy, the finest medical school in the
country. He received "modest wages" but, according to the local
officer of the Gendarmerie, "enjoyed a very high reputation" in his
central Russian town. When his son quit his studies and returned
home in the spring of 1874 to participate in the "to the people"
movement, "his father gave him a beating, since this did not please
him."[51] The son disappeared from town and was not seen again. Intellectual protest was a luxury such families could ill afford or tolerate.

Entry into the secondary or higher educational system was difficult
for people from these classes. Their families could offer no aid in
their preparation for rigorous intellectual studies. The schools were
frequently in distant towns; the fathers could not furnish the required
funds for food and lodging. Some students had to support their fam-

49. O. Aptekman, "Avtobiografiia," *Entsiklopedicheskii slovar' Granata*
(Moscow, 1927), XL, 648.
50. TsGIAL, f. 1282, o. 1, d. 339, ll. 287–88.
51. TsGAOR, f. 109, tr. eks., d. 144 (1874), ch. 1, l. 3.

ilies on the small stipends they occasionally obtained for their studies. The most extraordinary story from those years of the struggle for education was that of Sergei Nechaev. His father was from the petty bourgeoisie and worked at various times as housepainter and waiter in the textile center of Ivanovo, northeast of Moscow. Nechaev later made much of his lower-class origins. In an *émigré* paper he referred to people of his background as "children of starving fathers oppressed by privation, . . . raised in the midst of filth and ignorance, . . . for whom the family was the gateway to penal labor, for whom the best years of our youth were spent in a struggle with poverty and hunger."[52] This may have been true for others, but not for Nechaev himself.

He had begun working at an early age as a waiter, like his father, then as a clerk in a factory. He had a few years of elementary education, which was all most children of his class received. Somehow, perhaps through the influence of a few educated friends, he determined to acquire a higher education. Letters written when he was sixteen and seventeen years old show him struggling to learn French and German, Russian history and literature, geography, rhetoric, and more still. He was attempting to learn the entire *gymnasium* program of studies in the hope of passing the final examination and entering Moscow University. These plans were incredibly ambitious for a youth in his situation. He wrote plaintively to a friend that "in Ivanovo it is very hard to study alone without assistance, especially mathematics."[53] He continually begged for books from Moscow, promising to pay promptly. At the age of seventeen, he finally decided to go to Moscow to try to gain admission to the university. His father was not opposed to these plans, according to Sergei's sister, though he had to support his son completely in those years. He gave Sergei both money and new clothes before the departure for Moscow.[54]

Nechaev resented his dependence and suspected his family of despising him for his idleness. He wrote in the letter quoted above

52. Cited in B. Koz'min and B. Gor'ev, eds., *Revoliutsionnoe dvizhenie 1860-kh godov* [The revolutionary movement of the 1860's] (Moscow, 1932), p. 222.

53. N. Bel'chikov, "S. G. Nechaev," *Katorga i ssylka*, No. 14 (1925), 151; this article includes the complete copies of the letters.

54. *Ibid.*, p. 154.

that his reliance on their aid was "for me very regretable," since it seemed to him that "in my family I am regarded as a drone."[55] His aspirations far exceeded anything his family had ever attempted. It is not surprising that he should have felt hypersensitive in his relations with them. He was very fortunate to enjoy the support, or at least tolerance, of his father, but still was resentful, undoubtedly heightened by the extreme difficulties of the dream he was pursuing. In fact, he never was able to enter Moscow University. A year after leaving home, he was in St. Petersburg working as a teacher in a church-run primary school. He had passed the state teaching examination, but the climb up from his lower-class origins had fallen far short of his goal. He was a man of energy and ambition. The physical description given later by the police mentioned his "sharp, animated eyes, . . . high-pitched voice, awkward and impetuous movements."[56] But his dynamism was stifled and his expectations frustrated. His letters do not suggest that he saw education as the path to lucrative work or to social advancement. He seems to have been lured by student life and the temple of learning, the university.

Thus education brought tensions as well as hope to those few lower-class Russians who even dared aspire to advanced schooling. Nechaev could have spent his life as a waiter or clerk, unhappy but resigned, had it not been for the attraction of learning. His first revolt was not directed against the class system of Russia, but against the humble and ignorant environment in which he was raised. Another man who sought to receive higher education but suffered from frustrated ambitions was I. Myshkin, one of the populists in the famous trial of the "193 propagandists." The son of a soldier, he spent three years in a new military school. In a bitter statement to the examining magistrate before his trial, he outlined why he felt his life had led him to total struggle against the old order. He had been an excellent pupil in the school, where he had first thought of becoming a teacher as the "means for personal struggle." This required further education, but the path was blocked by his lowly origins. Unable to enter a military *gymnasium,* he attempted to complete studies in a military normal school. He was "ready to reconcile myself to my fate" and accept work as a poorly paid primary school teacher; his

55. *Ibid.,* p. 151.
56. TsGIAL, f. 1282, o. 1, d. 292 (1869), l. 2.

activities would be "useful to that class of people like ourselves." His "sole thought" was to be "useful to others, to live and to work for the people." To improve his poor education, he even began a special program of reading in addition to classwork. Then a ruling came from the War Ministry excluding lower-class children from these teacher-training classes for military schools, and "that dream was destroyed." He was the best student in his class, felt "absolutely no distinction" between himself and the sons of noblemen, only to be thrown back on his humble origins. "One had to see how many bitter tears were shed by us, the poor students, to understand what anger and hatred we felt."[57] The class hierarchy of his society stood in the way of his dream of a teaching career open to all, like himself, with talent. His revolt represented social protest of a special sort.

The profile of the class origins of the Petersburg radicals justifies classifying their families among the elite of the empire. The poor such as Nechaev and Myshkin were the exceptions. The class providing the personnel to run the political and military affairs of the country was also producing the cadres of the revolutionary counterelite. There was logic to this ironical situation only in that a noble upbringing was more likely, by virtue of its training in leadership, to develop the qualities necessary for the first recruits in the radical movement than was the education of the nonprivileged families. The landowning nobility was experiencing the disruptive effects of its own economic decline and of the increasing power of the state bureaucracy. Yet this potential conflict had no direct impact on the radical revolt. Some landowning nobles were in fact attempting to cope with the crisis by seeking positions for their sons in the bureaucracy.

Education was indispensable for such plans, just as it fitted in with the career expectations of men already in the bureaucracy and of any socially mobile family. It stands out as the single factor that touched the widest range radicals, from the countryside and cities, from wealthy nobility to poor clergy. There is, however, no reason to suppose that the educational aspirations of the families of radicals differed from those of families in which the offspring actually pursued the careers for which schooling prepared them. The social profile of the families of the radicals deviates in no striking manner from what

57. "Zaiavlenie I. Myshkina" [The statement of I. Myshkin], *Revoliutsionnoe narodnichestvo*, I, 183–85.

one might expect of students in mid-century Russia. The hypothesis suggested at the beginning of the chapter appears correct, but this merely shifts the problem of the recruitment of the radicals from the family environment to the schools. Somehow, some of those young people were divested of the special loyalties and attitudes of their disparate social classes to become members of the radical community. In those years, social traditions and old patterns of behavior disappeared. Alexander Herzen interpreted in poetic language the potentially overwhelming impact of higher education when he wrote that "teachers, books, and the university said one thing, and [our] heart and mind understood it. [Our] fathers and mothers, relatives and social peers said something else, with which neither [our] heart nor mind could agree."[58] The roots of radical revolt lay in the educational experiences of the student youth of the country.

58. Gertsen, *Byloe i dumy,* I, 367.

3 | Education of the Elite

Secular schools came to Russia relatively late. Prior to the reign of Peter the Great, education was primarily an affair of the Orthodox church. It served the liturgical needs of the church and benefited above all those charged with defending and preserving the faith. Peter attempted to create educational institutions for secular learning, as was his custom, by decree, over the opposition of a population who regarded schools as alien and harmful. The curriculum came straight from Western Europe and emphasized practical knowledge of immediate use to the state such as artillery and navigation. Within one hundred years, the state had developed a network of secondary and advanced educational institutions. The pattern set by Peter remained —Russian education depended on Western learning and pedagogy and on the needs and good will of the Russian state.

Russia's rulers paid public homage to the ideals of the Enlightenment. Catherine the Great promised that her Statutes for Public Schools of 1784, modeled on the Austrian school system, would "enlighten the mind" and "purify the soul."[1] Alexander I's modified educational plan of 1803 put the schools under the control of the new Ministry of Popular Enlightenment, a grandiloquent title suited to the style of the time but not to the actual operations of the ministry. The universities enjoyed some authority over their own affairs, but the professors held official bureaucratic rank, an honor implying continued dependence. The graduates found positions in the state administration. The Education Act of 1809 required that all bureaucrats of middle rank or above receive the equivalent of a university educa-

1. Quoted in William Johnson, *Russia's Educational Heritage* (New York, 1969), p. 50.

tion. The requirement later was dropped, but the hope that education would somehow improve the abysmal quality of state service remained so the state could assure the proper functioning of its vast bureaucratic system, staffed by men lacking real unity of outlook. Education was to provide the basis for competence and cooperation among the state servants, instilling in them a service ethic.[2]

The educational advisers of Alexander I had pointed out in an official report that the men running the private schools in the late eighteenth and early nineteenth centuries were frequently foreigners "unacquainted with our language which they scorn and unattached to our country which for them is alien." They naturally misused their positions of intellectual authority to "spread scorn for our language and encourage disregard for our customs [*vsemu domashnemu*]." The young Russian students were "transformed into foreigners."[3] Alexander's state-run school system stressed patriotism and national loyalty. It took on as well the task of instilling in upper-class Russians an active sense of civic responsibility. A Moscow University professor, speaking in 1842, alluded discreetly to the "failings and shortcomings quite common in the family environment" which apparently neglected the values of "duty, necessity, and social obligation." Fortunately, however, the schools could compensate for the cultural inadequacy of the family, thereby bringing "into unity and conformity the great variety of private backgrounds and attitudes" of Russian society.[4]

The minister of education had primary responsibility for elaborating this distinctly Russian education. Nicolas Uvarov, minister under Nicholas I, made the most concerted effort in his policy of "Official Nationality." Uvarov frankly spoke of his program as a weapon in the struggle against intellectual subversion by Western values. In his report for the year 1837 he declared that the "highest goal" of his ministry was "to remove the antagonism" which existed between "European education" and "our needs." He would base "secular education

---

2. This is the implication of a comparative study of the patterns of service of French and Russian provincial administrators (John Armstrong, "Old Regime Governors: Bureaucratic and Patrimonial Attributes," *Comparative Studies in Society and History*, XIV [Jan. 1972], 2–27).

3. Quoted in I. Aleshintsev, "Soslovnyi vopros i politika" [The estate question and politics], *Russkaia shkola*, Jan. 1908, pp. 14–15.

4. Quoted in N. Riasanovsky, *Nicholas I and Official Nationality in Russia, 1825–55*, (Los Angeles, 1959), p. 93.

and the awakened forces" of the country on one "standard," the "triple concepts of Orthodoxy, Autocracy, and Nationality."[5]

Uvarov's ambitious program disappeared when Alexander II supported expansion of the whole educational system. The Crimean War forced the tsar to recognize the military superiority of the Western powers, whose economic and social organization was distinguished by a comparatively high level of education. The self-assurance of "Official Nationality" seemed out of place. The new minister of education traveled around the country repeating the message that "learning [*nauka*] has always been for us one of the most important needs, *but now it is the first*. If our enemies possess a superiority over us, it is solely by virtue of knowledge."[6] He did not mean abstract rational pursuits, but the needs of the state. A few years later, when the state leaders became aware that the learning they were encouraging led to dissent and revolt, they reverted to the old pattern of rigid controls over the substance and organization of education. Alexander stressed this fundamental rule in his instructions to the new minister of education following Karakozov's attempt on his life in 1866. He expressed the wish that education "be conducted in the spirit of religious truth, respect for the rights of property, and observance of the basic principles of public order."[7]

The schools were protected from subversive Western ideas by controls on curriculum and on publication and importation of books. Their organization and system of honors followed the same type of hierarchical subordination as did the bureaucracy. The students found there a far more rigid and structured life than with their families. Though Uvarov's program did not endure, the Ministry of Education continued to stress religion and loyalty to the state.

Despite the emphasis on nationalism, Russian educational policy was strongly influenced by the Prussian model, in which the "initia-

5. Quoted in V. Charnoluski, "Narodnoe obrazovanie" [Public education], *Istoriia Rossii v XIX veke* (St. Petersburg, 1909), IV, 101.

6. Quoted in K. Timeriazev, "Probuzhdenie estestvoznaniia" [The awakening of scientific studies], *Istoriia Rossii v XIX veke*, VII, 2. The word *nauka*, often mistranslated "science," actually conveys the sense of all knowledge which is clearly and rationally understood. It is much closer to the German *Wissenschaft* than to "science," which in contemporary English and French designates only the natural sciences.

7. Quoted in M. Kovalevski, "Srednaia shkola" [Secondary schools], *Istoriia Rossii v XIX veke*, VII, 170.

tive of the bureaucracy" protected the universities from outside pressures while allowing them to develop one of the finest systems of higher education in the West.[8] There had been trouble in these schools in 1848, but these youthful revolutionary illusions seemed dead by the late 1850's. The Prussian educational system, operating within an authoritarian society, produced no large-scale revolt. In Russia the situation was different.

Evidence for the malfunctioning of the institutions of learning appeared in numerous reports of the secret police. A statistical report covering the period 1873–1877 revealed that a majority of those convicted of political crimes belonged to the country's "student youth." The same findings appeared in a study covering the period 1873–1879 and including a much larger number of people.[9] Data on the educational experience of these criminals made the problem seem even more disturbing—they had passed through some of the finest educational institutions of the country.

The single largest group of convicted political criminals with secondary or higher education came from the Petersburg Medical-Surgical Academy. Other institutions contributing large numbers of radicals were the Technological Institute, the Petrovsky Agronomy Academy, and Petersburg University. In the group of Petersburg radicals whom I studied (see Table 1, p. 37), the university led in numbers until the 1870's, when it was eclipsed by the Medical-Surgical Academy and the Technological Institute. These institutions represented the best Russia could offer in higher education, offered to the country's best students. Most radicals had thus been part of the elite student group of the empire, having advanced beyond the secondary schools into these elevated spheres of learning. It seemed as though the very excellence of education stimulated radical dissent.

The quality of the radicals' previous formal training was equally high. The majority had received the most difficult secondary training offered by the state, that of the *gymnasia*. I could obtain information on this question for only 295 of the total group. Of these, the *gymnasia* had trained over one-half (156, including the 9 who went no

---

8. See Fritz Ringer, *The Decline of the Mandarins: The German Academic Community, 1890–1933* (Cambridge, Mass., 1969), pp. 14–42.

9. N. Sidorov, "Statisticheskie svedeniia o propagandistakh" [Statistical information on the propagandists], *Katorga i ssylka*, No. 38 (1928), 32; Itenberg, *Dvizhenie*, p. 376, table II.

further with their education). Another 22, all from the period of the 1840's through the 1860's, had received their secondary schooling at the elite Alexandrovsky Lycée in St. Petersburg (located until 1844 in Tsarskoe Selo, just outside the city), whose program included the equivalent of the first years of university training. The religious seminaries had turned out only 26 individuals (almost all during the 1860's and 1870's), less even than came from the military schools (52 in all). The educational pattern followed by the radicals was the *gymnasium* and then professional school or university, the very path laid out to prepare the educated leadership of the country. The system of state schooling was functioning in a bizarre manner, one not at all to the taste of the country's leaders.

Schools for the Elite

From the time of Peter the Great, state educational policy had favored a small number of elite schools rather than elementary education for the rural and urban lower classes. Russia had an Academy of Sciences before a university, and this preceded a secondary school system. The reason was partly for prestige, since the higher institutions promised greater glory to Russian learning than the others, and partly practical considerations of economy of investment. The cost of educating a student in a university or professional school was high, but upon graduation he could begin a career in state service. The return was immediate and—in theory—appreciable. Elementary education, on the other hand, was of little evident benefit to the state and might actually stir up trouble by giving inferiors an exaggerated sense of their importance.

This attitude gradually gave way to a more generous—and in the long run realistic—policy of allowing the lower classes educational opportunities. Alexander I viewed his school system as open to all classes. Nicholas I reverted to a restrictive policy of limiting education by class origins. In Uvarov's elegant language, a proper system of public education should "offer opportunities to each one to receive that education which would correspond to his mode of life and to his future calling in society." Obviously, "the difference in the needs of the different estates and conditions of people leads inevitably to an appropriate delimitation among them of the subjects of study."[10] The total number of pupils grew by 40 percent between 1834 and 1856,

10. Quoted in Riasanovsky, *Nicholas I*, p. 141.

when 450,000 were enrolled in Russian schools. The benefits went mainly to the urban population, which accounted for two-thirds of the 1856 total. Only in two Baltic provinces and in Petersburg province did the number of pupils exceed 2 percent of the population.[11] Since these areas were also the most highly urbanized of the empire, the effects of education were extremely limited within the total population.

The state's educational responsibilities were divided among several agencies and ministries. In 1834 the Ministry of Education was responsible for only one-third of the pupils in the country, the Orthodox Church for another 23 percent, and the War Ministry slightly over 20 percent. The proportions changed later in favor of the Ministry of Education, but it never eliminated its rivals. There was thus considerable diversity within the system.

The Orthodox Church trained its own clergy. Until the 1860's the priesthood was a closed estate. The sons of priests provided the new recruits, daughters frequently married within the estate, and transfer to another estate required special permission. In the 1860's priests' children were freed to leave their estate. Religious education at the primary level included children of other classes and was the only one judged fit for the lower classes in the reign of Nicholas I. As in Prussia, the state preferred church-controlled primary education because it would "spread and confirm good character in the rising generation and . . . order and obedience—this . . . necessary moral discipline in social and family life."[12] Above the primary level religious training was only for the sons of clergy. The secondary schools, called seminaries, gave a general and superficial training in the humanities, followed by specialized instruction in religious subjects. After reforms in 1867, the program improved substantially, becoming very similar to the first four years of *gymnasium* studies with expanded training in science and mathematics. More and better qualified teachers were required. These schools never rivaled the *gymnasia* in quality or prestige, and because they did not accept children from

11. A. Rashin, "Gramotnost' " [Literacy], *Istoricheskie zapiski,* XXXVII (1951), 55–7; see also Arcadius Kahan, "Social Structure, Public Policy, and the Development of Education in Czarist Russia," in C. Anderson and M. Bowman, *Education and Economic Development* (Chicago, 1965), pp. 363–66.

12. "Obozrenie upravleniia Gosudarstvennykh imushchestv" [Survey of the administration of state domains], *Sbornik imperatorskogo russkogo istoricheskogo obshchestva,* XCVIII (1896), 481.

other estates, they did not influence the intellectual life of the country as the Jesuit schools, for example, continued to do in France. They did not train a large number of students, for the size of the clergy was not increasing. Between 1834 and 1878, the number of seminaries increased from 41 to 53, but the total student body declined slightly from 13,400 to 12,900.[13] Compared with the military or secular schools, the church schools occupied a relatively small place in the educational life of the country. Religious conformity was expected of all Russian subjects. Instruction in the Orthodox faith was required in all the educational institutions of the Russian parts of the empire, but there was no active religious life in the schools. The educational vocation of the church was restricted to the utilitarian function of training future clergy.

The military schools were concerned with the needs of the army, so were as specialized as the seminaries. Before the reforms of 1874, the soldiers in the Russian army were recruited from the lower, servile estate for a period of time equivalent to life service. Most of the officers were nobles though many nonnobles became officers through in-service advancement. The schools of the War Ministry catered to two separate social groups and occupational needs. The "cantonist schools," for the offspring of the soldiers, did little more than teach the basic skills of reading, writing, and arithmetic and were not meant to be the first level of an educational ladder leading into the officer corps. The schools for officers were restricted until the 1860's to the sons of nobles. There were twenty "cadet schools" and two technical schools, the engineering and artillery institutes in St. Petersburg. In addition, the elite regiments and officers attached to the imperial court had their own schools, such as the Corps of Pages where Peter Kropotkin received his education. The cadet schools, graduating yearly about five hundred, furnished the bulk of the trained officers for the army. A few went on to receive advanced education in the specialized institutions run by the War Ministry, chief among which were the War Academy and the Mikhailovsky Artillery Institute.

The total educational impact of the War Ministry was very strong under Nicholas I, who transferred a number of civilian institutions to military control. Generals appeared as school administrators. The civilian director left the Alexandrovsky Lycée to be replaced by a

13. Leikina-Svirskaia, *Intelligentsiia*, pp. 101–4.

Baltic German, General Golt'gner. His major task was to remove the liberal influences left behind by those Decembrists who were graduates of the school. Absolute obedience to the emperor constituted the very core of the military code of these schools. In 1834 the War Ministry had 22,000 elementary pupils and 33,000 students in its secondary and advanced institutions.[14]

The reforms of Alexander II tended to remove the military imprint from education by transferring a number of professional schools back to civilian control. His minister of war, Dimitri Miliutin, sought to raise the educational level of the whole army, soldiers as well as officers. He undertook a program to teach reading and writing to all army recruits—the first massive literacy drive in Russia. In 1863 he began to transform the cadet schools into military *gymnasia* with a program quite similar to the regular *gymnasia* and of the same quality. By 1880 there were eighteen military *gymnasia* with over 8,000 pupils, including nonnobles.[15]

The development of the professional schools directly reflected the changes in the Russian economy and the rise of new occupational needs. Many professional schools originally were part of the military educational system. Their graduates were needed by the army. The growth of artillery, for example, demanded a large armaments industry, which depended on the Ural mines. The Institute of Mining Engineers, founded in 1773 under military control, was the first technical school. The urgent need for army doctors led to the establishment of the Medical-Surgical Institute in 1783, which was made an academy in 1799 and put under the supervision of the Ministry of War in 1838. Maintenance of the system of roads and waterways became the responsibility of a special corps of engineers, trained in the Institute of the Corps of Transportation Engineers, also administered as a military school.

The rising pressure of economic growth and the increasing complexity of government operations together produced a sudden increase in the number of such schools. The administration of the vast plots of state land, mainly forests, became a specialized occupation with the founding of the Forestry and Survey Institute in 1811. The Ministry of Finances prepared specialists in mechanical and chemical

14. Rashin, "Gramotnost'," p. 15.
15. Leikina-Svirskaia, *Intelligentsiia*, pp. 92–5.

engineering after creation of the Practical Technological Institute in 1828. The need for legal specialists led the Ministry of Justice to open a special school of law in 1835, shortly after the completion of the monumental code of Russian law. The reign of Nicholas I saw also the founding of an institute for civil engineers and architects and an agronomy school, transformed into an advanced institute of agronomy in 1864. The reforms of the 1860's touched many of these institutions mainly by emancipating them from military control. They became institutions of higher education offering advanced instruction to a much larger number of students than before. During the reign of Alexander II technical education finally appeared as a necessary and important aspect of the educational efforts of the state in response to the needs of the economy and society as well as to its own interests. The students who flooded into these institutes in the 1860's and 1870's were interested in social and economic development, but many came to understand the character and direction of that development very differently than did the state.

The Medical-Surgical Academy was by all reports the single most important center of radical agitation in those years. Still under military administration, it offered the finest medical training in the country. It had developed slowly in the early part of the century as demand was small until the 1840's for medical personnel. The War Ministry needed only fifty graduates per year and the civilian ministries only ten. Private practice was virtually nonexistent. The school also had difficulty recruiting qualified students, probably because of the low level of science studies in the *gymnasia*. As a consequence, it took one-half of each entering class from the seminary graduates, who knew well the language of medicine, Latin.

The situation changed in the 1840's after the imposition of military control over the school. In 1838 a Polish student had slapped the director. The tsar took personal charge of the affair, sentencing the student to run a gauntlet of five hundred soldiers three times in the presence of the entire student body and putting the academy under the administration of the War Ministry.[16] The latter action was punitive in intent, aimed at extirpating the spirit of rebelliousness from the school. But the ministry improved the curriculum by introducing more

16. S. Svatikov, "Studencheskoe dvizhenie" [The student movement], *Nasha strana,* Jan. 1907, p. 170.

natural sciences and gave graduates the same privileges in state service as university students.

By the 1860's, the school had become the outstanding center for medical studies in the country. It still depended partly on German professors to staff its faculty, but an increasing number of Russians were also teaching. One student who transferred to the academy from a provincial university said that it was "one of the finest institutions of higher education" in Russia, attracting "the most learned elements" among student youth by its "outstanding facilities."[17] Enrollment grew rapidly. In the early 1840's the academy had only 327 students; by 1854 the number had risen to 900. The great pressure on enrollment came in the following two decades. By the early 1870's the first-year class alone numbered 500 students and the total student body was 1,600.[18] In 1872 women appeared for the first time as official students in a special course to prepare midwives. Despite a difficult entrance examination, 90 women entered the program of the 109 examined. It was the first institution of higher education to accept women as regular students, and its "co-eds" created a sensation as emancipated women.

The medical training consisted of a rigorous, five-year course. Medicine acquired a new reputation in the years of Alexander II as being scientific, practical, and progressive. Chernyshevski chose as two of his main characters in the novel *What's to Be Done?* students from the academy. The rising interest coincided with an increased demand for doctors, mainly in state service. Medical students were mobilized to fight epidemics, beginning in the 1848 cholera epidemic. Invariably some of the student volunteers never returned from these hazardous expeditions, but few apparently refused this extraordinary service. Both the state and the students recognized medicine as a cause worthy of support.

The same popularity touched the Petersburg Technological Institute. Its first years had not been very successful. The Minister of Finances, wishing to encourage the growth of trade and industry, had tried to obtain the support of the Moscow merchants for the

17. S. Chudnovski, "Iz davnykh let" [From long ago], *Byloe,* Sept. 1907, p. 281.

18. *Istoriia imperatorskoi voenno-meditsinskoi akademii za sto let (1798–1898)* [History of the Imperial Medical-Surgical Academy for 100 years] (St. Petersburg, 1898), pp. 454–55.

creation of an institute to prepare technicians for industry, but they were not interested. The school finally was created in the capital. Intended for the sons of poor urban families, it offered in its early period a mixed secondary and advanced program lasting six years, followed by two years of factory apprenticeship. The students received room and board, upon graduation were freed from all servile impositions such as conscription and corporal punishment, and obtained a lifetime internal passport. For the petty bourgeoisie this was an attractive inducement to send their sons to the institute. It continued to function until the 1860's as a narrowly professional school for the urban classes.

The educational reforms of the 1860's raised the Technological Institute to an institution of advanced education. The quality of instruction improved, and a secondary education was required for entrance. Graduates could hope, if they did well in their studies, to receive the legal status of personal honorary citizens. These reforms indicated the desire of the government to encourage technical training while actively pushing industrialization. In the 1860's the institutes of mining engineers, transportation engineers, and civil engineers became civilian institutions offering advanced education. In every case, the size of the student body was expanded and the students had the right to live in their own lodgings instead of in school dormitories. Paternalistic technical training for narrow segments of the population was not adequate for the needs of a developing economy.

The new opportunities for training in engineering, as in medicine, met a rising interest in such studies. Enrollment in the Technological Institute rose rapidly. In its earlier, quiet days, it included at most 140 students. In 1865 the student body numbered 665, and by 1871, 968. There were too few professors, classrooms, or scholarships for the students who came to study.[19] The director reported in 1872 that he had been forced to create parallel classes to meet the demand. He saw the reason for the sudden success of technical education in the changes occurring in the Russian economy. He noted the "success of industry, the development of a widespread railroad network re-

19. Ministerstvo vnutrennykh del, Tsentral'nyi statisticheskii komitet [Ministry of the Interior, Central Statistical Committee; abbreviated MVD-TsSK], *Istoriko-statisticheskii ocherk obshchego i spetsial'nogo obrazovaniia* [A historical-statistical study of general and specialized education] (St. Petersburg, 1883), pp. 138–39.

quiring a large number of specially trained technicians, and constantly increasing penetration of scientific elements in industrial production." He was impressed, and apparently somewhat bewildered, by the newly acquired prestige of his institute among young people who previously would have disdained such studies. He remarked that "in the last years, the student body has come almost exclusively from the *gymnasia,*" that is, from the best secondary schools in the country.[20]

Among these highly qualified students, however, were some who sought scientific knowledge as a tool to change the entire system, not to support economic development. The student disorders of the late 1860's and early 1870's invariably included students from the institute. As a result, the government brought out in 1872 new measures to restore order to the school. The program of studies became more difficult than before, and enrollment fell to five hundred. Those few who passed through the five-year program could look forward to high social position and good salaries, but technical training was not for the multitudes.

The attraction of professional schools sprang in part from an intellectual fad. All of these institutions offered training in subjects based on the physical and natural sciences. Their avowed aim was to prepare specialists with an understanding of scientific knowledge and the ability to use that knowledge to help solve serious human problems. Both characteristics appealed to those youth looking for a meaningful goal in life and to those dissatisfied with the traditional order, the idealistic and the discontented. Both could quickly become disillusioned by the difficult, prosaic, and generally uninspiring course of studies presented them. Only the most determined and the best prepared could last out the trials of professional higher education. These schools were by the 1860's as much a part of the elite education of the country as the universities.

Dominating the educational system of the empire were the schools of the Ministry of Education, especially its universities and its secondary schools that prepared for the universities, the *gymnasia.* In theory these gave the best schooling in the country. Petersburg and Moscow universities shared the glory of being the centers of scholarship. The network of schools was new by European standards. The

20. TsGIAL, f. 733, o. 158, d. 127, ll. 37, 47.

real beginning of the *gymnasium* system dated from the early nineteenth century. Moscow University was founded in 1755 and Petersburg University in 1811. By the last half of the nineteenth century,
professors in these institutions, such as Dimitri Mendeleev in chemistry and Ivan Pavlov in psychology, had attained an intellectual
stature equal to the best of European scholars. A century and a half
after Peter's modest reforms, Russian education had come of age.

The ministry lavished its care on the upper levels of its system. In
the 1870's a primary schoolteacher might hope after years of teaching
to earn 300 rubles per year; university professors could reach 3,600
rubles. Among the 72 regular members of the teaching staff of Petersburg University in 1869, 27 were full professors receiving 3,000
rubles or more. Their eminent position gave them official rank in the
middle or upper ranks of the bureaucratic hierarchy. As could be expected, they were predominantly of noble origin.[21] By contrast, the
primary schoolteachers were mostly from the lower classes. The
enormous gap in income and social status dividing the lowly schoolteachers and the august university professors indicated the great distance separating the base of the educational structure of the ministry
from the top. Russian education was an intellectual giant with feet of
clay.

The real efforts of the ministry began with the *gymnasia*. These
secondary institutions were modeled on the Prussian system, from
which the very name was borrowed. The years of study they offered
provided a ladder straight into the universities. Like the Prussian
schools, they emphasized training in the humanities, particularly
classical studies. Science and mathematics occupied only a small part
of the curriculum. In the *gymnasium* statute of 1828, these two disciplines received only one-tenth of the total weekly study time, while
over one-half was taken up by language alone. German and Latin
were both required subjects, as was Greek or French. This training
sought moral improvement as much as intellectual skill. The foundations of morality were to be found in religion and the study of the
classics of Latin and Greek literature. In this respect, the *gymnasia*
literally carried on the work of the Italian Renaissance. After a
brief effort in the 1860's to offer more preparation in science, the old
policy reappeared in 1871 in yet another statute relegating the sci-

21. *Ibid.*, o. 203, d. 208 (1869), ll. 70–89.

ences and mathematics to a modest place in the *gymnasium* curriculum. Dimitri Tol'stoi, minister of education, emphasized the moral advantages in the study of languages and literature. These disciplines, he argued, "influence all sides of the human spirit, elevating and ennobling it." The study of science, like that of law or political economy, was much less beneficial. Pupils received a "one-sided" development which left out "both their moral and their aesthetic education."[22] To insure that these schools had time to exert their full moral influence, the period of schooling was extended from seven to eight years. The pupils who had endured this long period of trial could at last gain access to the pinnacle of learning, the universities.

During the reign of Alexander II those youth seeking a secondary education with emphasis on science had to turn to a separate set of schools, the *progymnasia* (slightly altered in 1871 and renamed *realschulen*). Prussia again provided the model. In Russia, however, these schools did not open the door to the university. They provided training suitable only for lesser centers of higher education such as the professional schools. This dual track for secondary education preserved the sanctity of humanistic learning of the *gymnasia*.

Practical considerations of the relative utility of scientific and humanistic studies in secondary education did not greatly concern the Russian educational authorities. In their minds—as in those of the radicals—the best education was one in which students found the truth, the sole guide to moral action. This attitude justified the pride with which the inspector of the Petersburg educational district pointed in the early 1870's to the decline in his *gymnasia* of "immoral offenses," by which he meant any breach of school discipline. This proved, he concluded, that these schools were "educational-corrective [*vospitatel'no—ispravitel'nyi*] institutions in the true sense of the word."[23] Scientific training, though needed for the professional schools, did not provide proper moral inspiration. In fact, it appeared closely connected with the immoral behavior of the "nihilists." Those secondary schools stressing scientific learning could not turn out graduates worthy of direct access to the universities.

22. Quoted in Allen Sinel, *The Classroom and the Chancellery: State Educational Reform in Russia under Count Dmitry Tolstoi* (Cambridge, Mass., 1973), p. 145; Sinel's book provides an excellent survey of educational policy in the 1860's and 1870's.
23. TsGIAL, f. 733, o. 202, d. 5, l. 34.

The secondary schools for men grew steadily in size during the middle decades of the century. Under Nicholas I, enrollment in the *gymnasia* grew from 7,700 in 1825 to 19,500 in 1856. Expansion was more rapid in the next two decades. By 1880 there were 45,000 *gymnasia* students plus another 13,000 in the *realschulen*.[24] Among these pupils were the future intellectual and political leaders of the country.

The ministry also made a discreet provision for women seeking intellectual training. The first women's secondary school opened in St. Petersburg in 1858. Within ten years of its opening these schools, some of which received the title of *gymnasium,* numbered 125, with over 10,000 pupils. Since women remained barred from the universities, these institutions offered them the highest level of public schooling. Intended to be nonclass, they attracted primarily women from the upper classes.[25] From this group came the small cohort of *nigilistki.*

Pressure for higher education for women kept building throughout the 1860's, largely from the feminist movement, which was in close touch with similar groups in western Europe. Russians founded their first feminist journal, *Rassvet* (The Dawn), in 1859, only six years after the first such English journal. An editorial in the first issue called on women to become the "main force for all that is pure" and expressed the hope that its articles would "arouse the sympathy of young feminine readers" for emancipation.[26] A principal goal of the movement was the expansion of educational opportunities for women. For a brief time in the early 1860's women auditors were allowed in Petersburg University. Conservative professors tried by various subtle means "to expel [them] from the auditorium." Dimitri Pisarev, who witnessed such scenes, regarded the conflict as one between "diametrically opposed principles—the Domostroi [sixteenth-century handbook on family life] *versus* the nineteenth century."[27]

After the privilege of auditing was withdrawn, a campaign began

24. Rashin, "Gramotnost'," p. 51; MVD-TsSK, *Universitety i srednye uchebnye zavedenii* [The universities and secondary educational institutions] (St. Petersburg, 1888), p. 19.
25. E. Likhacheva, *Materialy dlia istorii zhenskogo obrazovaniia* [Materials for the history of women's education] (St. Petersburg, 1901), pp. 38–39.
26. Quoted in *ibid.,* pp. 457–58.
27. Pisarev, *Izbrannye sochineniia,* I, 39.

to open the universities officially to women. It failed. In 1868 four hundred women, many from the high society of St. Petersburg, signed a petition requesting the rector of the university to hold public lectures open to women. At the same time, a small group of intellectuals organized a private preparatory program of evening courses for women interested in higher education. The teachers, all contributing their services without charge, included university professors. The public lectures began in 1870 with an enrollment of 900, of whom almost 800 were women.[28] These lectures plus the special midwife program at the Medical-Surgical Academy constituted the only higher education available to women until the end of the 1870's. The only other alternatives were self-instruction, alone or in women's circles, or education abroad.

By the end of the 1860's a few young Russian women were pursuing advanced education in European universities. The University of Zurich was particularly popular, since it did not require a secondary school degree for admission and it offered to men and women a full program of medical training. By 1873 over one hundred Russian women were studying there. One of these was Vera Figner. Daughter of a noble landowner, she interrupted a traditional upbringing when at the age of seventeen she decided to study medicine. In a letter written in early 1871 she indicated that her aim in life had become "economic independence, the training of my mind, and public welfare, that is, usefulness to others." She was convinced that "in order to be more useful one should know more." Quiet provincial life was no place for such aspirations. "Only the university is worth so much that a woman could sacrifice all for it." She had heard of others with similar ideals who had entered medicine. She saw opening before her an active, constructive life in which she would "organize a hospital, open a school or a trade school." She was resolved "never to stop for anything" in the pursuit of her goal.[29]

Young men who completed their *gymnasium* education were not confronted with such dramatic choices. They had the option of higher education or privileged access to bureaucratic service. If they chose the latter path, they could begin at the fourteenth rank rather than at a nonranked, secretarial position. Nothing in the *gymnasium* curricu-

28. Likhacheva, *Materialy,* pp. 514–22, 538–52.
29. V. Figner, *PSS* (Moscow, 1929), V, 38–39.

lum was specially designed to prepare competent bureaucrats. The general moral and intellectual qualities of the successful graduate should serve to make him an exemplary state servant. The new bureaucrat had spent much of his time in the *gymnasium* poring over the classics of Roman literature. He had learned nothing about the traditions and behavior of the subjects of the Russian empire in the mid-nineteenth century.

The most elaborate training for state service took place in the Alexandrovsky Lycée, founded by Alexander I as an elite school for some of the nobility. A boarding school in which the pupils spent the greatest part of six years, it replaced the family as the center of existence for the one hundred boys, aged twelve to twenty, who attended. After Nicholas I introduced a military regime in the school, life became rigorous and disciplined. Its program of study remained similar to that of the *gymnasia,* but the quality of the teachers and the intensity of the studies made it superior. Some of its instructors came from Petersburg University, and many were western Europeans who scarcely knew Russian. At one time in the 1840's, an Englishman was teaching Russian history, a Frenchman Greek literature, and a German zoology, each in his native language.

The curriculum provided intensive exposure to Western culture, but much less to Russian institutions and life. The courses in Russian language, literature, history, and law constituted a relatively small part of the studies. Emphasis was on ancient and Western literature, world history, and Roman law. One eminent graduate of the 1830's, Nicholas Giers, recalled that "at that time, the lycée was regarded as the best school in Russia, and it enjoyed exceptional privileges."[30] Chief among these was the chance to enter the bureaucracy at the tenth rank upon successful completion of studies, with the likelihood of rapid advancement within a few years into the upper ranks. The pupils of this preparatory school for bureaucratic service received an education in Western learning, put to the service of the Russian state.

The universities were the top rung in the educational ladder of the Ministry of Education. Each university was the center of an educational district with jurisdiction over all the ministry's schools in that territory and theoretically set the model of academic excellence. It

---

30. Nicholas Giers, *The Education of a Russian Statesman*, trans. Charles and Barbara Jelavich (Berkeley, 1962), p. 49.

provided the bulk of the teachers for its district's *gymnasia*. To centralize the system, in 1834 Nicholas I gave each university a curator (*popechitel'*), appointed by the Ministry of Education, who was the chief administrative officer for the district. In his reign the country had six universities; Alexander II added one more in 1865. The reform of 1863 gave the university professors the right to elect their own rector and to administer their own affairs. But their institutions were too prominent and too visible from St. Petersburg to escape the tentacular controls of the state.

The universities offered courses in all the major areas of knowledge. All possessed schools ("faculties") of liberal arts (history-philology), science (physics-mathematics), and law. All had schools of medicine except Petersburg, which had the only school of Eastern (Asian) languages. Most had been created in the reign of Alexander I, and in their early years lacked trained Russian professors, so many foreigners, mainly Germans, held the teaching positions. An effort to train Russians as university professors finally began during the years of Nicholas I. At that time, the ministry began to send qualified university graduates to study in Germany or in Dorpat University in Estland, nominally a part of the empire but in reality as much a part of the German intellectual world as any German university. Dorpat became the center for the training of Russian scholars in the years that followed. Before 1860, 170 of its graduates became Russian university professors or members of the Academy of Sciences.[31] Among the foreign-trained scholars were the most famous professors of the 1840's, such as Timofei Granovski in history at Moscow University and Nicholas Pirogov in chemistry and Viktor Poroshin in political economy at Petersburg University. The Russian educational leaders wished to create advanced institutions on a par with their German counterparts. This striving for cultural elitism left a permanent mark on Russian scholarship and on the attitudes of the students. It succeeded remarkably well. The new scholars returning from the West represented the first generation of serious Russian learning. This was the beginning of the universities as part of the intellectual life of Russia.

Of the four years of study, the first two were devoted to "general lectures" and the remainder to advanced courses in the student's field.

31. Leikina-Svirskaia, *Intelligentsiia*, p. 175.

The cause of learning was only one function of the universities. From the student body came recruits for state service. The schools of law were primarily concerned with the preparation of men for the bureaucracy and had consistently the highest enrollment in the entire university system. The universities were also the source of the best teachers, including the next generation of university professors, available to the Ministry of Education. Despite these needs, their role remained ambiguous. They depended for much of their learning and scholarly traditions on western Europe, where freedom of inquiry was deeply ingrained in social and political life. Russia had no such tradition. In the revolutions of 1848 university students in the West were active in the uprisings. Though Russian students remained perfectly disciplined, Nicholas took immediate steps to forestall similar occurrences in his realm. He limited enrollment to three hundred students per university (medical schools excepted) and eliminated philosophy from the university curriculum. Rumors circulated that he was considering closing Petersburg University. These were probably false, but the very fact that educated Russians believed them indicates the precariousness of higher learning in the political order of the country.

Russian students began to justify Nicholas' fears in the early years of his successor. Following the disturbances in Petersburg University in the fall of 1861, it closed for two years. The Russian state shared with the radicals the conviction that knowledge was power. The universities were a dangerous cultural innovation precisely because their Western heritage stressed secular learning and the search for empirical truth. The Russian state had no comprehensive ideology to counter or stifle these aspirations which could sow doubt and create dissent. The requirement that every student receive instruction in Orthodoxy did not solve the problem. Tinkering with the curriculum could not guarantee political loyalty from the student body.

The actual number of university students did not reflect the importance accorded these institutions. The educational elite was a very small group of individuals, though growing throughout the nineteenth century. In 1826 there were 2,600 students in the six universities. By the end of Nicholas' reign the number had risen to 3,700 and by 1875 to 5,200. Moscow University was the largest, followed by Petersburg, which had over 700 students in 1847, 1,100 on the eve of its closure in 1861, and 1,200 in 1875. The growth of university enrollment did not exceed the rate of expansion of the Russian population and was considerably less than that of the *gymnasia*. Throughout the mid-nineteenth century university education was a privilege restricted to a small group of Russian youth.

The state's total educational effort represented a considerable investment of money and manpower. The school system increased in scope and numbers throughout the first half of the nineteenth century so that by the reign of Alexander II it was roughly comparable to that of Austria-Hungary. Its curriculum and organization were based largely on the Prussian educational model. Though it was an alien import, the upper classes of Russia appeared to have assimilated its methods and goals with relative ease. The old, church-dominated culture had declined with hardly a struggle. The school system, benefiting only a tiny minority of the population, was firmly and irrevocably committed to a Russian adaptation of Western secular learning.

School Days in the Russian Style

In the first half of the nineteenth century a classical education was the privilege of very few Russians. The youth moving into the *gymnasia* found themselves intellectually in alien territory. They were required to memorize a body of knowledge which they scarcely understood and which overwhelmed most of them. The authorities considered them under state tutelage and expected them to behave as exemplary subjects. Nicholas' use of military control in secular institutions was the low point in their treatment. Alexander II's reign opened with the promise of a better life. The spread of student disorders led by the 1870's, however, to the imposition of a regime of surveillance comparable in effect, though not appearance, to Nicholas' system. The role of the student was as ambiguous as that of the educational system. On the one hand, he belonged to an elite in society; on the other, he was isolated by the small size of his group and by the exotic character of his studies. The situation gradually improved in the course of the century as the numbers of students and educated Russians increased. The student who could overcome all the obstacles to the attainment of higher education demonstrated special ability and determination.

The *gymnasia* and other secondary institutions of the Ministry of Education required the ability to master rote learning. The overall emphasis on discipline and moral behavior was accompanied in classes by pedantic teaching. One Saratov *gymnasium* pupil of the 1850's remembered his education there as a "regime under which the pupils had to submit to harsh controls and to cram their heads with ancient classics." For the school authorities, the ideal of learning was "to make youth aware of, acquainted with, and meekly submissive to all absurdities."[32] Pupils were required to memorize a certain number of pages of the lesson and recite in class word-for-word exactly what they had read. For the recalcitrant, the remedy was stern punishment, including whipping.

Some change for the better came in the late 1850's and early 1860's when school authorities attempted to introduce intellectual content into the studies and remove some of the brutality from school discipline. Some young teachers attempted to reform teaching methods and arouse the curiosity of the pupils. These reforms were most apparent in the *gymnasia* of the larger cities, especially St. Petersburg. Peter Tkachev was a pupil in one of the Petersburg schools in the late 1850's, when "suddenly the entire climate unexpectedly changed." The school authorities became friendly, the birch whips disappeared from the classrooms, and teachers talked of abandoning "old methods of teaching" to allow "the widest possible reforms."[33] There is little evidence that innovative teachers filled the schools. The system itself was a major obstacle to change, particularly the emphasis on the classics. Science and contemporary literature aroused the greatest interest among the pupils, and neither had a large part of the *gymnasium* curriculum.

The pupils became adept at the skills necessary for survival. Tkachev recalled that his school comrades spent most of their time "thinking up and developing means for 'self-preservation'". Their ranking of important activities included "getting good grades, avoiding whippings, and keeping out of the way of the tough boys in the class."[34] Most schools probably remained strict in spite of occasional reforms and softening of discipline. Surveillance of the pupils' actions extended beyond the school walls. One report in 1870 to the Ministry of Education noted the "special care" being taken of the students in a provincial *gymnasium*. The school authorities "watch closely the

---

32. I. Voronov, "Saratovskaia gimnasiia" [The Saratov *gymnasium*], *Russkaia starina*, CXXXIX (1909), 356.
33. Quoted in B. Koz'min, *P. N. Tkachev* (Moscow, 1922), p. 12.
34. *Ibid.*, p. 13.

life of the pupils in their apartments and write down the results of searches of these apartments in a special book." This policy had a good influence on "the parents of the boys and landlords who, observing the care taken by the school administration, themselves treat the boys with special attentiveness."[35] Other schools probably used similar methods when judged necessary.

On fundamental questions of curriculum and school life, the pupils were extraordinarily submissive. A reinforced classical program was introduced in the early 1870's. The reform went counter to the tastes and capacities of most pupils and could have aroused considerable protest. One provincial inspector did report some resistance in advanced classes of one *gymnasium*. A university student in the town appealed to the pupils to "abandon those studies which they consider useless" in order to "remove the rot of antiquity."[36] The only obvious result was a rush by the schools to institute more classical studies so their pupils would not lose university entrance qualifications. These schools were only a step to the institutions of higher education or the bureaucracy. They shared in the aura of sanctity that enveloped higher education and made the pupils who admired learning feel part of a larger enterprise. One graduate of the 1850's affirmed that the *gymnasium* was "for every intelligent boy the symbol of knowledge, intellectual culture, the threshold to the university."[37] Their rigorous and uninspiring training served mainly to turn minds, like that of Goncharov's Oblomov, into "a complicated archive of past deeds, persons, figures, epochs, religions, of disconnected economic, mathematical and other truths, problems, contentions, etc."[38] Their pupils were taught—most of them successfully—to submit to established truth and to an established educational system.

Those youth who found intellectual excitement in their *gymnasium* years did so on their own. The energetic pupil could confront the world of Western literature. One adventuresome youth who followed this path in the late 1830's read the works of Pushkin, Lermontov, and Gogol, and also German and French novels and poetry in the original. The poet Schiller was his "friend and comforter." But his independent reading unsettled his view of life and the established

---

35. TsGIAL, f. 733, o. 202, d. 251, l. 13.

36. *Ibid.*, d. 252. Alston claims "public resentment" did exist (Patrick Alston, *Education and the State in Tsarist Russia* [Stanford, 1969], pp. 100–1).

37. P. Boborykin, *Za polveka* [For a half-century] (Moscow, 1929), p. 21.

38. Goncharov, *Oblomov*, p. 63 (pt. I, ch. 6).

order without providing any answers. "My ideas were in a terrible mess and I felt only that everything was horribly bad, that life was miserable and I could not understand why."[39] This was precisely the attitude which the educational authorities sought to discourage.

By the late 1850's groups of pupils began pursuing their own learning with the aid of the literary journals and publications and the support of former *gymnasium* pupils who were in higher education. In one Petersburg school the most effective stimulus to this "intellectual awakening" came from "old school comrades, already students, who came back on their own to their *gymnasium* during off hours, even for tea and dinner."[40] These intellectually more mature youth brought copies of the journals, such as *The Contemporary,* which preached in veiled tones moral and social emancipation. Peter Tkachev vividly recalled the new "spirit" which contrasted so sharply with the school's intellectual diet of "old textbooks," outside of which all knowledge was forbidden fruit. In the new atmosphere, articles, books, and ideas moved freely to create an "intellectual alertness [*trevog*] to new ideas."[41] These "new ideas" even penetrated the thick walls of the secluded Smolny school for girls, where the talk of relatives from the outside world stirred up flurries of amazement. Such talk might not go far in Smolny, but in other schools it encouraged the formation of small circles of pupils, united by dissatisfaction with their scholastic fare and by interest in new ideas. The intellectual development of younger generations of pupils quickened under encouragement from the older generation.

There were isolated incidents of resistance to the disciplinary regime to which the *gymnasium* students were subjected. The records of the Ministry of Education reveal six cases of disorders in *gymnasia* between 1863 and 1865. The various reasons for unrest included "suspicion of spying on the part of the school inspector, tactlessness . . . of the inspector or director, dismissal from the school of a favorite teacher."[42] In 1862 two pupils suspected of "political unreliability" were expelled from a provincial *gymnasium*

39. D. Akhsharumov, "Avtobiografiia," *Filosofskie i obshchestvenno-politicheskie proizvedeniia petrashevtsev* [Philosophical and social-political works of the Petrashevtsy] (Moscow, 1953), pp. 680–81.

40. V. Ostrogorski, *Iz istorii moego uchitel'stva* [The history of my studies] (St. Petersburg, 1914), p. 19.

41. Quoted in Koz'min, *Tkachev,* p. 14.

42. I. Aleshintsev, *Istoriia gimnazicheskogo obrazovaniia* [The history of gymnasium education] (St. Petersburg, 1912), pp. 276–77.

and ordered by the police to return to their families. The day of their departure, classes were empty while pupils accompanied their carriage to the edge of town. Later some pupils insulted the school director and broke windows in his house. Ten more were expelled.[43]

By the early 1870's a few pupils had adopted the techniques earlier developed among students in higher education to pursue their own radical readings and activities. Close-knit groups, called "circles" (*kruzhki*), were active in at least a few *gymnasia*. A circle in Kursk, in central Russia, consisted of fifteen pupils who had a good library with many forbidden publications, and assisted the populists in the "to the people" movement.[44] A small number of such young men ended their schooling at this point. Government statistics on people sentenced for political crimes between 1873 and 1877 indicated that 21 were pupils in secondary schools of the Ministry of Education and another 18 had dropped out of school, presumably to participate in the radical movement.[45] These figures are small compared with the numbers of students from universities or technical schools. Only an exceptional pupil might actually interrupt his secondary schooling for the sake of revolution. Even those who were drawn to the movement still desired higher education. The Kursk circle broke up, not because of arrests, but because its members had graduated and left for more advanced educational institutions. The participant quoted above, an outstanding pupil, was admitted to the school of natural sciences of Petersburg University and apparently never thought of turning down the opportunity.

Only a very small number of those pupils who entered the first year of secondary education reached the eighth year and received their degrees, fittingly called the "certificate of maturity." The *gymnasia* exercised a ruthless selection of pupils from one year to the next. An official report of the early 1870's estimated that one-third of the pupils entering *gymnasia* actually completed their studies; most took longer than the allotted eight years.[46] The middle years of study were the hardest. The inspector of the Petersburg educational district investigated the scholastic performance of his *gymnasium*

43. TsGAOR, f. 109, o. 85, d. 27, l. 38.
44. M. Timofeev, "Perezhitoe" [The past], *Katorga i ssylka*, No. 56 (1929), 94.
45. Sidorov, "Statisticheskie," pp. 48–49, table 4.
46. *Istoriia Rossii v XIX veke*, IV, 138; VII, 184.

pupils in 1870. He found that the percentage refused advancement from one class to the next was highest between the third and fourth years, when it reached 45 percent. He explained that this was the time of "transition from elementary teaching to more serious and scholarly [*nauchnomu*] teaching." By serious studies he meant classes such as elementary Greek, which failed up to 70 percent of its pupils, Latin which gave up to 55 percent failures, and mathematics which failed as high as 50 to 60 percent. A pupil who failed any course had to repeat that year's entire program. During the first five years the percentage of failures was one-third or higher.[47] As a result, some pupils remained two and three years in the class before advancing or abandoning school.

Living expenses presented another serious hurdle. One Petersburg *gymnasium* pupil from the 1850's remarked later that "the majority of the pupils were poor." He knew of one pupil who, on his scholarship of nine rubles per month, provided for his own needs and those of his widowed mother and five brothers and sisters. These meager scholarships were all that kept the poor pupils in school. A mediocre performance on the examinations at the end of the year deprived them automatically of this financial aid. The "outcome of the examinations was a question of life and death."[48] Only the most energetic and capable among the poor could possibly survive.

The total effect of difficult studies compounded by financial hardship made survival in the secondary schools a matter of wealth as well as fitness and hence automatically favored the upper classes. The records of the Petersburg educational district (virtually all northwestern Russia) indicated that in 1854, 152 pupils graduated from the *gymnasia* of the area. A majority were from the hereditary or personal nobility, that is, from landowning nobility, the officer corps, or the middle and upper bureaucracy.[49] This situation in the Petersburg district in the mid-1850's was typical of later periods and of other districts. In the 1870's the yearly number of graduates in that district was about the same. Throughout the country many more pupils dropped out of the *gymnasia* than graduated.

The total number of *gymnasium* graduates in Russia in any one

47. TsGIAL, f. 733, o. 203, d. 200, ll. 23–25.
48. A. Vereshchagin, *Doma i na voine* [At home and at war] (St. Petersburg, 1886), p. 111.
49. TsGIAL, f. 733, o. 95, d. 157, ll. 45–46.

year was very small. In 1869 they numbered only 1,690. They were already far up the ladder of the educated elite of Russia and usually went on into higher education. They had left behind most of their comrades from the early classes and had survived difficult examinations in dull subjects; frequently they suffered financial hardship. Those who had shown this endurance and skill—including the great majority of Petersburg radicals—could feel that they had been tried and had proved their fitness. Most chose to prepare themselves for ordinary careers as professionals, bureaucrats, or teachers. A few decided that they were competent to judge the established order in Russia. In most cases their intellectual awakening was still ahead, but their sense of pre-eminence was already in place. The conditions under which they had received their schooling could do no less for their character.

The juxtaposition of elite education and radical commitment first appeared in the Alexandrovsky Lycée, one of the first schools to contribute sizable numbers of youth to the radical movement. From here came the nucleus of the Petrashevtsy circle. Of the fifty Petersburg radicals from the 1840's in my group, twelve were from the lycée. They were noticeable as well among the radicals in the late 1850's and 1860's (9 out of 153). Their presence was particularly remarkable since the school was very small. As an exclusive training school for the upper bureaucracy, it attracted the sons of some aristocratic families. Like Nicholas Giers, they kept a proper distance from the less distinguished pupils, were respectful toward their superiors, and passably good in their studies. Giers, a pupil in the 1830's, later became minister of foreign affairs. The class of 1839 included a future minister of finances and a minister of education.

Within the institution, the pupils duplicated some of the conditions they would find in state service. The older and stronger boys from the upper classes had a circle of followers from among the younger pupils who acted as servants and received in return aid and protection. A strict code of honor ruled their behavior more closely than the surveillance of the school administration. Dimitri Tol'stoi, the future minister of education, publicly accused one of his classmates in the early 1840's of "immoral behavior." When this pupil was expelled, the rest of the class judged Tol'stoi responsible and ostracized him for the whole year remaining until graduation. Tol'stoi, convinced of the injustice of their decision, ceased speaking to them.[50] The same code could unite the pupils against the administration when they felt it had acted unjustly. On the eve of graduation the class of 1838 organized a collective protest because a surveillant had confined a class member to the punishment cell for refusing to cut his long hair. This small revolt brought an immediate visit from the grand duke, whose threat to send the leaders to an infantry regiment as common soldiers produced an apology from the entire class. These "noble sentiments" accompanied by pleas and tears from the eighteen- and nineteen-year-old nobles softened the heart of the duke. He forgave the class and allowed graduation to proceed.[51]

The atmosphere in the lycée stressed, far more than in the *gymnasia*, the building of character in preparation for state leadership. Despite the semimilitary regime, Nicholas Giers looked back on his years in the school as the "best years of my life." From his studies he retained an appreciation for the "usefulness of knowledge" and a "desire to learn." "Most important, I acquired the characteristics of honor and nobility of mind which were at the heart of the lycée education."[52] On these moral principles the school based its ethic of state service.

The pupils were interested in literature and the philosophical and social writings from the West in the 1830's, before any other educational institution in Russia except perhaps Moscow University, offered such a varied intellectual diet. The courses stressed a broad knowledge of Western culture. Not all the pupils appreciated this program. Mikhail Saltykov, a pupil in the 1840's, wrote later with scorn of "all that encyclopedic rubbish crammed in our heads."[53] Outside the classroom reading was varied and intensive. The school had a tradition of literary excellence dating from the time when Pushkin passed through its program. Russian literary magazines circulated freely, and pupils in the third and fourth years had the right (an exceptional privilege in that period) to use the school library. Some of the teachers showed an interest in their pupils, an attitude which did not begin

50. P. Semenov-Tian'-Shanski, *Memuary* (Petrograd, 1917), I, 129.
51. A. Iakhontov, "Vospominaniia" [Memoirs], *Russkaia starina,* LX (Oct. 1888), 120–23.
52. Giers, *Education,* p. 57.
53. M. Saltykov, *PSS,* IV, 181–82.

to appear in the *gymnasia* until the 1850's. Many of the pupils were from highly cultured and Westernized families, who provided them with varied reading material.

Their taste for the latest word in intellectual adventure led them to the writings of the utopian socialists, Henri de Saint-Simon and Charles Fourier, whose works were just beginning to attract attention in the West. The memoirs of the pupils from the 1840's repeatedly mention the ease with which literature that was strictly forbidden by the government circulated within the school. Perhaps, as Saltykov recalled, most of the students wanted mainly to "have a good time," but he developed his "taste for reflection" in his school years when he "explored the theories of the utopian socialists."[54] The problem was important enough to attract the attention of an agent of the secret police, who, writing in 1844, stressed the "lack of religious sentiment" and the "mood of irritability" in the lycée. "The indiscriminate reading of books," he warned ominously, "is the ruin of all young people," and the lycée pupils "more than others have the means for this."[55] The school's emphasis on intensive learning in humanistic disciplines seemed to stimulate the pupils to explore forbidden Western ideologies. Encouraged to master the most difficult fields of knowledge, they included in their own studies the most radical subjects.

There was a strong element of intellectual dilettantism in this interest in Western radical theories. Reading forbidden literature had its own special attraction, while an ostensible concern for social justice put an aristocrat's son in an exciting position of revolt against paternal authority. The ease with which the socialist books circulated suggests that few took the ideals seriously. In that training school for the future bureaucratic elite, strong forces pulled the pupils toward acceptance of the status quo. By the 1860's, in fact, the "radical years" of the lycée had ended. For the rest of its existence, it was a center of loyalty and obedience to the regime.

The role of the school was thus fairly brief, but still crucial, in the origins of the radical movement. When students from few other institutions showed any hint of subversive thoughts, the lycée had its contingent of the dissatisfied and disaffected. These few were taking

54. *Ibid.*, IX, 415.
55. TsGAOR, f. 109, pervaia eks., d. 215 (1844), ll. 5, 8.

upon themselves a role of leadership, though not that intended for them. Perhaps the school's emphasis on character building provided encouragement to rebel. The Third Section agent who observed the school life in 1844 was struck by the emphasis with which the teachers reminded the pupils of the important political role awaiting them. He observed that most boys eagerly looked forward to the time when they would "govern society, opinion, and the state." This propensity to "childish self-esteem" was "deep-rooted." Feeling so important, the pupils rebelled at the "slightest severity" on the part of the administration.[56] As already seen, such protests usually were short-lived.

By the 1830's the lycée pupils possessed a sense of self-importance and group solidarity. These conditions, which did not appear in the universities until the late 1850's, were highly conducive to intellectual dissent. The school had already been indirectly implicated in the Decembrist movement, since a few of the participants received their education there. The introduction of military control in the 1830's had failed to produce a spirit of obedience and discipline. Within the walls of the school, radical dissent seemed a suitable path of revolt. The most vivid illustration of the connection between "childish self-esteem" and the "mood of irritability" noticed by the police agent comes in a letter from one of Petrashevski's later comrades, Nikolai Speshnev. While still a lycée pupil, he recounted to his father the extraordinary rebirth he had felt when "at the age of sixteen I became quite different. For the first time I fell under the spell of pure learning, plumbed its depths and went so far that I understood clearly and absolutely that learning is one whole, one truth. . . . I lived in a different world, apart from my comrades."[57] Shortly afterward the school authorities expelled him from the lycée. The causes of his expulsion are not known and may have had nothing to do with his new ideals. His letter indicates that Speshnev carried away with him a sense of personal superiority which was an intimate part of the education provided by the lycée.

The absence of such an intellectual and social atmosphere effectively discouraged radical protest. This, not the social composition of the student body, was decisive. By the 1860's even institutions catering to nonnoble youth, which had been models of submission, began

56. *Ibid.*, ll. 3–4.
57. "N. A. Speshnev o samom sebe," *Katorga i ssylka*, No. 62 (1930), 95.

to feel the ferment of student agitation. The Main Pedagogical Institute of St. Petersburg remained a quiet center for the meek until its dissolution in 1859. It trained teachers for the elementary and secondary schools of the Ministry of Education. Offering the prospect of a less glorious career than the university and well provided with stipends for its pupils, it attracted a high percentage of *raznochintsy*. Over one-half of the students were sons of priests and of nonnoble bureaucrats. The course of studies was less demanding and "encyclopedic" than in schools like the lycée. Consequently, the institute accepted graduates from the lowly district schools (*uchilishcha*) and seminaries as well as from the *gymnasia*.[58] The presence of large numbers of poor students, many sons of priests educated in seminaries, did not strengthen the potential for protest in the school. The school authorities tried to keep the humble scholarship students in their place. According to one, they were told that "we were nonentities, that the government had showered us with its favors in accepting us in the institute." The director deserved their "eternal thankfulness" for his "unbounded paternal love" which assured them "all these advantages" in the school.[59] The poor students could prove their gratitude by excelling in their studies and obeying all the rules.

Only the exceptional student could break this paternalistic pattern. Nikolai Dobroliubov was a seminary pupil forced by his parents' lack of means to accept the "favors" of the institute. His remarkable talents and will power made little impact on the student body. One year after his arrival in 1853, he organized a collective protest against the oppressive policies of the director, but was forced to make a public apology for disrespect toward his superiors. Later he formed a small circle of friends for reading and discussion of books on social and political issues, most of them forbidden by the censor. This modest action represented a significant act of defiance among the submissive students of the institute. By comparison with the Alexandrovsky Lycée, this school was a fine example of discipline.

Similar conditions reigned in the seminaries where no hint of political dissent appeared until the 1860's, when the model of radical protest was well established in the institutions of higher education. The education offered by the seminaries resembled in many respects

---

58. TsGIAL, f. 733, o. 95, d. 66, l. 43; d. 74, l. 60.
59. M. Shemanovski, "Vospominaniia" [Memoirs], in *Literaturnoe nasledstvo*, XXV–XXVI (1936), 272–73.

that of the Jesuit schools, on which the church educational system was modeled when set up in the previous century. It offered little intellectual inspiration in spite of the secular courses in its curriculum that were strengthened and augmented by the reforms of 1867. One pupil in a provincial seminary complained in a satirical poem written in 1869 of the "dull, joyless life of the seminary pupil" who "vainly seeks the truth from pedants and clear knowledge from ancient books."[60] Nikolai Dobroliubov recorded the same impressions in his diary while in a seminary twenty years earlier. He stood out from his schoolmates by his exceptional intellectual abilities, and described himself as a "bibliophile." By the last months of his schooling, he was burning with impatience to leave behind the "mediocre" studies and "pedantic" clerical teachers.[61] The pursuit of real learning led, as in the case of the *gymnasium* students, to the centers of higher education, of which St. Petersburg was the most important. One of these individuals left his seminary in 1875 at the age of twenty with the firm determination "to become a revolutionary." He also felt a variety of hopes and desires which he anticipated would lead him to a "new, exciting life." His first move on graduation was to enter the Medical-Surgical Academy.[62] His enthusiasm for scientific studies lasted only a short time, but the order in his choice of activities was significant. Between the seminaries and the radical movement stood true knowledge and a student youth culture that provided the real school for the radical movement. The seminaries were channels which could lead a few of their pupils toward the new life without themselves serving as the crucible for this transformation.

The universities played the role of incubator for radical protest on a large scale in the late 1850's, followed by some of the professional schools in the late 1860's and early 1870's. To the extent that it is possible to circumscribe the formal educational locus for this youth revolt, these schools were the major centers. They provided the peculiar combination of intellectual and social conditions to crystallize latent disaffection and encourage a new style of life. As the movement developed, such protection became unnecessary, but in the first

60. Quoted in Nechkina, "Iunye gody Kliuchevskogo" [The youth of Kliuchevski], *Voprosy Istorii*, Sept. 1969, p. 80.

61. Dobroliubov, *Dnevnik*, pp. 78–80, 87.

62. M. Chernavski, "Demonstratsiia 6 dekabria 1876 goda" [The demonstration of December 6, 1876], *Katorga i ssylka*, No. 28 (1926), 7–8.

stages it was crucial. Just as the Alexandrovsky Lycée had had an important part in the dissent of the 1840's, these institutions set the tone for the later movement. The student agitation in the late 1850's, culminating in the Petersburg University demonstration and strike in the fall of 1861, indicated clearly the new conditions in the universities. The disorders in the professional schools in 1869 showed similarly the changed atmosphere there. The educational training of the Petersburg radicals was by the 1870's predominantly in the professional schools, whose percentage rose steadily from the 1840's at the expense of the university and lycée (see Table 1).

The student movement displayed certain characteristics which differentiated it from radical protest. The rise of militant student solidarity in defense of corporate rights reflected unique conditions in the educational institutions. The origins of the radical recruits lay partly within these schools, partly in the ferment of ideas among groups of rebels on the fringes of formal educational life. The distinction between political dissenters and other groups was occasionally blurred by common causes uniting large numbers of people, some times coming from outside the educational community. This was the case, for example, with the movement for literacy schools in the early 1860's. The process of radical recruitment nonetheless had its roots primarily in the social and intellectual life of the student youth in higher education.

The advanced institutions of learning acted as filters in the selection of political dissenters as well as approved graduates. Their rigid standards of admission and difficult studies cut out many who might otherwise have joined the movement. Rebels from the system in every other respect, the young radicals still shared the high intellectual expectations of the most ardent scholars. Many of them had not completed their studies, not because of inability to succeed but of a conscious choice to put their mental energies to better use. They were not "drop-outs" in the usual sense. The young women, deprived of formal education in most cases, set their own rigorous intellectual standards in what schooling they could find. The intellectual world of mid-century Russia was small, confined by the limited means of communicating ideas, by the highly theoretical character of intellectual pursuits, and by the small size of the educated community. The educational experience, particularly in the advanced institutions, provided the logical skills and criteria of intellectual excellence that appeared among the radicals. Deprived of this opportunity by academic failure, a young man had little alternative but to return to his family or begin working, effectively ending his life of learning. The schools were influential both by their process of recruitment and their training.

Favored by their rigorous secondary training and by admissions standards, the *gymnasium* graduates constituted the chief reservoir of students for advanced learning. Almost all chose to pursue further schooling. By the 1860's they constituted the majority of students in the institutions of higher learning in St. Petersburg and Moscow. They were invariably the largest group of Petersburg University students between the 1840's and 1870's. In 1841 they made up 60 percent of the student body; in 1879 they were 69 percent.[63] The same situation existed in the professional schools, such as the mining, technological, and agronomy institutes. In all of these more than two-thirds were *gymnasium* graduates and university transfers.[64] The seminaries had only a small representation in these schools. Their graduates gradually became more numerous in the university, where they made up one-fourth of the student body in 1879. In the Technological Institute, they were only 4 percent of the student body.

The secondary education of the Petersburg radicals was a close duplicate of that of all students; over one-half (53 percent of the known total) of the radicals were *gymnasium* or *progymnasium* graduates. The similarity of educational preparation indicates how closely the recruitment to the Petersburg radical group depended on the larger community of those admitted to the institutions of higher education.

The students' trials began when they entered the classrooms. Many did not have adequate funds to pay for their tuition and living expenses. Hardship was not widespread during Nicholas I's reign, when enrollment in the universities was small and the professional schools operated as boarding schools providing for the basic needs of their students. Increases in tuition came in both 1845 and 1848 as part of a government effort to purge the universities of their nonprivileged students. The rapid expansion of student bodies and the transformation of many of the professional schools into open institutions like

63. TsGIAL, f. 733, o. 95, d. 110 (1841), ll. 115–16.
64. *Ibid.*, f. 908, o. 1, d. 125, l. 88.

the universities created an acute and visible problem. Living on their own, many students struggled on virtually a starvation level. Scholarships and other forms of financial aid did not keep up with the increased demand. In 1873 the Technological Institute gave financial aid to one-third of its students, the Agronomy Institute to one-half, and Petersburg University to one-half. The proportion increased later in the decade. Even this aid frequently consisted only of tuition exemption.

As a result, poverty among the student youth was widespread. There were some possibilities for outside work, particularly tutoring, but the chance of finding such work diminished as the numbers of students in the capital increased through the 1860's. The director of the Technological Institute reported in 1869 that a "very large number of young men already prepared for higher education came to the capital counting on finding the means with which to live while they continue their education. . . . A large proportion of them" discover this to be impossible.[65] This school probably had one of the largest concentrations of students living in poverty, for the sudden rise in its enrollment in the late 1860's far outstripped the financial aid available. But the situation was general. The first student-conducted survey in Russia, organized in 1870, found that in Kiev University 143 of the 355 respondents (only 38 percent of the student body) had no support from parents, the university, or the state. Estimating the yearly income necessary for student living expenses, the authors concluded that over 70 percent of their group lived on a less-than-adequate income.[66] The students had to have high expectations from their education to accept, in increasingly large numbers, these difficult material conditions.

The first-year students were under particularly heavy pressure. If they did not do well on the examinations at the end of the year they could not hope to receive financial aid, and at worst might have to leave school. This situation probably explains why the most active and numerous participants in the student disorders came from this group. During the unrest of March 1869, a university student issued a statement of grievances that emphasized the frustrations of these

65. *Ibid.,* f. 733, o. 158, d. 103, l. 2.
66. M. Benasik, *Studenchestvo v tsifrakh* [Statistics on the student body] (St. Petersburg, 1909), pp. 8–10.

struggling youth. "We want to study," he argued, "but every possibility for this is taken away from us." Around him were poor students who "came here without a penny, not infrequently from 200, 300, even 1,000 versts away." They had to work to live, which took time from their studies, but "to get a good scholarship one must have good grades."[67] The dilemma was disastrous for many. A poor student named Nadutkin in the Medical-Surgical Academy that year was in his second year of studies but still working to complete the first-year program. Much of his time went into the struggle to survive, the means for which he found in tutoring and proofreading. In March his professor informed him that he had failed his first-year examination and refused to discuss the matter further. Nadutkin protested angrily and was expelled immediately.[68] His classmates organized a collective protest, which spread to the other schools. The student disturbances of that year had begun, though they were of no use to poor Nadutkin.

The head of the Third Section, investigating the causes of this unrest, thought that poverty had produced a revolt of the student proletariat. He was very impressed by the miserable living conditions his agents had discovered while searching student quarters. He concluded that this "poverty, with its accompanying physical and moral suffering," combined with "the sight of the city's luxury," was producing embittered young men. Instead of admitting that they had "chosen the wrong path," they became rebels. They were a "half-educated proletariat who upon their very entry into adult life carry in themselves hatred for the existing political and social order."[69] The argument was attractive, though dangerously oversimplified.

The fact that these students lived in poverty did not destine them to become rebels; on the contrary, the most young men such as Nadutkin could accomplish was participation in a student demonstration before disappearing back into the provinces. A student career cut short so quickly gave little chance to build up the commitment and circle of comrades to carry over into the radical movement. By the same token, a good scholarship was no guarantee of political reliability. Many sacrificed promising studies and financial comfort to join the dissenters. Lazar Gol'denberg was one of the fortunate

---

67. "Proklamatsiia S. T. Enisherlova," in Svatikov, "Studencheskoe dvizhenie," *Nasha strana,* Jan. 1907, p. 206.
68. Chudnovski, "Iz davnykh let," p. 287.
69. "Revoliutsionnoe i studencheskoe dvizhenie," pp. 113–16.

students in the Technological Institute in 1869 with a generous scholarship. Yet he was also one of the activists in the student agitation that spring and soon afterward severed his ties with formal learning to work for the cause.[70] Student hardship remained an issue capable of touching off disturbances and mobilizing large numbers of supporters. But it was not the catalyst that united the students in the first place nor could it furnish the inspiration for the new life of the radical community. Poverty was a condition of life, for students as well as radicals.

The program of studies in the institutions of higher education provided the most effective device to separate the desirable students from the dross. The examinations which came at the end of each year represented an impressive hurdle. Until the late 1860's the most difficult ones came at the end of the second year, prior to entry into specialized studies. In 1867 the university council took note of the "sad fact that a very insignificant number of students" even attempted these examinations. They decided to advance the crucial examination to the end of the first year, "as a result of which the young men entering the university will be obliged to study zealously in their first year." That year the university graduated 72 students, but lost another 245.[71] The Technological Institute at the end of the 1860's and early 1870's failed a sizable proportion of the new students. Large numbers enrolled, but they were poorly prepared for the difficult engineering and science courses. In 1872–1873 the first-year class had over 600 students out of the total of 1,130 in the institute, but almost one-half of the class had failed their examinations the year before. By comparison, the third-year class had only 121 students.[72] This remarkable attrition testified to the rigors of a system of elite education.

The wholesale failure spared no class of Russians, even the nobility. The sons of nobles had a slightly better chance of graduating than priests' sons, but the difference was not great. In the early 1870's a government committee made a study of the social composition of the graduates of several institutions of higher education. Its report showed that there were a higher proportion of nobles among gradu-

70. L. Gol'denberg, "Vospominaniia" [Memoirs], *Katorga i ssylka,* No. 10 (1924), 99–103.

71. TsGIAL, f. 733, o. 203, d. 207 (1867), ll. 20, 58.

72. *Ibid.,* o. 158, d. 127, ll. 129–30.

ates than among the student body as a whole in Moscow University (62 as opposed to 53 percent), but in the Technological Institute the proportions were exactly the same (53 percent). The offspring of clergy had the worst chance of survival. Their proportion of graduates was consistently lower in all the schools than in the student bodies. All other estates, grouped in one category, did neither much better nor much worse than could have been predicted by enrollment. In the Technological Institute, for example, they constituted 41 percent of the student body and 44 percent of the graduates.[73] There was scarcely any discrimination by class in these schools, for all suffered heavily.

The *gymnasium* graduates had the best chance of graduating from the educational institutions surveyed in the early 1870's. In spite of the handicaps, those without the *gymnasium* certificate continued to try to break into the system. For a period, they could attend Petersburg University as "auditors" in the hope of ultimately passing the entrance examination and attempting to survive as regular students. The minister of education suppressed this right in 1866, declaring these unofficial students (among whom just recently had been Karakozov) to be "the most dangerous and unreliable element among the student youth."[74] His assumption seemed to be that real learning necessarily eliminated dissent. The right to audit continued to exist in the professional schools. A student was allowed to repeat the same year once or twice. This option, added onto the long years of schooling already spent by the *gymnasium* pupils, produced a student body in higher education which was scarcely youthful. In Petersburg University, 85 percent of the students in 1880 were twenty-one years of age or older.[75] The "student youth" of Russia were literally in a state of prolonged adolescence.

In a country whose population was largely poor and illiterate, the demand for educational excellence was likely to produce conflict. To work properly, the system had to provide satisfactory alternative employment for the "drop-outs" and the rapid assimilation of the lucky few who completed the program of studies into the existing so-

73. *Ibid.*, f. 908, o. 1, d. 125, l. 89.
74. Quoted in A. Georgievski, *Kratkii ocherk pravitel'stvennykh mer i prednachertanii protiv studencheskikh bezporiadkov* [A brief study of government measures and plans against student disorders] (Stuttgart, 1902), p. 3.
75. MVD-TsSK, *Universitety*, p. 5.

cial hierarchy. By the 1860's this was no longer happening. The government's response consisted of strengthening even further the elitist character of higher education. A commission investigating the student disorders of 1874 sharply criticized the easing of entrance requirements in the late 1860's and early 1870's. The "artificial expansion" of the numbers of students had created "overcrowding" in the schools. Instead of seeking ways to expand the capacity of the system of higher education, the committee focused on the imperfections of the students. They saw "on the one hand, a contingent of young people who, sooner or later, will abandon studies as a result of inability, and on the other hand, a contingent of young people without any material support, often without any family aid." In their view, higher education formed part of a society of the well-born and the able. Those who had problems with advanced learning must be lowly and unfit individuals obviously not deserving the privilege of knowledge. One member qualified such people as the "intellectual proletariat."[76] He feared them as much as radicals such as Pisarev welcomed them. Neither side questioned the necessity of giving those who entered the system the rigorous, exacting training suitable for an elite.

These state officials saw higher education through a special prism shaped by their own conception of society and by their admiration for the Prussian system of education. Educational reformers since the time of Peter the Great had shaped and molded a hierarchy of schools which demanded intellectual discipline and the assimilation of a curriculum largely determined by Western models. The schools controlled by the Orthodox church, the War Ministry, the Ministry of Education, and the other governmental agencies provided for the needs of a developing state and society. On the whole, they appeared to perform at least adequately. The entire network of schools was by the mid-century extensive and complex. At the top its elite schools offered the finest training available in the country to a small group of select youth.

These same channels were followed by the radicals in their educational careers. One after another, the Alexandrovsky Lycée, the university, the professional schools all began contributing to the supply of intellectual rebels. Something within those institutions was de-

76. TsGIAL, f. 908, o. 1, d. 125, l. 76.

flecting a small percentage of students away from their designated path of social promotion.

These disruptive conditions existed in some sort of symbiotic relationship with the educational institutions themselves. The radicals were young people who for the most part could have succeeded in their schooling, not those who failed. Their biographical characteristics revealed them similar in educational background and social class to the student bodies of the most advanced institutions. Thus the harsh selectivity of the school system must also have operated on the composition of the radical group. Education in Russia represented one aspect of the social inequalities of a rigidly hierarchical society. The protest of the radicals originated among those privileged to receive this training and also privileged to be born noble. Men such as Nechaev and Myshkin were exceptional, not typical. Most of the rebels had successfully survived the educational trials set in their path thanks partly to their class advantages but mainly to their own intellectual capacity. They were typical of the educated class in Russia in every respect except their refusal to accept the system that had nurtured them.

4 | Recruiting the New People

The Russian system of higher education brought together a diverse student body and offered an intellectual training on the basis of which they were to become constructive members of the state apparatus or to enter professional occupations. This process of social fusion depended upon a set of inducements and constraints in which the schools provided the intellectual formation and moral instruction to prepare the country's elite. They awarded the diplomas which were the permit to entrance into rewarding and highly regarded occupations. Yet the government was disappointed that the system did not function as well as expected: By the 1860's the schools had inexplicably become the chief recruiting area for the radical movement. Students in the capital pursued activities undesirable to the authorities and organized their own affairs in a manner which the state found unacceptable. The demonstrations and strike of 1861 in Petersburg University furnished vivid evidence of active student solidarity in defiance of established rules and traditions.

The student movement had its own distinct interests. It was concerned with fees, student body organization, and status, all of which sprang from the immediate needs and aspirations of the students. The demonstrations which broke out sporadically in the 1860's and 1870's were the direct product of this environment. Many of those active in this movement felt no desire to follow the much more dangerous path of political revolt, but large numbers of young people otherwise disunited in the schools were brought together. Their autonomous organizations provided the institutional experience for common living which became the basis for the life of the new radical community. This unique student experience was never the sole training ground for radical revolt. Some recruits sought entry after years at established occupations, while others trained themselves in relative isolation. But by the late 1860's the schools were the source of the single largest group of radicals. What had involved small groups in the 1840's had become a mass movement by the middle of the 1870's.

The example of Prussia gave educational authorities a model for proper social promotion. Great respect was accorded government service in Prussia, and its schools prepared young men from all classes for entry into administrative positions. This career preparation was so attractive that in the 1830's and 1840's the universities were turning out more graduates than there were openings.[1] Prussian society incorporated the prestige of learning into the system of social promotion. Their schools apparently acquired a hold over social mobility which the Russians sought but never fully achieved. The primary schools trained the lower classes, and advanced education was restricted to a small elite whose elevated position in society was guaranteed upon graduation. As a result, "the segmentation of the educational system probably had more to do with German social stratification than any other factor." Advanced training conferred special qualities of wisdom and virtue through moral development, all of which were incorporated in the concept of *Bildung* (untranslatable in its real sense, usually given as "cultivation"). The acquisition of this virtue placed a man, as much by public regard as personal capacity, among the elite of Germany. "Academic values bore the stamp of public and official recognition. . . . The mandarin aristocracy of cultivation had become the functional ruling class of the nation."[2]

The Russian educational leaders very much desired the same result. They maintained rigid standards in their secondary and higher schools and attempted to weed out the dross by a process of moral and mental purification. The training they provided was far more alien to their students than in Prussia, and their society did not possess the strong sense of class prestige conferred on the Prussian educated class. The Russian system worked for the majority of youth who passed through it into professional occupations or state service. Only

1. Lenore O'Boyle, "The Problem of an Excess of Educated Men in Western Europe, 1800–1850," *Journal of Modern History*, XLII (Dec. 1970), 475–78.
2. Ringer, *Mandarins*, pp. 30, 38, 85–87.

a small group disrupted the process, but their presence was highly disturbing in a society unprepared for dissent and extremely sensitive to political opposition. The schools were not achieving the desired level of social homogeneity to permit smooth promotion of youth from diverse social backgrounds into the upper classes.

Education and Social Promotion

As in Prussia, social promotion through education was a class policy. The admission into institutions of secondary and higher education of individuals from diverse social strata assumed that these youth would be able to fuse into new occupational groups upon graduation. The process was fairly easy in an elitist institution like the Alexandrovsky Lycée, which absorbed many sons of upper bureaucrats and aristocrats. It was more difficult to take a son of the petty landed nobility, whose father had received only rudimentary education, had served as an army officer, then retired to his estate, and to prepare him as a bureaucrat. Thus the spread of learning and the rise of professional groups resulted in a restructuring of part of the upper classes. As in Prussia, the title of nobility remained, but the social composition of the noble estate altered in occupation and training. The state had only to tinker somewhat with its system of honors and prestige to provide for new occupational groups in the upper ranks of society. It created a new estate in the 1840's partially to accommodate the professionals. The "honorary citizens" were distinguished by economic enrichment or by graduation from an institution of higher learning, but were excluded from the nobility. After the training of engineers in the Technological Institute was improved, its graduates with good academic records entered this estate. These were only minor adjustments to a social hierarchy that continued to reward social prominence with the title of noble.

As a result, advanced education opened bright perspectives of individual upward social mobility. It provided a path by which the offspring of middle and lower classes might obtain access to the nobility. By traditional standards these individuals of low birth were potential troublemakers. While still students, they had either to change allegiance rapidly to accept their own good fortune in anticipation of social promotion or to be expelled before stirring up trouble. For the sake of social stability, integration within the schools was a necessity, but this created the possibility, unanticipated by the educational authorities, that a new student group would appear which denied the very foundations of class society and organized its own internal life on nonclass, egalitarian principles.

Student and radical protest in and around the schools immediately aroused visions of class protest. The head of the Third Section stressed this motive, as already noted, in discussing the student agitation of 1869. The theme attracted radicals as well. It had the virtue of associating the revolt of intellectuals with the deeper forces of class conflict, personified by the poor, *raznochintsy* students. Peter Tkachev defended this theory in his later writings. He had attended a Petersburg *gymnasium,* then was admitted as a first-year student in the university in the fateful year of 1861. Though he never completed a formal course of higher education, he was around student circles until the late 1860's. On the basis of this experience, he argued that social oppression was the key to understanding the revolutionary potential of Russian students. "Our student youth," he wrote in 1874, "find themselves in conditions suitable for the development of a revolutionary attitude . . . not by reason of their knowledge, but by reason of their social position." He believed that "the majority are children of proletarian parents or of people very recently risen from the proletariat." Once they had begun "to reason intelligently," they came "automatically and inevitably" to accept "the necessity for the revolution."[3] For the sake of this argument, Tkachev had to disregard his own background, for his father had risen from the merchant estate to noble rank as an architect. For him to visualize students in the ranks of the socially oppressed justified his revolt and reassured him that the radicals such as he were only the vanguard of the social revolution.

This theory of radical and student protest offered both the police and the radicals an intellectually satisfying picture of a phenomenon difficult to understand. It assumed that the process of social fusion within the schools was not working. The authorities knew the figures on the social composition of the students in various educational institutions. They did not make any serious effort to compare these data with the statistics they possessed on the social background of arrested radicals, or to compare the change of student social origins

3. P. Tkachev, *Izbrannye sochineniia* [Selected Works] (Moscow, 1933), III, 71–72.

over time with the appearance of student agitation in various schools. These comparisons provide simple if crude evidence on the social roots of radicalism among student youth.

The educational institutions assumed a slightly mixed-class character at the *gymnasium* level. Nicholas I had favored the nobility, partly by encouraging the creation of noble institutes whose educational function was similar to the *gymnasia,* but whose enrollment was restricted to sons of nobles only. In addition, in 1845 the Ministry of Education placed special restrictions on the admission of sons of merchants and petty bourgeois. The minister commented that "the *gymnasia* will become mainly the place for the education of noble and bureaucrat children while the middle estate will turn to the district schools."[4] In fact, the new policy had hardly any effect on the estate distribution of the pupils. Throughout Nicholas' reign, the nobility and bureaucracy (usually put together in one category in official statistics) provided almost four-fifths of the enrollment, the rest being filled mostly by the urban estates. The Russian state found, as the French in the same years, that the middle classes could overcome considerable obstacles to send their sons to schools offering substantial promise of social mobility.[5]

By the mid-1870's the noble-bureaucrat group had declined to one-half of the total enrollment, and the urban group had risen to over one-third.[6] In 1880 the hereditary nobility contributed only 20 percent of the *gymnasium* youth, while the personal nobility (middle bureaucracy and lower officers) and lower bureaucracy were 30 percent.[7] This represented some decline in the proportion of the "official classes," remaining nonetheless greatly overrepresented in comparison to their percentage of the total population. As already indicated, sons of nobles had a greater chance of graduating than did other classes, accentuating even more the continued congruence of elite education and enrollment based on social privilege. The ideal of Nicholas I was thus still partially respected. This fact did not prevent some of the pupils from becoming active in the radical movement, nor did it alter the potential for disruption which these pupils showed upon entering higher education.

4. Quoted in I. Aleshintsev, "Soslovnyi vopros i politika" [The estate question and politics], *Russkaia shkola,* Jan. 1908, p. 47.

5. On France, see O'Boyle, "Educated Men," p. 492.

6. Rashin, "Gramotnost'," pp. 72–73.

7. MVD-TsSK, *Universitety,* p. 122.

The institutions that appeared most susceptible to corruption were the technical and professional schools, attracting large numbers of students of nonprivileged origin. They were, of all the schools of the country, the most democratic in social composition. The Petersburg Medical-Surgical Academy was typical of this type of educational institution. In 1857 its students included 38 percent from the nobility and the bureaucracy, 27 percent from the clergy, and 19 percent from the petty bourgeoisie. Eight years later it contained 36 percent sons of nobles and bureaucrats, only 15 percent priests' sons, and 12 percent from the petty bourgeoisie. The numbers of *raznochintsy,* mainly sons of soldiers, rose from 6 to 15 percent in those years.[8] Thus the trend of social composition of the student body was not toward a rise of lower classes, but a readjustment of lower-class representation. The sons of nobles, bureaucrats, and merchants were proportionately as numerous in the mid-1860's as earlier. The trend probably continued in much the same direction in the years that followed, at the very time when the institution was becoming one of the centers of student agitation and of recruitment into the radical movement. In the 1850's school life had been virtually without incident. One of the few radicals there recorded his profound disillusionment at the political immaturity of his schoolmates. He found a large number of Poles, who kept completely to themselves, and a group of Germans hardly speaking Russian who talked "chiefly about potatoes." The rest were "blessed Orthodox Russians," whose "sole aim was to study zealously, and who explained naively that everything outside their circle [of immediate interests] concerned them hardly at all."[9] By the late 1860's the institution was not substantially altered in social composition, but student interests were very different.

One new element among the students was a small group of Jews. They had first been allowed to enter in 1849. By 1865 they numbered 46, 6 percent of the student body. Their status within the academy might have been unpleasant had social origins counted, since they were religious outcasts as well as social inferiors (mostly petty bourgeois by birth), but neither characteristic seems to have affected their lives. One of these young men was Mark Natanson, son of a Jewish merchant from western Russia. He kept notes of his first impressions

8. *Istoriia imperaterskoi voenno-meditsinskoi akademii,* pp. 568–69.
9. Letter of January 21, 1859, in TsGIAL, f. 1282, o. 1, d. 71 (1862), l. 195.

of the student body. Nowhere in these pages is there a single reference to social standing or class hostility.[10] Within a year of entering the academy, he was an active member of the radical community. The forces attracting him to this new life appear unrelated to any movement of social protest or conflict reflecting the presence of large numbers of *raznochintsy* in the school.

The universities favored the upper classes in the composition of their student body to a greater extent than did any of the professional schools. In the years of Nicholas I, the sons of nobles and bureaucrats made up slightly more than two-thirds of the total enrollment. This constituted social favoritism for the privileged classes but not exclusion of all others. The proportions had hardly changed in the mid-1860's, when the sons of the clergy were 10 percent of the total university students and the city estates 9 percent. The decline of the elite began in the years that followed. By 1880 the nobility and bureaucracy made up slightly less than half (47 percent) of the student body, while the clergy and urban classes were each approaching one-quarter (23 and 21 percent, respectively).[11] Petersburg University followed the evolution of the total university enrollment fairly closely. It too was largely monopolized by the official classes of nobility and bureaucracy until the 1860's. In 1859 (as indicated in Table 2), hereditary nobles constituted 58 percent of its 1,026 students, the sons of bureaucrats 22 percent, and sons of clergy another 9 percent; only 11 percent came from the remaining nonprivileged and lowly classes.[12] Yet this was the very period of rising agitation among the students of the university. By 1879 these other groups had increased to one-half of the student body, including 30 percent sons of priests.[13] Thus the evolution of the social composition of Petersburg University provides no evidence of a sudden rise in representation of the *raznochintsy* at the same time as student radicalism spread. Application of these vague class explanations to both the student and radical movements has only obscured the true problem of the origins of dissent in mid-century Russia.

The educational atmosphere of the university acted as a catalyst to break down old patterns of behavior. After a student entered the

10. Cited in Koz'min, *Revoliutsionnoe dvizhenie,* p. 82.
11. Rashin, "Gramotnost'," p. 78.
12. TsGIAL, f. 733, o. 95, d. 172, ll. 333–34.
13. *Ibid.,* o. 203, d. 213, l. 10.

walls of the temple of learning, the prospect of a career seems to have played a much greater role than social traditions in determining his goals. Because it was not reserved for the privileged, the university gradually instilled in its student body a sense of corporate pride and solidarity. This process of social fusion took place slowly, but had touched a large number of students by the late 1850's. The rise of student radicalism coincided with the weakening of class consciousness within the university.

The one social group that did not respond to the pressures for integration was the Polish students, who came to Petersburg University in fairly large numbers following the closing of Vilno University in 1831. They represented almost one-fourth of the student body in 1841 and nearly one-third in 1859. They remained together, did not frequent the Russian student organizations or participate in their activities, and observed their national traditions. The tormented history of the Polish national movement in those years made them feel isolated. Though a few did move into the Russian community, most probably looked on their years in St. Petersburg as a painful period which would end only on their return to the Polish provinces. In a report written in 1856, a Russian official attacked the Polish group in the universities for "their rigid outlook, their stupid illusions of an uprising in Poland," which "filled their hearts with hatred toward Russia."[14] Polish national loyalty created bonds which neither the elixir of learning nor student brotherhood could weaken. An activist Russian student of the late 1850's noted that the large group of Poles in Petersburg University "kept absolutely aloof from the Russians, with whom no intimacy existed."[15]

The Polish students' solidarity and militancy might have attracted the less organized Russians, but were founded on a different set of values. Before the uprising of 1863 some Poles attending the university became active in the political opposition, but they did not join the activities of the Russian students. The new university regulations of 1861 hit them severely by reducing the number of tuition exemptions,

14. *Ibid.*, f. 735, o. 10, d. 305, l. 5.
15. L. Panteleev, *Vospominaniia* [Memoirs] (Moscow, 1958), p. 169; also, T. Snytko, "Studencheskoe dvizhenie v russkikh universitetakh" [The student movement in Russian universities], in V. Korluk and I. Miller, eds., *Vosstanie 1863 goda i russko-pol'skie revoliutsionnye sviazi* (Moscow, 1960), pp. 176–322.

granted them in earlier years fairly generously. They participated in the agitation that fall. In the preparations for the demonstration and strike, their representatives declared that the Polish students "would not refuse" to aid the student movement.[16] They suffered the same penalties for agitation as the Russians. The Ministry of Education figures show that almost two hundred Poles were expelled from Russian universities in the early 1860's.[17] Contrary to the suspicions of the Third Section, the Poles did not subvert the Russian students. The two groups were separated by national and cultural differences effectively blocking borrowing and assimilation of practices and beliefs.

The Student Corporation

Class and estate distinctions among students gradually gave way to a consciousness of the unique calling of learning, at least among the active students. This transformation came most easily to those who enjoyed the leisure and advantages of wealth. It is no wonder to find Alexander Herzen, amply cared for by his aristocratic father, praising Moscow University in the 1830's as "a great reservoir into which poured from all sides, from all estates, the young forces of Russia." With the means to pursue his education in the best conditions, he could easily join those who "cleansed themselves of the prejudices acquired at home, fraternized with one another and reached the same level."[18] The very fact of poverty made the poor students more conscious of their origins. Herzen had pitied the sons of clergy in the university who obviously did not fit into his new community. Twenty years later they continued to stand out by "their excessively long coats, strong local accent in conversation, their snuff pouch, and clumsy movements."[19]

Money helped overcome these idiosyncrasies of the lowly, but so did the respect for and pursuit of learning. This latter factor played the major role in solidifying the increasingly large number of students in Petersburg University in the late 1850's. They were probably less well off on an average than those of earlier years, but had a greater consciousness of learning as a sacred cause in itself. This was the

16. Panteleev, *Vospominaniia*, p. 84.
17. TsGIAL, f. 733, o. 147, d. 785, ll. 212–17.
18. Gertsen, *Byloe i dumy*, I, 109.
19. R. V., "Russkii vrach" [The Russian doctor], *Sovremennik*, No. 89 (Oct. 1861), 582.

hope of one student activist, who made a speech in 1858 to his fellow students proclaiming that "in the face of learning, there are no estates, or titles, or uniforms." The university could not consist of "petty bourgeois, merchants, bureaucrats, officers, or well-born Russian nobles. . . . There should be only adepts of learning." He felt that this process was complete in Petersburg University. "Thank God, that there has already formed among us that atmosphere in which the external condition of a man does not devour the man himself."[20] There was a strong element of wishful thinking in his comments, for his speech sought to achieve that very solidarity in defense of student interests which he was proclaiming already in existence.

The data on student agitation suggest that social solidarity was a reality among those youth involved in protest action. The Third Section kept records, in conjunction with the Ministry of Education, of the expelled students involved in undesirable agitation. Their records were incomplete. The disturbances of 1869 produced a list of students expelled from Petersburg University for involvement in the agitation. The profile of those eighty students is a faithful reproduction of the composition of the student body of the university and shows no bias toward the less privileged and lowly. The sons of nobles and bureaucrats were in a majority (56 percent), though there were a significant number of priests' sons (19 percent). The school of law was most heavily represented (59 percent), followed by the school of science.[21] This evidence suggests strongly that social origins played no major role in the unrest. A random sampling of the student body would have produced approximately the same proportions. The use of estates to measure social origins leaves much to be desired since it cannot reveal actual economic conditions or occupations of the families. As the only available quantitative data, it must be used with the more impressionistic evidence of memoirs as proof of the new social conditions in the institutions of higher education. New bonds of student loyalty were supplanting class consciousness to unite large numbers of students in open protest against the authorities. This was no "proletarian" revolt.

The data I was able to collect on the social origins of a part of

20. Cited in B. Modzalevski, "Iz istorii . . ." [From the history . . .], *Golos minuvshego*, Jan. 1917, p. 141.
21. TsGIAL, f. 733, o. 147, d. 785, ll. 57–66.

the Petersburg radicals, displayed in Table 2, suggest a heavier weighting from the upper classes even than in the institutions of higher education, their principal area of recruitment. My figures cover only a portion of those active in Petersburg and make no pretense to describe the character of the radical movement throughout the country. Unfortunately, the statistics of the Third Section are quite worthless, since they never examined separately the estate background of those arrested on suspicion of political activity who had a secondary education or above.

The real significance of the data on the Petersburg radicals appears when my figures of social origins are compared with the enrollment figures of the educational institutions of St. Petersburg. If the non-privileged educated youth really did constitute a significant element in the radical movement, their proportion among the radicals should have been greater than in the schools. Just the opposite is true. Consistently from the 1840's to the 1870's, the distribution of radicals by estates resembles most closely the university, the major institution which most favored the upper classes. In the 1840's approximately 70 percent of university students came from the nobility and bureaucracy; the figure for the radicals is even greater, 88 percent. In the late 1850's this group represented 80 percent of the student body and slightly more among the radicals. By the 1870's they had declined to 60 percent among the latter, but had fallen even lower (approximately 50 percent) in the university. The percentage of priests' sons had risen by then to 30 percent in the school and to 15 percent among the radicals. There is no basis in fact for the theory that the evolution of the radical movement between "fathers" and "sons" over the decades of the mid-century reflected the influx of large numbers of *raznochintsy*. Tkachev, son of a successful architect-nobleman, was a more accurate representative of the "men of the 1860's" than the "proletarian student" of whom he later dreamed. But class was not a real factor. Put figuratively, the educational institutions had become a crucible for the tempering of radical revolt among students for whom social origins had lost real meaning.

Radical recruitment grew out of the restructuring of student loyalties to produce what was called at the time a "student corporation." This development too presented the government with an unexpected effect of elite education. Under Nicholas I it regarded the elevated calling of student as an official category within the hierarchy of estates. The more influential the school, the greater was the emphasis on the prestige of the student body. The university, like the smaller Alexandrovsky Lycée, occupied the uppermost rung of this social ladder, fitting preparation for future cultural and political leaders. Its students held a position in society resembling that of bureaucrats or army officers. Like the latter, they enjoyed special rights and duties. The outward symbol of this status was the student uniform, including three-cornered hat, sword, and coat, which all were required to wear whenever they were outside the university. Within the institution they received special care and surveillance. In some respects, these practices resembled the corporate traditions of the universities of western Europe, but they were conferred by the state. They represented, to use the medieval term, the university corporation.

The effort to elevate the university student body seems to have borne fruit. One student of the early 1850's remembered that "the university attracted us above all because it was the symbol of our liberation from the restrictions and dependence of the life of 'children,' from the humiliating status of pupils, from family control."[22] One envious student in the Pedagogical Institute believed the university had an "entirely different spirit" than his school. "There is the real life; the students study what they please. They are not school children, but work independently."[23] Their role was pursuit of true learning, which enjoyed the respect previously given to study of the Holy Scriptures. Other schools could not possibly compete. Nikolai Shelgunov, a pupil in the lowly Forestry Institute in the 1840's, recalled that the pupils in military schools considered the university students "an object of envy," though their jealousy was weakened by "a trace of a certain holy fear of higher education." It seemed to him that Petersburg society "loved and respected the students. . . . There were few of them and they were highly valued."[24] A committee of Moscow professors, evaluating the cause of the unrest in their university in 1861, echoed a similar opinion. They found that "Russian society inspired students with a feeling of dignity such as hardly exists in other countries. These young men are filled with the consciousness of their high calling [and] in the eyes of many . . . represent the

22. Boborykin, *Za polveka*, p. 57.
23. Panteleev, *Vospominaniia*, p. 129.
24. Shelgunov, *Vospominaniia*, p. 123.

future hope of Russia."[25] Such expectations guaranteed that university corporate life would transmit to the students a sense of special honor.

The government wished to control the students in their years of study while preparing them for assimilation into the upper levels of society upon graduation. Its draconian regulations served to unite the students by creating a potential for resistance from pampered juveniles. Punishment for infraction of the rules in these schools was severe. The Third Section reported one incident in 1848 of a sort which probably occurred frequently. The school inspector judged that a university student had "rudely answered" his command and ordered the youth arrested. A classmate tried to organize his comrades to protest the inspector's insulting behavior and "rude language." Rumors circulated of a collective protest.[26] Nothing came of the agitation. In those years the students were incapable of uniting in opposition to the authorities. They disliked but still obeyed the daily inspection of rooms and ban on smoking, the restrictions on long hair, and the requirement to salute school officials. Liberation from this enforced university corporation had to await the swelling of enrollment and the new liberal spirit of the early years of Alexander II's reign.

Behind the façade of prestige and privilege, the students' lives seem to have been quiet with little concern for larger issues. They divided among themselves partly according to social background, partly according to career expectations. The future historian Nikolai Kostomarov found this state of affairs on arriving in Kharkov University to begin studies in the late 1830's. The students seemed to have "no common interests among themselves beside listening to lectures, and thus formed no ties which might have created a spirit of comradeship." Those of wealthy parents did not mix with the poor, the sons of nobles stayed away from the nonprivileged, and the scholarly students striving for teaching positions had nothing in common with the bureaucrats-to-be who only wanted their degrees as quickly and painlessly as possible.[27] Conditions in Petersburg University were probably similar. This disunited mass of students could pose no serious problem for the authorities, for whom isolated cases of individual insubordination were a natural reflection of juvenile immaturity. They were incapable of defending their own interests and even less of de-

---

25. Quoted in I. Borozdin, "Universitety v Rossii" [The universities in Russia], *Istoriia Rossii v XIX veke*, IV, 189–90.

26. TsGAOR, f. 109, per. eks., d. 255 (1848).

27. N. Kostomarov, *Avtobiografiia* (Moscow, 1922), pp. 142–44.

veloping traditions of dissent and resistance which might prepare for radical revolt.

Like the Alexandrovsky Lycée, the university student body contained a peculiar mixture of elitist attitudes and egalitarian habits. They were a chosen few living in a little world apart from other Russians. Both social expectations and intellectual tastes dictated the emphasis on moral improvement. In the 1840's the student body lacked a sense of common interests and the means to express their solidarity, but the elements of egalitarianism and elitism contained the formula to mold a unified student body.

In the first few years of Alexander II's reign the universities created a model for the student corporation which spread to the professional schools to become an integral part of higher education for the next half-century. The atmosphere in Petersburg University altered suddenly and radically. The size of the student body expanded rapidly from 476 in 1855 to 1,026 in 1859—a greater increase than over the entire thirty years of Nicholas' reign. Old class distinctions disappeared readily and new forms of association developed. The sudden change in scale was accompanied by greater willingness to innovate. The "thaw" which touched all aspects of the official life of the country affected the students and school administration. The new students seemed of a different character than the older classes. Dimitri Pisarev, who entered the university in 1856, considered his classmates "timid, inclined to humility," and awestruck by their professors. Those who came in two and three years later were "daring and unrestrained" and within a few months became the "masters of the university."[28]

The rigid controls governing the university corporation could not continue into the new reign. A report on the student disorders of 1861 argued that "from the moment after the Crimean War, when Russia began its renovation, the university rules of 1835 could no longer be effective." The "police character of the rules . . . served only to provoke continual clashes between students and the university administration."[29] Some of the school authorities were eager to es-

28. D. Pisarev, *Izbrannye pedagogicheskie sochineniia* [Selected pedagogical works] (Moscow, 1951), p. 116.
29. K. Kavelin, "Zapiska o bezporiadkakh" [A note on the disorders], *Sobranie sochinenii*, II (St. Petersburg, 1900), 1191. An original of the report can be found in the Valuev archives (f. 908, o. 1, d. 140). The author was professor in the university at the time, classified as a "liberal."

tablish new, freer relations with the students and to disregard petty regulations. Smoking became common in the university buildings in flagrant violation of the rules, student uniforms were disregarded or altered, and mustaches appeared on previously shaven lips. The university students adopted a new style of life which no official rules could repress. It reflected a consciousness of collective rights and a willingness to defend these rights. This attitude led to public protests against professors felt unworthy of the privilege of teaching.[30] Established authority in the university was no longer sacred, either within the classrooms or without. Paternalism in the universities disappeared. One unhappy Moscow University professor wrote that the students in those first years of Alexander's reign "did as they pleased."[31] No foreign universities set the model for this new life. The Russian students were developing a pattern of collective behavior unlike anything western Europe had seen.

Their most important innovation was the student assembly (*skhodka*) for collective decision making. The assembly defended student interests in dealing with the authorities, yet it possessed no rules or formal procedure and no regular leadership. Any group could call an assembly; attendance fluctuated wildly as interest in issues waxed and waned. There was no agenda and no rules for voting. After a long period of talk among the participants, someone usually presented a proposal to try to crystallize the mood. Nicholas' ban on collective student activity was still in effect, but the school authorities could not and in some cases would not enforce it. The increase in numbers and the rising agitation among students made it impossible to block meetings by any means short of confrontation. In the late 1850's the practice of holding assemblies became part of student life. They regarded the meetings as their "private affair," seeking no formal permission or official supervision. Petersburg University authorities at times took advantage of this new institution of student solidarity to deal with the militant youth who periodically presented new demands. A Petersburg professor noted in a report on the disorders of 1861 that "when the students came in a crowd to request something, they were told: 'Choose your delegates and send them in-

---

30. William Mathes, "The Origins of Confrontation Politics in Russian Universities," *Canadian Slavic Review*, II (Spring 1968), 34–36.
31. B. Chicherin, *Vospominaniia* [Memoirs] (Moscow, 1929), p. 16.

stead.' " The assemblies thus provided the means for selecting student representatives. As long as the government took no action on the
old regulations, the university administration "tolerated" the assemblies and officially "as it were took no notice of them."[32] The student
corporation had found its collective voice.

Learning meant more than ever before, but true knowledge came
most often from outside the classroom. It was symbolic of the intellectual concern of these students that the first open violation of the
old regulations in Petersburg University was a public debate in 1856
on the existence of God, with many students supporting the antireligious, materialistic position against the right-thinking professor
defending Christian theology. No punishment followed, as would
have immediately occurred in earlier years. The concern for learning
is clear in the proposal made in 1857 by Petersburg students to pub-
lish a yearly journal of student articles selected from the various
schools of the university. The administration accepted this request
and allowed the students to elect their own editors and to hold private meetings to select the articles. Student-organized libraries appeared in several universities. Efforts were made to find means of
aiding the poor students. Cafeterias were set up to provide cheap
food, and student-aid funds, financed by public activities such as
concerts, offered loans to the needy. When the Petersburg students
discovered in 1861 that their treasurer had embezzled much of their
loan money, they organized a public trial. With a law professor serving as judge, they conducted the proceedings according to the strict
rules of Western jurisprudence—four years before the Russian courts
were reformed along similar lines. This flowering of collective interests and activities proved the extent of student involvement in advanced learning.

Activism was probably not to the taste of many students, who found
it a totally new experience. A Petersburg student leader delivered a
speech in 1858 lamenting the unsatisfactory state of the marvelous
new institutions. "The [student-aid] fund is empty, the assemblies and
literary readings have been abandoned!" It seemed to him an utter
waste of time and effort for "all the youthful ardor" of the students
to go into "street scandals or the base acts of unworthy comrades"
or other "personal affairs." He wanted a collective demonstration to

32. Kavelin, "Zapiska," p. 1194.

protest the mistreatment of some students by a group of soldiers, but this would be impossible for lack of "unity, crushed under petty factions, split by mutual misunderstandings."[33] His appeal was successful. The lapse of activism, if it really was as bad as he said, lasted only a short time. But the student corporation probably remained the work of only a part, perhaps a minority, of the student body and did not interest those concerned solely with social advancement and professional careers.

All were equal in the student community no matter what their estate. It was completely unlike the German model of student organization. The Russian manner of organization, especially in the assemblies, resembled the egalitarianism of the peasant communes, whose meetings also had the name of *skhodka*. This fact led Dimitri Kavelin, Petersburg history professor, to conclude that the student community forming around him had somehow found inspiration in Russian cultural traditions. He argued that "educational institutions, especially universities, assume a form like their contemporary social institutions."[34] Western medieval universities had developed as guild-like corporations, resembling urban society of the time. The German student fraternities preserved some of these traditions, but Russia had not followed this social path, and its universities could not reproduce the same social patterns. Its students, whose concern for social prestige faded as their interest in learning increased, expressed egalitarian sentiments as did the peasantry. The two communities had nothing in common except a disdain for any authority but that emanating from the group. The students, privileged by official educational policy, denied any privilege among themselves. In an authoritarian society their style of life was anarchistic.

Conflict with other groups and with the authorities was inescapable. Students now had the means of collective defense against slights to their dignity, of which they were as conscious as before. The police could no longer manhandle them like ordinary subjects without provoking large-scale protest. After one clash in Kazan University between students and police over an "affair of honor," a professor commented that "for the first time there has appeared among the students a consciousness of their solidarity and their community of

33. Cited in B. Modzalevski, "Iz istorii," pp. 144–45.
34. Kavelin, "Zapiska," p. 1193.

interests." The incident typified for him the transition "from the roudy, dissipated time to the period of more serious agitation."[35] This ferment had no political overtones. The issues involved questions of pride and honor and originated in the position of privilege accorded these students in Russian society. The authorities were disturbed by their collective character. Acting together the students found the strength to resist and set a model of insubordination. During a fire in a student's apartment in St. Petersburg in 1858, a brigade of soldiers under the command of an officer mistreated some students trying to save the belongings of their comrade. The action became a public incident, provoked student assemblies, and led to more agitation. The student solidarity producing these collective protests was leading, according to a report written in early 1861 on student unrest, to "conflicts with the police, the breach of discipline within and outside the university walls. Any personal insult, often imaginary, any violation of the rights of one individual, very frequently wrongly understood, arouse agitation in the entire mass of students." Despite repressive measures, this "corporate spirit remains."[36] This revolt against authority occurred without conscious plan or political aims.

Another result was increased interest in dangerous intellectual activities. Student solidarity made learning a cause which the youth could pursue without professorial guidance. Freedom to learn meant freedom to dissent as well. The student journal of Petersburg University published scholarly articles written by talented students. Dimitri Pisarev had an article in it. But the meetings of the editorial committees of the various schools quickly turned into centers for discussion of forbidden literature.[37] The interest in intellectual debate led some of the more daring students to produce "underground" newspapers.

The limits of the permissible were still vague, and the students were not agreed among themselves how far they should go. Pisarev himself was a modest student liberal at the time. He spoke out against action that would produce conflict with the school administration and end the period of uneasy tolerance of student initiative. In a let-

35. Quoted in S. Ashevski, "Russkoe studenchestvo v epokhu 60-kh godov" [Russian students in the 1860's] *Sovremennyi mir,* Sept. 1907, p. 50.

36. TsGIAL, f. 908, o. 1, d. 125, l. 7.

37. A. Skabichevski, *Literaturnye vospominaniia* [Literary memoirs] (Moscow, 1928), p. 101.

ter to the editor of one of the papers, he warned against excesses which would injure "the privileges, the rights, and the liberties of the entire university." He feared that "as a result of a daring word," the authorities would end the publications, forbid the assemblies, "prevent the students from coming together, destroy, in a word, everything that is in the process of being born."[38] His was the voice of moderation and protection of student interests against acts of political dissent. The same theme echoed repeatedly in later years as the schools felt the tension between two paths, one in the pursuit of learning and careers, the other of resistance and political dissent.

The new social atmosphere in the universities incited greater interest in public issues. The student activists could form a nucleus and their activities serve as a point of attraction for the less dynamic and committed students. At Kazan University a student library and reading room appeared with the stern warning that alcohol was strictly forbidden on the premises. The library was not purely for relaxation but a center for the pursuit of knowledge. It appeared to one student "a marvelous means to attract students away from bars and bordelloes and to school them in social theory,"[39] by which he meant radical literature. Through these activities the school of dissent could become part of the educational institutions.

Students inevitably exceeded the limits of academic learning. This "willfulness" bothered the head of the Third Section. In his report to the tsar in 1858, he warned that "in recent years" the university students had begun "to show dissatisfaction with the existing order, to desire a transformation, . . . and claim the right to judge themselves as well as their teachers."[40] His misgivings were well founded. The old system of control in a semiofficial university corporation had collapsed. The students had created in its place, in the words of an official report, a "distorted student corporation."[41] Some felt themselves part of a larger intellectual world, elevated to a position of importance by sharing in its privileges. They were among the searchers for truth and had the right and obligation to defend their position against interference or oppression.

38. "Pis'ma D. Pisareva" [Letters of D. Pisarev], *Russkaia starina,* CIV (1900), 111–14.
39. I. Khudiakov, *Zapiski Karakozovtsa* [Notes of a Karakozovets] (Moscow, 1930), pp. 38–39.
40. TsGAOR, f. 109, d. 23 (1858), l. 13.
41. TsGIAL, f. 908, o. 1, d. 125, l. 7.

This attitude led directly to the first major public clash between students and authorities, the Petersburg demonstrations and strike of the fall of 1861. A variety of issues were involved, but many students probably felt that their cause represented much more than resistance to higher tuition. A student proclamation, distributed just before the unrest, stated that "we are legion, because behind us are common sense, public opinion, literature, the professors, the countless circles, critically thinking people, western Europe; all that is best and progressive is for us."[42]

The disturbances that hit Petersburg University and in a milder form the other universities were vivid proof of the new student spirit. Within a few years, similar unrest would appear in the professional schools. The immediate issues always involved student concerns, but some participants quickly went on to total opposition to the autocratic regime. The student community developed in close contact with the new radical community and became a regular source of recruits experienced in opposition and independent action. The students never united around political protest, though they were thought at times to have done so. The two communities never fused, but the cultivation of independent learning and the training in revolt made the student body the most fertile recruiting ground in the 1860's and 1870's for the radical movement.

The sudden conflict in 1861 resulted from a polarization of forces, with the students less and less inclined to accept tight controls over their actions, and the political authorities more and more intolerant of the flagrant violation of university regulations and public order. In the spring several incidents revealed the undisciplined and rebellious sentiments among students in various universities. The growing agitation provided grounds for the dismissal of the liberal minister of education, replaced by a conservative, and the imposition of severe restrictions on the students. The authorities also used the old policy of financial pressures to cut out undesirable poor students, raising tuition to 50 rubles. The sum was large enough to pose a serious hardship for many. All the corporate privileges won by the students in the previous six years were eliminated, including calling assemblies without official permission. The attack on student power and the increased cost of university education united the student body in opposition. The conflict in Petersburg University focused on the student

42. TsGAOR, f. 109, per. eks., d. 277 (1861), ch. 1, l. 363.

handbook (*matrikul*), which spelled out the new regulations and which all had to sign.[43] In the new atmosphere of student solidarity, collective action was inevitable.

Student assemblies began in mid-September, culminating in a meeting on Friday, September 23. The doors of the university were locked, for registration was not to begin until the next week. The students broke into the building and held their assembly, as usual in one of the big amphitheaters. According to a secret police report, over a thousand youth met to discuss the new university policies. The collective decision was for protest. "The assembly decided that any student who accepted the rules would be ostracized." Everyone could sign the booklet but would not obey the rules. A public burning of the booklets was planned.[44] In response, the authorities kept the doors of the university locked the next Monday, September 25, the day of registration. A crowd gathered outside, then the leaders selected at the assembly proposed that they march through the center of the city to the house of the university curator to demand the opening of the university. Such a demonstration had never before occurred in Russia. One professor hurried to the scene to warn the demonstrators that they were, as he noted in his diary, "harming the university and the cause of learning." A student answered: "What do we care for learning [*Chto za nauka*] . . . ! We're dealing with up-to-date issues!"[45] Troops quickly arrived to disperse the students and that night police agents arrested the suspected leaders. But the struggle was just beginning.

The university was to open for classes on October 11. By then a total of 673 of the estimated 1,400 students planning to attend had actually signed the handbook. Student agitation had continued since the demonstration. On October 10 a new assembly met and resolved to boycott classes. The ubiquitous police agents noted that the next day students stood in front of the university buildings urging those coming to classes to destroy their handbooks and to stay away. Police again dispersed the demonstrators, but only seventy students ap-

43. See Thomas Hegarty, "Student Movements in Russian Universities, 1855–61 (Ph.D. dissertation, Harvard University, 1965), pp. 110–40; this work contains the most complete account available in English of the student agitation in the 1850's and early 1860's.

44. TsGAOR, f. 109, per. eks., d. 277 (1861), ch. 1, l. 41.

45. A. Nikitenko, *Dnevnik* [Diary] (Moscow, 1955), II, 213.

peared that day for classes. The same incidents recurred on the following day, this time with a larger crowd outside, including students from other schools. When soldiers arrested some of the demonstrators, police agents reported that others "heaped insults [on the soldiers], called them scum [*podlets*], and accused them of attacking helpless people."[46] The massive arrests of late September and early October filled the prisons to overflowing and forced the police to send some prisoners to the naval fortress of Kronstadt.

The strike was a success. A police report at the end of October reported that only 20 percent of those who had enrolled were attending classes. Many of the professors were not giving their lectures, some pleading illness, others stating that they had no students. Not all those students who appeared in the university attended classes; some just wandered around in the corridors, talking among themselves. "In a word, the university is not at present an educational institution; it is nothing at all, except a place for relaxation."[47] In December the government abandoned hope of restoring normal university life and closed Petersburg University for an indefinite period. It did not reopen until two years later.

The students had shown their power. Their solidarity had made possible massive public defiance of authority. Nothing like it had happened since the Decembrist uprising in 1825. Most of the students had joined the demonstrations and strike to express their opposition to government restrictions on their privileges and to protest the financial hardship imposed on them. But their rebelliousness stimulated political unrest as well. They could be inspired by this action to take up the defense of human rights against the same oppressive regime. In this sense, student agitation crystallized latent opposition and brought to life intellectual dissent. The Land and Liberty party recruited several of the leaders of the Petersburg University agitation. Others joined the movement later. Peter Tkachev, a first-year student that fall, was arrested in the October 11 demonstration and released soon afterward. He quickly reappeared in opposition circles, moving further and further into the radical community. Student solidarity provided the training for resistance. Dissent had found solid institutional foundations.

46. TsGAOR, f. 109, per. eks., d. 277 (1861), ch. 1, ll. 297–300.
47. *Ibid.*, l. 522.

This extraordinary display of student militancy convinced the government to make a major reversal of policy. New regulations in 1863 offered corporate privileges to the professors, but forbade student autonomy. The hurdles of strict academic standards and controls still stood in the way of all the students. The technique of social promotion did not change, but the student body lost most of its special privileges. It came more and more under the control of the city police, first outside the university then within its walls. It lost all the rights gained in the late 1850's, for the regulations forbade student assemblies, the election of delegates, reading rooms, or any other uncontrolled activities. Officially, the student corporation did not exist.[48] The students were not ordinary private citizens either, for they were part of an elitist educational system and were preparing for occupations in the upper classes.

They continued to keep alive the traditions of student solidarity. Though forbidden, assemblies continued to meet. The university students had developed a sense of their collective identity and the method of protest in gatherings that preserved equality but still permitted leaders to appear. Student circles continued to search for independent learning which libraries and reading rooms had earlier stimulated. Most of the students did not have interests much beyond their university life and only a few were willing to run the risk of oppositional activity. Only rarely did open clashes with the authorities occur after 1861, usually the work of a small part of the student body. Not until the end of the century did a massive student movement reappear like that of 1861. Still, the institutional activities and group solidarity of the students provided an alternative educational experience that could lead directly into the radical community.

The example of the universities spread within a few years to the professional schools. Until the 1860's these institutions had been conspicuous by the absence of corporate student life or activities. Occasional protests against the severity of the school regime only emphasized the powerlessness of the students. One activist student found on his arrival in the Medical-Surgical Academy in 1859 "constant police surveillance and petty tutelage on the part of the administration." These policies appeared to him an "insult to the human

---

48. See William Mathes, "N. I. Pirogov," *Slavic Review,* XXXI (March 1972), 44–50.

dignity of the academy students." Few others felt strongly enough to protest.[49]

Student life and attitudes had to change before collective action could become possible. These changes appeared in the mid-1860's, when most of the professional schools had become institutions of higher learning. Their enrollment was increasing. The key once again was the development of student solidarity within the institutions. It came partly by borrowing. The contacts among schools were frequent. No distinction was made now between university and professional students. In St. Petersburg all were part of the city-wide student body. Within the educational institutions, willingness to submit to petty controls decreased as the prestige of learning and the sense of collective pride spread.

The Medical-Surgical Academy remained a military institution, but was so pre-eminent in medical studies that its atmosphere resembled the civilian schools. Enrollment grew in the mid-1860's. The new students were no longer willing to tolerate the military regime and set out to manage their own affairs. They set up a cafeteria, first mentioned in police reports in 1865. They rented a floor in a house near the academy, part of which became sleeping quarters, the rest used for the cafeteria. The funds came from voluntary student contributions. The very successful cafeteria provided cheap food—20 kopecks for a three-course meal, 10 kopecks for a bargain, two-course meal—for students struggling to survive the harsh life in the capital. Up to three hundred ate there, a sizable part of the academy.[50] The students received permission to set up in the academy their own library and reading room. They included among the publications medical textbooks, general literature, and occasionally illegal works. They had an abundant supply of newspapers; the subscriptions were provided free by the publishers. The walls of the room were covered with notices of apartments to rent, clothes to sell, and so on. It was so much a student sanctuary that the inspector made a point of staying away "to avoid unpleasantness." It became the center for the new student life and was the gathering place for assemblies.[51] This corporate

49. Quoted in R. Taubin, "Obshchestvennoe dvizhenie v Rossii v 50-kh godakh XIX veka" [The social movement in Russia in the 1850's] (Doctoral thesis, Institute of History, Academy of Sciences of the USSR, 1965), p. 303.
51. *Istoriia imperaterskoi voenno-meditsinskoi akademii*, p. 656.
50. TsGAOR, f. 109, o. 1, d. 1322, ll. 8–11.

spirit developed student agitation and brought to the sedate neoclassical buildings in the Vyborg section of the capital just that type of youth predisposed to a new life. It gave them good training.

Mark Natanson entered the academy in the fall of 1868. The brief outline he wrote later of his life there suggests that his first months were spent finding his place among the students. Though his "ideal of man" did not correspond to the prevalent vulgar tastes among students, he quickly found a circle of sympathetic comrades. Soon he was a leader of the first-year class, elected to be one of the two delegates to the library committee.

That fall he was "enthused for learning." This included illicit reading, for he devoted some time to putting together a "revolutionary socialist library," perhaps as a part of the student library. He participated in the "class, academic and general student assemblies" and joined his "first little circle." Though he apparently took no part in organizing the spring 1869 disturbances in the academy, he was sufficiently active to be expelled from school and arrested.[52] He had assimilated the new student style of life augmented by a growing involvement in political dissent and resistance to authority. He borrowed directly from his school experience in founding the Chaikovtsy circle and developing the first "self-education" circle. His experience in the corporate life of the academy provided crucial elements in his maturation into a radical.

The power of the medical students to manage their own affairs was exceptional among the educational institutions of the capital and was the envy of youth in the other schools. That winter of 1868–1869 saw the development of a student corporate spirit that transcended institutional limits. The Medical-Surgical Academy and the Technological Institute had undergone the same internal transformation as the university and students from the three institutions began to meet in assemblies in their living quarters. When Vera Zasulich came to the city in the fall of 1868 to escape the life of a governess, she found student assemblies everywhere. Up to one hundred participants gathered in apartments. Most appeared to her to be first-year and second-year students. A few came from outside the educational institutions. Peter Tkachev, at the time a writer, was there, as was Sergei Nechaev, working as a teacher in a church-run primary school.

52. Cited in Koz'min, *Revoliutsionnoe dvizhenie*, pp. 182–83.

There were even a few women, like Zasulich, who "sympathized with this burgeoning youth movement."[53] The cohorts of the student community were growing in numbers.

Their principal interests were student rights and the need for political action. In their memoirs participants in the meetings all agreed that the most frequent subject of discussion was the relative importance of student interests as opposed to larger political issues. The point of departure for the debates was the development that year of student activities, such as the cafeterias and reading rooms. The St. Petersburg educational institutions were not treated equally. The Medical-Surgical Academy granted far more liberty than either the Technological Institute or the university. Students of the latter two felt they were unjustly deprived of equal rights. Led by a first-year university law student, Stepan Ezerski, one group urged that they all concentrate on the gradual development of independent student activities. In opposition to this "moderate" faction, a group of extremists called for "agitation in response to the obligation to work among and with the people."[54] The latter valued the student movement only if it could produce recruits for the radical movement. In the words of a police report on the factional struggle, these youth believed that the dissatisfaction created by "shortcomings in the situation of the student body have served and can serve in the future as an excuse to incite action among student youth."[55] Sergei Nechaev was the most anxious to manipulate the student movement. He called for a public struggle in favor of student rights and circulated a petition to protest student oppression. He had obtained almost one hundred signatures before the moderates forced a halt to what they feared was a provocative action.

The great majority of the youth active in the meetings were probably moderates. They supported agitation solely for the sake of the movement in defense of greater student privileges. They were not drawn by visions of a greater struggle nor did they see themselves as new people striving to bring a new life to Russia. An extremist medical student, Zemfiri Ralli, admitted that "a majority of the students" did not want a "large movement." Even the group of *nigilistki* audit-

53. Zasulich, *Vospominaniia*, pp. 21–22.
54. Chudnovski, "Iz davnykh let," pp. 284–85.
55. TsGAOR, f. 109, o. 85, d. 34 (1869), l. 9.

ing medical courses sent delegates to the meetings calling for an end to the dangerous agitation.[56] The student movement was no more involved in radical revolt then than earlier when it was restricted to the university, but the organization and debate it cultivated were in open violation of the submissive behavior expected of students. It could produce conflict which, as Nechaev realized, might push individuals into irrevocable acts of defiance they might otherwise have avoided. The student community was inevitably associated by intellectual interests and action with recruitment into the radical movement.

The tense atmosphere in the schools that year needed only a spark to set off large-scale disturbances. Ironically, the conflict broke out in March 1869, in the Medical-Surgical Academy, the one institution with least cause to complain of repression. One poor student was harshly treated, then expelled for resisting, and his comrades united in collective action. Their noisy demonstrations in support of his cause provoked the closure of the academy on March 15. The tremors spread to the other institutions, where the students sympathized with the struggle of the medical students and had their own grievances as well. In both the Technological Institute and the university, students organized assemblies, disrupted classes, and presented protest petitions to the administration. Ironically, the leader of the university agitators was the same Ezerski who earlier had argued against open confrontation. The movement was a failure. None of the student demands was met. A disciplinary board finally handed out punishments to ninety university students, including Ezerski.[57] All those suspended or expelled were exiled by the police to other parts of the country. But the potential for further trouble remained. The strong ties of student solidarity guaranteed that some students would be ready to accept martyrdom. On the other hand, the suspiciousness of the authorities assured that conciliation would rarely be possible. As one rebellious student complained in a letter written in 1872 to a comrade, in his school "everything comes from the top down." He and his friends were prepared to "gather up their forces" to fight these conditions.[58] Incipient conflict reigned in the institutions of higher education of St. Petersburg.

56. Z. Ralli-Arbore, "Iz moikh vospominaniia" [From my memoirs], *Byloe*, July 1906, p. 141.

57. TsGIAL, o. 203, d. 208, ll. 55–57.

58. TsGAOR, f. 109, tr. eks., d. 63 (1872), ch. 1, l. 61.

Student Conflict and Radical Recruitment

By the early 1870's the pattern of student corporate life and activities was fixed. Open confrontation broke out periodically between students and authorities. The same style of agitation endured for another half-century. A government report in 1890 gave a vivid description of student unrest valid for earlier and later years. The trouble always began with "assemblies in buildings, grounds, and courtyards of educational institutions, occasionally in city streets and squares, accompanied always by noise, uproar, shouts, occasionally broken windows, often with public demonstrations." The students invariably showed "obvious disobedience to their own [school authorities], and at times to public authorities and even insulted officials by various words, occasionally by actions." In the end came "declarations of various demands, in a majority of cases absolutely unrealizable."[59] Resistance had become a part of the educational experience.

The response of the authorities to student unrest had become as stereotyped as the unrest—it was repression. Their own diagnosis stressed the expansion of student enrollments and excessive permissiveness in granting collective privileges. The Third Section report on the disturbances of 1869 singled out the "corporate spirit, that is, that unity of interests and academic commitment" among students which created excellent "grounds for agitation."[60] The state's task was therefore to dissolve that unity by severe controls and to insure that learning did not inflame the minds of the unworthy by limiting enrollments.

The restrictive measures put the students in the category of common citizens subject to arbitrary police controls. Regulations provided for close cooperation between the city police and school officials, who were to inform the police of any suspicious student actions. Expulsion from advanced educational institutions and even occasionally from *gymnasia* brought immediate exile and close police surveillance. Unauthorized assemblies frequently ended with police occupation of the buildings. The minister of war commented during the discussion on student unrest in 1874 that the institutions of higher education had become "open auditoriums, in which the students are private individuals." The state had taken the necessary steps to "re-

59. Quoted in Georgievski, *Kratkii ocherk,* p. 1.
60. "Revoliutsionnoe i studencheskoe dvizhenie" [The revolutionary and student movement], p. 112.

move from this mass everything which could serve in any way as a bond between private individuals. . . . The students have been transformed into city residents under the jurisdiction of the general police."[61]

As the agitation increased, so did the intensity of police surveillance. The university added a rule in 1872 specifically forbidding participation "in any secret society or circle whatsoever, even without criminal aim."[62] Fearing the recruitment of students into the radical movement, the authorities issued regulations that assumed all students were potential rebels. The police sought to enforce these restrictions by mobilizing the inquisitive janitors (*dvorniki*) as informers on students living in their buildings.

A report by Petersburg University professors in 1878 protested this "interference in the private lives of the students." It claimed that "any meeting of a few students in the apartment of one of their comrades immediately fills the police with exaggerated apprehension." The result was that "these gatherings are frequently dispersed by the appearance of police officials." Any individual who came to the attention of the police immediately lost all privacy. His landlord and janitor had to answer questions such as: "Where does he usually go? What does he do? When does he return home? What does he read? What does he write?" This extraordinary surveillance indicated the crucial role played by the student community in recruitment into the radical movement, yet it reflected the inability of the authorities to purge the student body of the spirit of subversion. The university report candidly noted that "the administration and a certain segment of society regard the students as politically disloyal." They thereby acquired "an opinion of themselves as outcasts and martyrs."[63] The author of the report made the optimistic assumption that the disaffection of student youth was due primarily to official oppression. However, the process of learning had diverged into two channels as the school of dissent developed alongside the formal system of studies. The former flourished in the new atmosphere created by the rise of student solidarity. It taught revolt; confrontation with the authorities could turn this dissent from intellectual exercise to real commitment.

61. TsGIAL, f. 908, o. 1, d. 125, l. 82.
62. *Ibid.*, f. 733, o. 202, d. 5 (1872), l. 27.
63. *Ibid.*, o. 200, d. 7 (1879), ll. 6–7.

The Petersburg University faculty were correct in protesting in 1878 that "the great majority of Russian youth are unattracted by revolutionary aspirations," which were "the affair of a few individuals."[64] Still, the advanced schools offered a protective environment around the school of dissent, provided a new life of student brotherhood and activity in preparation for open revolt, and created new forms of association which carried over directly into the radical community. In 1878 the minister of education had a good case in attacking the agitation in institutions of higher learning during the previous two decades for their contribution to the growth of political protest. He pointed to Petersburg University, where students had attempted before 1861 "to organize proper, quiet assemblies and to restrict the participants to the subject of so-called student life." But the meetings had often "acquired political overtones." The same had happened to the student reading rooms, which "became filled with forbidden books and proclamations."[65]

The student experience had become by the 1860's an exceptional and, by older Russian standards, unprecedented phenomenon. Leo Tol'stoi, at the time aristocrat, former officer, writer, and amateur pedagogue, felt revulsion and pity for the student, "torn away from home, away from the family, cast into a strange city full of temptations for his youth, without means of support . . . , in a circle of comrades who by their company only intensify his defects." He claimed to know "many students" who returned from their years of education "at odds with their families in nearly all their convictions, including marriage and honor." Such an unnatural upbringing could produce only disreputable bureaucrats or "sickly liberals."[66] Tol'stoi dreamed of an education combining the traditional home tutoring of the aristocracy with the cultivation of natural development preached by Jean-Jacques Rousseau. His dream was as remote from Russian reality as radical visions of an egalitarian society. Advanced education was by necessity a process of alienation from the family and social background, for recruitment into the small elite of the country required the creation of a homogeneous group of heterogeneous origins.

64. Quoted in Georgievski, *Kratkii ocherk*, p. 7.
65. TsGIAL, f. 1282, o. 1, d. 416 (1878), l. 21.
66. L. Tol'stoi, *On Education*, trans. Leo Weiner (Chicago, 1967), pp. 136–37.

Beginning in the early 1860's, tracts and appeals to students stressed a theme of revolt and lofty mission. One which appeared in Moscow in 1862 called on the students to "prepare for the future victories" by working for the revolution and acting as "an example of unswerving firmness worthy of imitation" for succeeding generations.[67] Personal dignity and student honor became justification for resistance against oppression within the school. The unrest in the Medical-Surgical Academy in 1874 produced an appeal, posted in the reading room, to the downtrodden of the school. "Comrades!," it began, "we are despised, we are laughed at, we are considered worthless, and we have tolerated this!" Student unity and struggle were necessary to avoid the "shame" of defeat.[68] The fact that confrontations with the authorities inevitably ended in victory for the oppressors did not diminish the appeal of this message as long as honor was at stake.

The tension between individual pride and institutional humiliation brought Alexander Mikhailov to his first open act of resistance. He had been one of the fortunate applicants in 1875 to pass the recently instituted rigid entrance examination to the Technological Institute. He was among the 140 accepted out of the 400 who applied that year and as a precocious *gymnasium* pupil had begun exploring literature of dissent in a small circle of comrades. For him, as for so many others, the juvenile exploits of the years in secondary school meant little next to the lure of advanced learning. He entered the Technological Institute ready for study, though probably uncertain where the knowledge he acquired would lead him. He came prepared as well to defend student interests. In his autobiography, he recalled how "within two months" he had organized a student-aid fund and formed a circle with students from other schools.[69] He possessed the qualities of an activist and potential rebel.

Events that fall determined his fate. New rules for students required regular attendance in lectures and obligatory laboratory work every two days. Mikhailov objected, asking "why should I bother with work in the institute, when that very school does not recognize me as an individual and considers violence and coercion the best

67. TsGIAL, f. 1282, o. 1, d. 68 (1862), l. 181.
68. *Ibid.*, d. 339 (1874), ll. 2–3.
69. A. Mikhailov, "Avtobiograficheskie zametki," *Byloe,* Feb. 1906, p. 162.

means for higher education." Other students submitted a collective petition protesting the new rules. The administration responded by expelling the entire entering class and demanding new applications including the promise to obey all the school regulations. The collective protest collapsed, and all but Mikhailov and one other youth submitted to the humiliating procedure. The police exiled him to his home town. A year later he received permission to return to St. Petersburg to begin again his scientific studies, but by then he was committed to another life. "The temple of learning no longer attracted me. . . . I had passed into the main camp of the martyrs for the great cause."[70] Few students were willing to carry their resentment to such lengths, but many more certainly shared Mikhailov's sense of personal dignity.

The intellectual and social conditions of student life nurtured and protected the standing of these youth as a special elite of the land. Their corporate life passed on to new generations the attitudes and habits of solidarity. The formula, simply put, was dignity plus student solidarity equals resistance. It did not work with equal force in all educational institutions. The largest and best schools seemed to provide optimum conditions. By contrast, the smaller institutions, particularly the military schools, retained firm control over the life of their students. A few individuals in these schools responded to the call of the new life, but they did so as individuals or small groups and primarily through a process of intellectual exploration. The minister of war complained in 1862 that "in the course of recent years the cadet corps, infantry schools, and even the [war] academy have graduated young officers with such a false and harmful outlook that they are a bad influence."[71] These were modest problems compared with those posed by Petersburg University or the Medical-Surgical Academy, where a factor of mass seemed to add to the volatile mixture of elitist education and student solidarity to produce the most active centers of resistance as well as the major sources of recruits for the radical movement.

By the late 1860's agitation among students had become the single most important precipitant in this strange chemistry of revolt. It

---

70. Quoted in M. Klevenski, *A. D. Mikhailov* (Moscow, 1927), pp. 11, 15.
71. Quoted in P. Zaionchkovski, *Voennye reformy 1860–1870 godov v Rossii* [Military reforms in Russia in the 1860's–1870's] (Moscow, 1952), p. 222.

brought out the potential for dissent and presented in dramatic terms the moment of decision between a normal life and one of opposition. The unrest of 1868–1869 appeared later to some who passed through it into the radical movement as the reason behind a "strong change in the mood of the best part of the [Petersburg] student youth." They had tried "to uphold their rights and freedom in the narrow bounds of one or another educational institution."[72] Having failed, some like Mark Natanson went on to more politically oriented activities. The atmosphere generated by these conflicts created a heightened political awareness and activism. One youth who experienced this training wrote that "any student movement created appropriate circumstances for the appearance and growth of circles and student assemblies and for the distribution of revolutionary propaganda."[73]

Officials feared the success of police repression created recruits for the radical movement. Punishments were sudden and harsh. The head of the department of police wrote in 1882 of the disastrous effects he saw from such punitive measures. Expelled students found their lives transformed, their prospects of careers terminated. "The disorders in higher educational institutions and the large or small numbers of expulsions which inevitably follow represent a sort of recruitment service, producing sedition in the ranks of student youth." Their hope for normal social advancement was "destroyed at its very beginning" as they were forced into "inactivity, hunger, and privation." If they were not already committed to revolt, they became likely candidates for subversion.[74] However, the records show that most former students returned to quiet, undistinguished lives. The leader of the unrest in Petersburg University in 1869, Ezerski, never reappeared among the activists after his exile. Such men were lost for the radical movement and for the government as well, since they would never hold professional occupations.

By the mid-century the elaborate system of educational advancement appeared to be working well. Graduates from the *gymnasia* entered the bureaucracy at the fourteenth rank. University graduates could begin at the tenth or twelfth rank, depending on their degree.

72. [Morozov], "Ocherk," p. 205.

73. O. Aptekman, *Obshchestvo 'Zemlia i Volia' 70–kh godov po lichnym vospominaniiam* [The Land and Liberty party of the 1870's according to my personal memories] (Moscow, 1924), pp. 48–49.

74. Quoted in Georgievski, *Kratkii ocherk*, p. 1.

Several professional schools prepared for service in specific ministries. The size of the bureaucracy was growing fairly constantly; in St. Petersburg the central and local administrative agencies numbered 11,500 in 1881. At least until the 1870's, graduates from *gymnasia* and universities had no difficulty finding work. In the discussion of the committee investigating the student unrest of 1874, the state comptroller declared that there were more requests for positions in general bureaucratic offices than available openings, but posts were still unfilled among the teaching and medical staff.[75] Employment outside of the state was available. Russia does not appear to have had a crisis of unemployed intellectuals in those years.

The possibility to advance even part of the way up the social ladder represented a powerful inducement to the lowly of the country who had access to the educational system. The government believed that the new careers opened up by the reforms of Alexander II helped create the rapid expansion of university enrollments. A committee in 1875 concluded that the new openings in the fields of judicial, municipal, and *zemstvo* administration made the university "more than ever before attractive to poor youth precisely because young people with a higher education have now open to them . . . a variety of enticing careers which did not even exist before."[76]

The government had some qualms about this process of rapid promotion through an elitist educational system. A report on the rising student unrest of 1861 stressed the "abnormal situation" in the universities created by the "granting to the students of service privileges and semimilitary dress." As a result, they considered the schools "not as a means of scholarly education, but as a position, through which they would pass to win something later on in service."[77] Similar objections reappeared in the mid-1870's, after student corporate status had officially disappeared. A commission studying disorders in 1877 found that this acquisitive attitude toward schooling had spread to a large number of "advanced institutions," where a "significant part of the students . . . seek not knowledge, but privileges and rights." As a result, the process of schooling was producing "a transfer from one class of the population to another rather than the

75. TsGIAL, f. 908, o. 1, d. 125, l. 59.
76. Quoted in L. Kamosko, "Izmeneniia soslovnogo sostava" [Changes in the estate composition], *Voprosy istorii,* Oct. 1970, pp. 204–5.
77. TsGIAL, f. 908, o. 1, d. 125, ll. 6–7.

acquisition of education."[78] These government leaders were searching for evidence that the Russian schools, like those in Germany,
were turning out youth with proper "cultivation [*Bildung*]." Social
ambition was in their eyes a dubious personal quality. The government adhered nonetheless to its policy of social promotion.

Those youth who refused to be "bought" found the system ab-
horrent and their schoolmates who chose the route ignorant or greedy
(or both). Dimitri Pisarev had nothing but scorn for his classmates
in the university in the late 1850's who sought "the shortest road to
rank, honor, large earnings, and consequently all the blessings and
enjoyments of life." These youth, among whom he picked out particularly the "poor and undistinguished," became, following graduation,
"civil servants, teachers, scholars, merged into the common mass and
showed nothing remarkable either in their personality or activities."
Their goals had "nothing to do with education."[79] They were lost to
the cause of liberation and to the radical community. Sergei Nechaev
took a particularly jaundiced view of the student youth with whom he
became acquainted in the capital in the late 1860's. He observed
that after an initial period of enthusiasm for organizations and agitation, the students "became accustomed to studying and in their last
years of study are absolutely tame." After graduation, the "former
rebels are transformed into completely loyal doctors, teachers, and
other types of bureaucrats, and become family men."[80] His solution
to the enticements of normal life was violent confrontation in the
schools, destroying these accumulated habits of conformity. He
dreamed of massive revolt by a unified student body. Despite his
hopes, the system continued to function as it was intended for most
Russian youth.

Material rewards played a large part in winning over the potential
rebels. During a discussion at one of the circles in the capital in the
1860's, one young man complained that he would have to enter the
bureaucracy since he had no special talents for writing or any other
"liberal profession" and had lost his tutoring position. "What else can
I do," he asked, "if outside of service I have no other means to provide for my family?" The outcry was immediate. One person insisted

78. *Ibid.*, f. 733, o. 158, d. 210, ll. 13–14.
79. D. Pisarev, "Nasha universitetskaia nauka" [Our university learning],
Izbrannye pedagogicheskie sochineniia (Moscow, 1951), pp. 125–26.
80. Cited in Koz'min, *Revoliutsionnoe dvizhenie*, p. 180.

that an educated man had "first of all to clarify what he lives for," while another pointed to the duty of the "young generation" to "search out new paths in conformity with new contemporary needs." His education and talents seemed to a third to make it "criminal" for him to follow "the old path," while another critic judged the bureaucracy fit only for those "with no energy, no initiative, no feeling of personal dignity, no realization that a new age had begun."[81] But none of this provided for his family. Russia was a poor country in which few people had the means to afford the luxury of a life of voluntary unemployment for the sake of the radical cause.

After joining the ranks of the regularly employed, few reappeared among the radicals. One who did, Wilhelm Bervi, had been drawn into government in the late 1840's since "outside government service the educated man had no other path by which to live from his own work." A decade later, stimulated by the example of student corporate life with its freedom and "self-rule," he believed that security counted for little by comparison with the cause of freedom and equality.[82] Men of his background were more numerous among the radicals in the 1840's than later, when the model of radical revolt had settled firmly into the student environment where it could skim off a part of each generation.

Consequently, recruitment into the radical movement represented a unique type of generational revolt. The range of ages of new recruits corresponded closely with that of the students in higher education, as did average ages of those arrested. In Petersburg University the student body consisted mainly of young men in their early twenties; only 15 percent in 1880 were below twenty-one.[83] The statistics collected by the Third Section on people arrested for political crimes in the period 1873–1879 showed that 70 percent of this group were twenty-five years of age or younger.[84]

These young rebels were conscious of a bond of unity, for each new generation experienced a similar alienation from the ties holding it to the "older generation." The simple fact that Peter Kropotkin was thirty years old when he decided to remake his life and sought to enter the Chaikovtsy circle made him suspect to some members.

81. Vodovozova, *Na zare zhizni*, II, 54.
82. N. Flerovski [V. Bervi], pp. 19, 140.
83. MVD-TsSK, *Universitety*, p. 5.
84. TsGAOR, f. 109, o. 1, d. 741, l. 26.

But nineteen-year-old Sofia Perovskaia justified his admission to a suspicious, twenty-two-year-old Mark Natanson by arguing that "he is completely young in spirit."[85] The new community was bound together by convictions, style of life, forms of association, and age. It possessed "common experience, common values, and mutual identification" and thus developed that "age-group consciousness" which one sociologist has argued is the chief characteristic of a generation as a social group.[86]

The similarity of age and upbringing between the radicals and students reinforced and reflected the importance of the educational environment in the recruitment of radicals. Peter Tkachev felt the generational bond in his own past. He was a university student in the circles of the early 1860's, joining in the demonstrations of the fall of 1861, and participating in the literacy-school movement. He was conscious later of having been one of "that generation" of student youth, sharing "its passions and mistakes, its beliefs and hopes, its illusions and disappointments." The experience was particularly vivid because "almost every blow of the reactionaries had an effect on me either directly, or indirectly through my close comrades and friends."[87] The crucial years for the radical movement were those when the educational institutions grew in size, the intellectual corpus of the literature of dissent became organized and accessible, and the bonds of student solidarity united youth within and among leading educational institutions. These made up the conditions for "a breakdown in the 'generational equilibrium'" of Russian society, but they cannot be described, as a sociologist would prefer, as a "sign of sickness."[88] On the contrary, they were an inherent part of the dynamics of an expanding educational system and of a peculiar Russian adaptation of student life. Against their will, the educational authorities had contributed to the creation of a two-track pattern of educational promotion, with one path leading to political revolt.

The institutions of higher education were the major culprits. In

85. Quoted in M. Miller, "The Formative Years of P. A. Kropotkin: A Study of the Origins and Development of Populist Attitudes in Russia" (Ph.D. dissertation, University of Chicago, 1967), p. 259.

86. Shmuel Eisenstadt, *From Generation to Generation: Age Groups and Social Structure* (Glencoe, Ill., 1956), pp. 170–74.

87. P. Tkachev, *Izbrannye sochineniia*, III, 58.

88. Feuer, *Conflict of Generations*, p. 11.

them the offspring of the upper classes mingled with common folk, and by the 1860's seemed unaffected by such mixing. The common bonds of learning and student solidarity brought to many of these youth greater meaning than did class privileges. The assemblies and circles, the cafeterias, student-aid funds, and reading rooms all embodied the new-found unity of the student corporation. Young men could enjoy these activities without putting in question the rightfulness of their career ambitions within the country's elite, for such privileges suited well their special educational vocation. Conflict with the authorities probably did not attract many, even in defense of the new institutions and liberties. It entailed serious risk of punishment and symbolized a definite step away from an orderly life.

Yet conflict was as inevitable as the new student community. It was no accident that Petersburg University, whose student body had played a key role in the corporate life, should be the first school in the capital to experience major unrest. It was natural too that the student customs should spread to the professional schools when, in the 1860's, they became real institutions of higher education. The entire student body of the capital thus became a source of recruits for the radical movement. These developments repeated themselves in other educational centers of the country. Youth revolt had found a secure place in Russian higher education.

5 | New Learning

The Russian government could no more control the learning available to its educated youth than it could discipline the students in its institutions of higher education. The two problems were closely related. The independence of the student corporation encouraged the search for unorthodox social and philosophical ideals outside the classrooms, while interest in the literature of radical dissent differentiated the new breed of students from the uninspired degree-hunters and pedants. The authorities tried to supervise the distribution of knowledge. The ubiquitous censor had a hand in every book published, though the restrictions in Alexander II's reign were somewhat looser than under Nicholas I. The educational curriculum received close attention from the Ministry of Education. School inspectors and agents of the secret police watched over the high priests (professors) and the lesser clerics of the temples of learning. By contemporary European standards, these controls were draconian and symbolized the oppressive power of the Russian autocracy. Appearances were deceiving, however. Despite strict surveillance and stern punishments, subversive knowledge spread widely in those very institutions intended to prepare the elite of the country.

The educational system functioned primarily to transmit a certain amount of information, part for vocational purposes, part for strengthening the moral fiber of educated youth. Many students probably never sought more. Knowledge for the real-life Oblomovs represented nothing more than random facts whose memorization was required for scholastic success, but which had no relevance to their personal lives or convictions. Extracurricular study of a literature of dissent required a special climate of opinion and a unique social environment if it was to attract large numbers of young Russians. The Westernized, alienated Russian intellectual had appeared by the 1830's in real life and in Russian literature. The behavior and writings of such men served as a model to others in later years and thus accelerated the process by which the radical community coalesced and recruited new members. The intellectual and social dimensions of radical revolt in mid-nineteenth-century Russia were mutually reinforcing. Their interaction produced a subculture able to survive and flourish under the harshest circumstances.

The writings of Western radicals were accessible to educated Russians inasmuch as their education invariably provided them with knowledge of at least one Western language. Many of these works were quickly translated, legally or not, into Russian. They spoke of profound transformations of human society which would assure, at some point in the not-too-distant future, real freedom and social equality for all mankind. Their messages differed widely, but all were the product of an intellectual community familiar with Enlightenment theories of progress, human perfectibility, and the powers of reason, and of societies where revolution had been either a real possibility or an actual experience. Russia lacked both characteristics. The only revolutions the country had known had been instituted by the state. Russian secular culture was still in its infancy at the time of the Enlightenment. There was no reason to expect that by the mid-nineteenth century some educated Russians would find in Western radical thought the final truth on the future of man in society.

Yet this was happening in major centers of learning and obscure corners of the country, wherever suitable conditions existed. There was no unity of views. Russian radicals repeated the bitter debates which divided Europeans and argued among themselves over the proper methods to adapt Western dreams to Russian realities. These revolutionary ideals defined for many an all-encompassing cultural system by which to guide their lives. This was a question of ideological truth.[1] Many Western and Soviet historians have studied this side of the Russian radical movement. Radical ideology also provided a form of learning by which young Russians could be converted from obedience to revolt. The chief obstacle to this proselytizing action was the inaccessibility to the uninitiated of much of Western radical

---

1. See Clifford Geertz, "Ideology as a Cultural System," in David Apter, *Ideology and Discontent* (New York, 1964), pp. 47–73.

literature. An informal school of dissent, with its own curriculum and methods of instruction, was needed as part of the intellectual environment in and around the institutions of higher education. The student corporation offered the only solid foundation on which such a system of alternative schooling could be built. It enjoyed the flexibility and relative freedom denied the formal educational system.

Dissent in the Schools

The teachers had very little to do with the disruption of regular learning and the rise of interest in the new, radical thought. The memoirs of the period indicate that few professors were capable of arousing interest in their subjects and even fewer sought to arouse in their students a vision of a better life for Russia. Their weak influence was partly due to the repressive power of the government. The most spectacular example of the subordination of learning to political power was the disappearance of the study of philosophy after 1848. Nicholas I considered the subject pernicious and politically dangerous. It did not reappear until 1856. Any professor could be punished, by the educational authorities or the police, for deviation from the strictly defined academic limits of his specialty. Peter Lavrov, in the early 1860's a professor of chemistry with a strong interest in intellectual freedom, publicly complained of the difficult conditions under which teachers had to work. Their "every word is listened to by unauthorized ears," he said. They needed "moral heroism not to suppress historical facts." Issues that were analyzed in "hundreds of courses" in other countries "cannot and must not be the subject of teaching by our professors."[2] If the police found incriminating lecture notes from a particular course in the possession of a suspected radical the career of that teacher could be threatened.

The very nature of scholarship also limited the impact of the teachers. Germany continued to be the major source of inspiration for Russian learning. Germans still taught in Russian schools and many of the young Russian scholars appearing by the mid-century had received their training in German universities. German scholarship stressed specialization and mastery of systematic factual knowledge.

2. Quoted in R. Eimontova, "Universitetskii vopros" [The university question], *Istoriia SSSR*, Nov. 1971, p. 153.

Students had the position of invited apprentices with no assurance of success and little direct aid from their mentors. One student from the Medical-Surgical Academy in the 1860's wrote later that the professors were good and their attitude toward students "tolerant and well-wishing," but, with a few exceptions, they "stood completely outside of involvement in public issues and even regarded rather indifferently the fate of the students."[3]

At their best, the professors symbolized pure scholarship, which for a time appealed to some of the future radicals. Dimitri Pisarev was attracted to Petersburg University by its high prestige and felt flattered to begin immediately working closely with one literature professor, under whose guidance he set to work in the field of philology, translating from German into Russian works he hardly understood. Over sixteen months of labor went into this task, which Pisarev later decided was actually worth about two weeks of his time. His mentor disillusioned him completely in the end by his timidity and concern "only for phrases." Pisarev was not satisfied to learn the slogan of one French poet that "ignorance is slavery and knowledge is liberty." He wanted to find out what that knowledge was and what liberty it would lead to, but he received no answers to these questions.[4] It was well for the career of his professor that he did not.

Some subjects lent themselves to interpretations whose significance exceeded the limits of the material. In the 1840's, T. Granovski's famous lectures in Moscow University on medieval Western history became a battleground between the supporters of the Westernizers and the Slavophiles. Similarly, in Petersburg University the lectures of V. Poroshin on political economy attracted students interested in the fundamental principles of social organization and the distribution of wealth, but also those eager to learn the socialist message. Poroshin himself was a respected scholar, a graduate of Dorpat University. He was a follower of Western economic liberalism, interested in the diffusion of more scientific methods of agricultural production, and a firm believer in the fine results of the spread of knowledge. In his eagerness to survey the entire range of Western views on ownership of property, he introduced into his course extended and detailed discussion of the writings of the utopian socialists. Though he included a

3. Chudnovski, "Iz davnykh let," p. 283.
4. Pisarev, "Nasha universitetskaia nauka," p. 80.

refutation of these theories, he showed great daring merely mentioning such radical subjects. Nowhere else in Russia could students obtain publicly information on the socialists, whose writings were banned by the censor.

One of his students, whose notes fell into the hands of the police, made special mention of the refusal of these theorists to recognize "the right of private property," which was a "violation of the general natural equality of men." The investigating commission charged with the Petrashevtsy affair of 1849 judged severely Poroshin's "detailed philosophical analysis" of utopian socialism. This discussion, they declared, was "not in a loyal spirit of conformity with monarchist principles, which should guide the Russian youth on the path to their future life."[5] Very shortly afterward, Poroshin went into an early and unwilling retirement.

The eagerness to find judgments on truth and social justice through academic study increased greatly in the early years of Alexander II. The military defeat in Crimea served as a public lesson in Russia's backwardness, with dramatic effect among educated citizens. One writer commented in 1860 that "intellectual activity" was spreading "everywhere." He found that "in the most unenlightened cities, where until now interest has been concentrated on cards, drinking, and partying, public libraries have appeared; people even want to have books at home." In the search for learning, "people who never read a thing have begun to study, to keep abreast of literature, to acquaint themselves with 'the fantasies of youth.' "[6] Students, young and old, demanded more of their courses than ever before. A retired officer recalled that he began auditing university lectures in those years in order to meet the "needs of the time," which demanded "not dry formal knowledge, but general ideas and universal principles."[7]

The contribution of the professors to this search for relevant learning was uneven. Those who were unwilling to introduce their personal convictions into their courses were regarded by students as pedants. Their popularity, according to an ardent student of the late 1850's, depended on their commitment "to apply knowledge to the solution of current problems, to the destruction of old evils." The

5. V. Semevskii, *M. V. Butashevich-Petrashevskii i petrashevtsy* (Moscow, 1922), pp. 32–38.
6. *Severnaia pchela* [The northern bee], 1860 (No. 1).
7. Shelgunov, *Vospominaniia*, p. 114.

words of teachers who accepted this challenge "opened up before us new, fresh ideals, whose rapid application, it seemed, would assure the happiness of our political, social, family and individual lives."[8] But most fell far short of satisfying the demands for intellectual emancipation. A report analyzing the reasons for the student unrest of 1861 found that the "weakening of the moral ties" between professors and students had played an important part in the "deviation of our universities from their original goal."[9] Intellectual erudition was no longer sufficient to maintain their authority.

The demand for new learning came from only a few students, the same youth who looked increasingly to their own activities as the source of true knowledge. The government could sense that its educational program no longer monopolized the instruction in proper ethical principles and that some youth had found intellectual guidance outside the classroom. A report on the student disorders of 1874 blamed the professors for having retreated into an ivory tower of scholarship, preferring to emphasize "educational" rather than "moral [*vospitatel'nye*] aims" in their work. They even showed at times "a tendency to attribute to student youth a civic maturity and civic importance which cannot exist."[10] The process of radical recruitment shifted moral and intellectual authority to new sources of learning, sufficiently impressive to constitute an informal curriculum in the school of dissent.

The elite schools of St. Petersburg, the summit of the rigidly hierarchical educational system, were the chosen centers for independent schooling. Since they provided the best instruction in higher learning, they should also be able to contribute, directly or indirectly, the intellectual keys to social and political emancipation. If their professors were not capable of this, students could take over the task themselves with the aid of writers from the capital and abroad. The intellectual reputation of the city was firmly established by the 1860's, as shown by the rising flood of students. One of those who came late in the decade explained in his memoirs that he had first tried the law school of the new university in Odessa, but had found there neither the "active life" nor the intellectual answers for which he was searching. He

---

8. L. Modzalevski, "Iz pedagogicheskoi avtobiografii" [From a pedagogical autobiography], *Russkaia shkola*, March 1897, pp. 22–23.

9. TsGIAL, f. 908, o. 1, d. 230, ll. 6–7.

10. *Ibid.*, o. 1, d. 125, l. 60.

turned to St. Petersburg like "all thinking Russians." Only in that "center of Russian intelligence" could he find "a solution to all the cursed questions." Three weeks after arriving in Odessa, he applied for admittance to the Medical-Surgical Academy.[11] The next spring, 1869, he was expelled for having participated in the academy's disorders. He had found the active life he wanted and was on his way to discovering the answers to the problems tormenting him.

Intellectual ferment in the capital took a variety of forms. Both the memoirs of Petersburg radicals and the records of the authorities point to certain sources for the new schooling in dissent. Particularly in the 1840's it came from courses of formal learning. Later it came most often from readings outside the classroom but discovered by and distributed primarily among student groups. The records are sparse as to which key elements raised the disturbing questions and provided the answers. There was no one path to dissent. Each individual found the "truth" in his own way, turning from factual information to abstract theory in what appeared a flight from everyday reality. Several important concepts seem to have played a major role in this process of disaffection.

In the educational institutions as well as in the published literature a comprehensive refutation of the inevitability and rightfulness of the social and political system of Russia could be found in subjects that discussed the life of man in society, past and present, and provided grounds for moral judgment. History was one of these subjects, though not the history of facts. It had to be, as Peter Kropotkin described it while still in the Corps of Pages, an account of "the reasons and the consequences of events," which for him required personal evaluation on the basis of "one's own political convictions."[12] On this foundation, history became a moral battleground directly involving the student. The history of the Western revolutionary movement was omitted from the schools' courses, which avoided discussion of the cause of freedom in the modern world. Readings of Rousseau and Montesquieu indicated the proper basis for judging history, according to the notes of a Petersburg University student. He found that the principle "men are born free" gave him the answer to world history and proved that "any people who do not govern themselves exist in a

11. Chudnovski, "Iz davnykh let," p. 280.
12. Quoted in Miller, "Formative Years," p. 105.

situation of slavery."[13] He read in history the confirmation and illustration of a philosophical truth valid even in his own country. Russian historical traditions and values paled to insignificance in the light of these ideals. The study of law could lead, like history, directly to the discovery of universal principles. A law course given in the 1840's in one of the officers' schools stimulated one cadet, later arrested in the Petrashevtsy affair, to consider the rights of the individual and to conclude that natural rights were inherent in the very nature of man, "gifted with mind and freedom." These unique attributes made "man an end in himself and permit him under no circumstances to be regarded as a means." Slavery represented a clear violation of natural rights, an injustice which arose only because of special conditions. He felt in conclusion that he had defined a new ethic based on individuality, which gave him the right to argue that "I can do as I please."[14] This was a daring statement for a young man in those years, but one that was repeated many times later on. He had defined for himself a position outside of accepted moral limits, though he was unsure how to use his new freedom. The investigating commission charged with the Petrashevtsy affair seized upon these notes as proof of his subversiveness. Their judgment was oversimplified and attributed to independent thought a force on behavior greater than it actually possessed, but they were correct that the principle of individual rights was incompatible with the political bases of the Russian autocracy.

The study of man in society figured prominently in courses on political economy, treated often as a part of law but closer in content to contemporary economics and sociology. It dealt specifically with economic activity and the social relations resulting from variations of economic organization. Of all the disciplines offered, it came closest to providing a theoretical foundation for the analysis of Russian society. Interpretations had to be drawn independently, since the discipline appeared in the schools divorced from any direct connection with Russian institutions. Its range in those years extended from the classical economists to, in certain cases, the utopian socialists. The professor of political economy at Petersburg University, Poroshin,

13. Quoted in V. Semevski, "Petrashevtsy," *Golos minuvshego,* Dec. 1915, p. 48.
14. Quoted in *ibid.,* Nov. 1915, pp. 13–15.

had sound academic reasons for discussing these latter writers, since they too were concerned with the principles of socioeconomic organization. Men such as Fourier saw the reform of social institutions as the key to the satisfaction of human needs and the hope for future happiness. In academic form the courses appeared merely as an abstract analysis of socioeconomic life; they were popular in the school of dissent because they suggested that traditional forms of social life were susceptible to radical improvement.

Political economy emphasized the problems of distribution of wealth and types of property. It provided a form of static economic analysis and neglected the issues of production and economic growth. By analyzing distribution, it suggested rational explanations of inequalities of wealth and property. This was only one logical step away from the conclusion that such inequalities were an avoidable misfortune. Once again, abstract analysis led to moral judgment. In 1848 the English liberal John Stuart Mill published his study of *Principles of Political Economy.* Thirteen years later Nikolai Chernyshevski translated and annotated a Russian edition, which quickly became popular. His interest, as that of many of his readers, did not spring from any admiration for economic liberalism, which he criticized as "incompatible with the demands of economic theory in its very essence," meaning "learning and the conditions of human well-being."[15] Mill's concise and thorough model of social analysis was helpful in the search for the perfect society. Chernyshevski explained that "the task consists only in the discovery of the means of economic organization which will achieve the demands of common sense," that is, the distribution to the laborers of the fruits of their work.[16] Beyond this point, ideological controversy obscured the precise form of the paradise on earth; still, political economy could provide the responsive student with grounds to believe that the traditional social organization of his country had no rational sanction for existence. Stripped of its appearance of inevitability, the established order lost the moral power of inescapable fate.

The study of philosophy and science was more abstract than law or history and could furnish a pure vision of new principles of life far more sweeping than anything available in the human sciences. The

15. N. Chernyshevski, *PSS* (Moscow, 1949), IX, 516–17.
16. *Ibid.,* VII, 44.

popularity of German idealist philosophy in the universities of the 1840's came from its internal logical integrity and comprehensiveness. It was one complete answer to the search for the Good, the True, and the Beautiful far removed from the ugly reality of Russian life. Friedrich Hegel offered the most powerful philosophical system in those years. His impact on young Vissarion Belinski was overwhelming. The famous Hegelian dictum that "the real is rational and the rational is real" caused the critic intellectual anguish as he sought to apply it to his understanding of Russian life. He resolved the apparent dilemma by interpreting the formula as justification for sweeping criticism of conditions in his country, a position to which he was already strongly drawn emotionally. He was only one of the men who used Hegel as a springboard to radical dissent.[17]

The influence of Friedrich Schelling's philosophy did not prove as enduring, but for a few years was equally as great as Hegel's. The most popular professor in the Moscow University school of sciences, M. G. Pavlov, preached Schelling's idealism under the guise of natural philosophy. His students, among them Alexander Herzen, found in his lectures a schematic but totally inclusive explanation of matter and reality with no foundation in empirical science. One of them declared himself "indebted to these lectures not so much for their scientific knowledge [!] as for their general philosophical ideas, which marked almost the beginning of my intellectual development." His *gymnasium* schooling had been "purely mechanical." Exposure to Schelling's philosophy "opened before me a new world of ideas, a new approach to knowledge." The great power of this new learning sprang from its apparently limitless scope and power of explanation. "I saw opened before me," he wrote, "a vast world of philosophical principles, which satisfied my young mind immensely."[18] But philosophical idealism was not destined to play a leading part in the new curriculum for radical revolt. By the 1850's it was supplanted by materialism as the last word in metaphysical truth.

The intellectual preconceptions of this early enthusiasm for philosophy never left the school of dissent. Real knowledge had to furnish

17. See Martin Malia, *Alexander Herzen and the Birth of Russian Socialism* (New York, 1961), pp. 202–5; Edward Carr, *Michael Bakunin* (London, 1937), pp. 61–63, 113–17.
18. Ia. Kostenetski, "Vospominaniia" [Memoirs], *Russkii arkhiv*, XXV (1887), 229.

final answers or it was not satisfactory. The break with tradition depended upon rational criteria for justification; absolute certainty was therefore indispensable. The emphasis placed on intellectual rigor in the school system carried over into the radical movement as an intellectual elitism of equal severity, but totally different aims. The revolt of these youth assumed the capacity to manipulate complex, abstract ideas with ease, for these defined the essence of their new beliefs.

Philosophy was a dangerous intellectual discipline. A half-century later, a Chinese scholar attempted to explain in his own terms Nicholas I's hatred of the subject. Western philosophy led people, he wrote, to "imagine a world different from this one, and to judge this one by the imagined one, so that the reader, roaming about in the rarified realms of thought . . . would inevitably lose faith in the Sages and the Sons of Heaven."[19] Most educated Russians never let their ideas become so elevated or their imaginations overcome their sense of reality. Those who did could build a coherent refutation of the moral authority and of the religious beliefs defended by the Russian church and state.

The new reality offered in place of old religion appeared by the 1850's under the guise of science and its related philosophical school of materialism. This new outlook on the universe struck the authorities as the key to the decline in religious faith and the rise of dissent among educated Russians. They set out to extirpate materialism from the schools and to restrict the study of science, but the sources of the new learning were mainly outside the schools. The state could not prevent illegal diffusion of books and literature presenting "scientific" proof of the nonexistence of God, of the laws of history, of social equality, and much more. Science was the key, and it gained the respect of almost all educated Russians.

Science became more than a search for precise explanations of the observable regularities of the physical and biological universe. It appeared a form of new learning, more in touch with modern needs and interests than law or the humanities. Interest in scientific study increased in almost all the educational institutions of St. Petersburg in the 1860's and especially the 1870's. The Petersburg University faculty noticed the rising percentage of students choosing the school

19. Quoted in Donald Price, *Russia and the Roots of the Chinese Revolution* (Cambridge, Mass., 1974), p. 162.

of science over the more utilitarian law school. In their report for 1875–1876, they concluded that the students were less motivated than earlier by "the desire for practical activity" and more by "the desire for significant knowledge."[20] Science was also a weapon against the rigorous system of classical learning zealously defended in the *gymnasia*. Study of either pure or applied science brought its own form of intellectual liberation and helps explain the popularity of the professional schools. One peripatetic student arrested by the police in 1873 for propaganda activities came to science on his way to political dissent. He had gone through six years of the *gymnasium* before failing Greek. He had had enough classical studies, whose only effect was to give him a "boundless revulsion for the study of ancient languages and a desire for varied experiences and a change of life." Another secondary school made him aware of "the inadequacy of my scientific knowledge," by which he meant the "basic sciences and mainly mathematics." As a result, in 1871 he joined the large number of youth entering the Technological Institute. After two years he decided that he had "no more use" for institute courses and dropped out to begin revolutionary activity.[21]

The hope that science could provide the knowledge needed to make one's life useful stimulated the sudden growth of interest in medical studies. Both in Russia and abroad, young Russians began seeking medical training in much greater numbers than ever before. Many went to the University of Zurich, where some found in the course of their educational experience that their real goal was radical reform of society. Vera Figner came ostensibly to study medicine, and went through considerable mental anguish as she sought to acquire both the basic scientific knowledge denied her in earlier schooling and medical training. Her original hope had been to find meaning and purpose to her life, an aspiration shared by other Russians she met there. "Essentially, we did not aspire for higher education as such," she wrote, "since we believed that one could develop one's mind and enrich it through self-education, without guidance by people in authority."[22] Medical training coincided with the crystallization of radical

20. *Protokoly zasedanii soveta Sanktpeterburgskogo universiteta za 1875–1876* [Notes of the meetings of St. Petersburg University for 1875–1876] (St. Petersburg, 1876), p. 60.
21. TsGAOR, f. 112, o. 1, d. 211, l. 93.
22. V. Figner, "Studencheskie gody" [Student years], *Golos minuvshego,* Jan.-Feb. 1923, p. 181.

social views and ambitions. Over one-half of this Zurich group came to the attention of the secret police in their drive against radicals. The Russian government viewed them as potential troublemakers and ordered all to return in 1873.[23]

The government was associating science and revolt, but what was the logical connection between study of the operations of the physical and biological world and dissent? When science was seen as an intellectual panacea in the 1850's and 1860's, it was expected to generate the fundamental answers to human development. One student in the Petersburg Mining Institute in the late 1850's explained how science served youth like himself in their "search for enlightenment." They expected it to provide "indisputable knowledge primarily in the sense that it left the least room for doubt." He admitted that this attitude showed a "naive faith in the sole saving power" of science, but the need was great for "something unequivocal to cope with the mass of problems which showered down on us."[24] The attitude that knowledge from science was the answer spread through radical literature in the writings of men such as Nikolai Chernyshevski, who took up the new source of hope with zeal. He believed that "all the diverse phenomena in the sphere of human motives and conduct spring from one nature, are governed by one law." Physiology seemed to be the crucial link. Western writers like Auguste Comte were arguing that careful study of the brain would soon reveal the fundamental principles of social life. The moral sciences, Chernyshevski admitted, had "not yet been worked out as fully as the natural sciences," but their problems would be resolved just as surely as older discoveries had brought the final answer to metaphysics.[25]

The ultimate metaphysical system for him had been scientific materialism. Though with nineteenth-century modifications, it remained an old philosophical school which reduced all reality of the universe to force and matter. A book by the title of *Kraft und Stoff* (Force and Matter) came to Russia soon after being published in Germany in 1855 by L. Büchner. By 1858 it was circulating among Petersburg

23. J. Meijer, *Knowledge and Revolution: The Russian Colony in Zurich* (Assen, 1955), pp. 140–42.

24. N. Mikhailovski, *Literaturnye vospominaniia* [Literary memories] (St. Petersburg, 1900), I, 307.

25. N. Chernyshevski, "The Anthropological Principle in Philosophy," in James Edie   *et al., Russian Philosophy* (New York, 1965), II, 49; A. Vucinich, *Science in Russian Culture* (Stanford, 1963), I, 15–16,

students as part of their underground literature. According to one university student, it hit his circle of friends like a "real bomb," destroying the "remains of traditional faith."[26] Peter Kropotkin's brother Alexander read this book and the works of the other German materialists and preached the new gospel in letters to Peter. "Now I am not in need of the nonmaterial," he wrote. "There is nothing except matter. Away with idealism!"[27] Materialism was the explanation given by hostile critics for the spread of godlessness and rebelliousness among student youth. The authorities saw it as all that had gone wrong in the upbringing of the nihilists. It was "the negation of religion, morality, family life and generally all civil and political principles on which modern society is based."[28]

Literature of Dissent

Though the schools contributed an environment and information capable of disturbing orderly minds, intellectual authority among critical students passed increasingly to writers outside the academic world. This special "school" came to function more and more on its own, with special methods, institutions, and sources of information from Western writings and from Russian publicists. In the 1840's the West contributed considerable numbers of books to student libraries. Though most were forbidden in Russia, they circulated fairly widely. An agent of the Third Section sent to Petersburg University in 1844 to investigate reports of subversive literature found among the students all the "foreign, forbidden, antireligious, and antisocial books" possible and imaginable. Such reading encouraged interest in "what they call cosmopolitanism," not in "their own fatherland." He did not feel that the problem was serious: "Fortunately, all this amounts to only impulses of youth and the desire for action, all of which lasts only until graduation."[29] The quantity of illegal literature increased in the years of Alexander II. The enthusiasm with which it was greeted testified to the importance of Western writings in the search for new learning.

Gradually certain Russian writers acquired a prominence and respect which made them the real teachers of dissent. The Russian literary world was expanding rapidly in mid-century both in quantity

---

26. Panteleev, *Vospominaniia*, p. 164.
27. Quoted in Miller, "Formative Years," p. 101.
28. TsGAOR, f. 95, o. 1, d. 459, l. 22.
29. *Ibid.*, f. 109, d. 206, (1844), ll. 27–29.

and in quality, but only certain subjects provided the inspiration and justification for intellectual and political revolt. A few writers were able to select these themes and present a picture of a better life as well as a condemnation of the old. The most important of the new writers were Belinski, Dobroliubov, Chernyshevski, Pisarev, Mikhailovski, and Lavrov. Their works reflected a sensitivity to the needs of the young public in part because each of them had experienced the search for a new ethical foundation for his life. Their skill and creative ability permitted them to become the intellectual mentors to these youth. Belinski, the first of the unofficial teachers, had found his audience by the early 1840's. His great admirer Herzen asserted that the university students "soaked up" his vitriolic articles "with feverish interest, laughter, and dispute—and three or four beliefs [and] honors had disappeared."[30] This circle of readers was not as large as Herzen implied nor could Belinski's views so easily prevail unless the ground were already prepared. Within a limited circle, he, like the others to follow, received the authority denied officially designated teachers.

The journals to which these writers contributed became the vehicles for the diffusion of this critical knowledge. Their reputations were made in articles which spread the new learning despite official censorship. *Otechestvennye zapiski* (The notes of the fatherland) published Belinski's works during most of the 1840's. His fame was primarily responsible for its jump in circulation from 1,200 subscribers in 1839 to 4,000 in 1847. The Russian reading public was small and the critical readers smaller yet. These latter were multiplying as the years passed. The most influential radical journal of the 1850's and 1860's was *Sovremennik* (The contemporary), among whose collaborators were Chernyshevski and Dobroliubov. It expanded from 3,000 to 6,500 subscribers between 1854 and 1861.[31] In the first half of the 1860's *Russkoe slovo* (The Russian word) published the attacks on Russian institutions and beliefs by Dimitri Pisarev, literary spokesman and educator for what hostile critics thought was subversive nihilism. By the late 1860's *Otechestvennye zapiski* as-

30. Gertsen, *Byloe i Dumy*, I, 359.
31. *Istochnikovedenie istorii SSSR XIX-nachala XX veka* [A guide to history of the USSR in the nineteenth and beginning of twentieth centuries] (Moscow, 1970), pp. 245, 279.

sumed prominence once again under the editorship of Nikolai Nekrasov. This was the last of the great radical journals, their golden age ending in the 1860's.

The one uncensored Russian journal of those years, *Kolokol* (The bell), occupied a special position. Edited in London by Herzen and circulated illegally in Russia, it gave critical factual information on the struggle between reform and reaction under Alexander II. Peter Kropotkin, whose aristocratic relatives had access to all Herzen's writings, wrote to his brother of his first contact with Herzen's work. "How good it is," he exclaimed, "so much bitterness free of charge. In it one can receive the most correct news of everything that is happening in Russia."[32] Herzen's writings suffered because of their factual content. The school of dissent required more philosophy and basic analysis than he provided. The Russian journals were more difficult to read, but richer in the methodology of intellectual protest. Their relative abundance aided immensely in the expansion of the radical community in the 1860's and 1870's.

Works of Russian fiction were used to analyze the ills of Russian life. Critics such as Belinski saw literature as a source of enlightenment as well as a work of art. The actual intent of the author mattered little. Belinski's review of works such as Gogol's *Dead Souls,* published in 1842, and Turgenev's *Huntsmen's Sketches,* which appeared in 1847, stressed their didactic use as a mirror of Russian reality. He transformed literary criticism into social criticism; his readers had to be aware of the techniques of social analysis. The task of the radical critics consisted thus of defining a critical method and using it to dissect specific works of literature.

Their choice of works to review was great. Russian writers were turning out an astonishing range of literary masterpieces between the 1840's and 1870's. The possible interpretations of this literature extended from amusement and escape to moral exhortation and instruction. Gogol's works appeared to some critics as humorous accounts of human foibles. Belinski took them much more seriously. He found in *Dead Souls* a clear picture of men's "pettiness" and "even more" a representation of "the phenomena of life in the fullness of their reality and truth."[33] Since his conception of truth was fundamentally

32. Quoted in Miller, "Formative Years," p. 81.
33. Quoted in A. Dement'ev, *Ocherki po istorii russkoi zhurnalistiki 1840–1850 godov.* [From the history of Russian journalism] (Moscow, 1951), p. 328.

hostile to life as he saw it, the novel *Dead Souls* became a condemnation of the landowning nobility and serfdom.

Belinski saw the didactic role of literature as a holy cause, the best means of opening men's minds to the truth. Works of literature were the "consciousness of the people."[34] He firmly believed that an author must assume the role of social analyst and moral leader. The great authors of the time ignored such exhortations, but Belinski's views did set a style for literary analysis among Russians searching for means of understanding their society. Works of fiction could divulge the basic defects of Russian life. The realism these critical readers came to expect from literature was not pure observation, but the ability to bring in focus moral issues.

Dobroliubov, Belinski's successor as radical literary critic, further developed this line of analysis. In an early literary essay, he stated that literature changed "according to the course of life." Literature, to be true to its nature, had to respect the realities of life. Aesthetic values had much less importance for him than for Belinski. He believed that the "mission" of fiction was "to serve as the expression of popular life, of popular aspirations."[35] The titles of some of his famous articles, such as "The Dark Kingdom" and "When Will the Real Day Come?" indicate the blatantly didactic purpose of his writing. To serve the people meant above all to show them the moral truth. He transformed Goncharov's novel *Oblomov* from a study of one man's failure to come to terms with life into a social criticism of "Oblomovism"—the inability of the older generation to set a personal model of wholehearted revolt and radical action. He used Turgenev's novel *On the Eve* to appeal for the rise of new people to hasten the coming of the "real day" of revolution in Russia. He did not write reviews in the usual sense. He used literary works that attracted his attention as an intellectual springboard for discussion of the personal qualities needed to produce a new man in a new society.

The contribution of these critics to the curriculum of dissent was great. Thanks largely to their efforts, by the 1860's a corpus of writing had come into existence which summed up the intellectual antagonism between accepted beliefs and the new faith. In 1867 the

34. Belinski, *PSS*, IV, 418.
35. Dobroliubov, *PSS*, I, 207, 237.

head of the Third Section laid special emphasis on the "harmful books" he felt were responsible for the unfortunate "moral direction of some youth." He believed that the serious trouble had begun in the late 1850's when the works of Büchner and Feuerbach had appeared in Russian translation and the writings of French socialists and positivists had become popular. These writings, "under the guise of a modern level of scientific knowledge, contained the basis of materialism." They created "hostile feelings toward the authorities" and "refuted the legality of the existing order."[36] They represented a syllabus of intellectual revolt over which the institutions of higher education and the state authorities had no control.

The radical critics drew inspiration from their own intellectual development and the experiences of their circle of friends. Hence, their writings tell us something of the formative influences in their lives. These works, in turn, provided a simplified prospectus in radical ideology readily available and understandable to student youth. They became the most important educational force in recruitment for the radical community.

Reason was crucial to the school of dissent. It provided the ultimate assurance that men could actually remake the social and political order. "Knowledge," wrote Pisarev, "constitutes the only key to broad and rational activity." It must reveal not "the exterior symptoms of evil," but the "true causes." Such insight was not available to all men, and circumstances might prevent them from attaining the goal. Pisarev saw no hope for the graduates of a seminary, scene of a novel he was reviewing, who were "badly educated men" incapable of real understanding or action.[37] Under proper conditions, however, success was guaranteed. The power of reason assured the attainment of truth. Of this the individual who dared challenge hallowed values could feel so sure that he could flaunt all hostile authority. Thus the test of reason stood by itself as a central tenet in the new learning, sanctioning the criticism of all established beliefs. Pisarev gave the most forceful expression of this credo in an article written in 1861, passed miraculously by the censor. He declared that all authority should undergo examination by reason. If it proved "necessary or useful," it would remain firmly in place, but if it turned out "false,

36. TsGAOR, f. 109, o. 85, d. 32 (1867), l. 14.
37. Pisarev, *Izbrannye sochineniia*, II, 454,

then doubt will destroy it and achieve something marvelous." This was the "ultimatum of our camp: what can be smashed should be; what stands up under the blows is acceptable, and what flies into a thousand pieces is trash." The rational critic could "strike out on all sides," for "harm will not and cannot result."[38] This message became a motto for radical youth. The police later discovered portraits of Pisarev with the slogan written underneath: "Words and illusions will perish, facts will remain." Others bore the assurance that "the work of destruction is done; the work of creation is ahead and will occupy more than one generation."[39] Reason had disclosed the laws of nature and would soon provide the solutions to the development of mankind. Serious effort and intellectual ability must be used properly in the elaboration of a new faith. This intellectual elitism, as has already been noted, was a central characteristic of the radical movement.

The powers of reason could be properly developed by new people whose presence the critics discerned already. The ideal of personal emancipation played a key role in the revolt of the radicals. They wished to create a new individual, whose conduct and convictions would differ from the customary standards of behavior. The publicists found the literary representations of such men and women and offered them to their public to be studied and imitated. The radicals of the 1840's had had no models for conduct. Their efforts at emancipation were occasionally successful, often hesitant and timid. By the early 1860's the public image of the new man was well fixed in literature and repeated many times over in reality. Reality and fiction were mutually reinforcing. Chernyshevski's characters in *What's to Be Done?* were all drawn from his acquaintances, mainly in St. Petersburg. By immortalizing and praising certain moral and personal traits, he and other writers multiplied immeasurably the attraction of individual emancipation.

Literature provided inspiration for the creation of the idealized new people, but it was a tool, to be used as the critics saw fit. They often seemed to be rewriting the novels or plays. Dobroliubov's articles were notably biased in accentuating certain characteristics of the personages in the literature he chose to analyze. His goal was clearly

---

38. *Ibid.*, I, 66.
39. These portraits were found in a package mailed by a suspected Petersburg radical in 1870. TsGIAL, f. 1281, o. 1, d. 69, ll. 491–92.

didactic. Other critics followed in his footsteps, and Chernyshevski completed the portrait in *What's to Be Done?*, a moral essay dressed up as a novel. Curiously, the most effective descriptions of new people were of women. The men seemed to possess superhuman qualities, like Rakhmetev, or else to be ordinary individuals lacking heroic stature. Dobroliubov in particular preferred to discuss heroines, underlining their tragic grandeur and their admirable strength of character.[40] As such, they could serve as ideals for anyone who was searching for encouragement and inspiration to escape the constraints of a former life.

To Dobroliubov social and family ties constituted the essence of personal slavery. He repeatedly sounded this pessimistic note in his articles. Before he found positive traits to praise, he damned the old life. He reviewed a series of plays by A. N. Ostrovski on the life of the petty bourgeoisie under the title "The Dark Kingdom" [*Temnoe tsarstvo*]. In that land so much like Russia, he saw "nothing sacred, nothing pure, nothing just." The dominance of "terrible, savage, unjust oppression" [*samodurstvo*] had removed "any consciousness of honor and right." He forecast that there could be no improvement until individuals could develop "human dignity, freedom of personality, faith in love and happiness, and the sanctity of honest work."[41] These qualities were linked in his mind with the emergence of the new people, whose traits he began to find in Russian literature by the end of the decade. He used Turgenev's novel *On the Eve* to proclaim the weakening of conditions which had "destroyed the determination and the energy of strong individuals." He saw that "children are being brought up in the hopes and dreams of a better future." When their turn came to "get to work," he expected them to show "an energy, stability, and harmony of heart and mind of which we can scarcely acquire a theoretical understanding." Their rise to dominance would bring the "real day" to Russia.[42]

Young rebels in Russia were attracted to this writer by his messianic call for complete moral renewal and destruction of the old bonds. Sergei Nechaev, biding his time in St. Petersburg in 1868 as a schoolteacher after failing to enter Moscow University, was con-

40. See Rufus Mathewson, *The Positive Hero in Russian Literature* (New York, 1958), p. 72.

41. Dobroliubov, *PSS*, II, 56.

42. *Ibid.*, p. 240.

vinced that his generation would answer Dobroliubov's appeal.[43] The critic found his ideal in Ekaterina, the heroine of Ostrovski's play *Thunder,* a woman of determination and courage seeking to escape her harsh life to find true love. Dobroliubov chose to dwell on her personal "devotion" and "idealism" as the committed fighter for a new life which would realize the "full harmony of ideas and the demands of nature."[44] This idealized heroine appeared in his article as the embodiment of the natural qualities of determination, commitment, and complete consciousness of individual dignity which he sensed were developing in Russia.

There was no equivocation in Chernyshevski's portraits of his heroes and heroine in *What's to Be Done?,* published in 1863. These "tales of the new people" contained a full program for the new life. The book acquired immense popularity among students as the finest portrayal of the sort of men and women they aspired to become. The plot consisted of the efforts of a young woman, Vera Pavlovna Rozal'skaia, to free herself from the yoke of petty-bourgeois family life. She found support from two medical students, Lopukhov and Kirsanov, and at critical moments from the awesome Rakhmetev. The author insisted that these characters were not "heroes, individuals of a superior nature." If they seemed that way, the fault was with the reader. "They do not stand too high, rather you stand too low." Chernyshevski was convinced that the reader "can be the equal of the men whom I portray, if you work on your development." Such efforts were the essence of "happiness."[45] Many young people agreed.

The optimistic message of the novel was an invitation to personal emancipation. Its confidence in the beneficial results of freedom provided encouragement for the hesitant and an ideal for the confused. Chernyshevski hoped to see his model for moral regeneration spread throughout society. He had written earlier that the personal example of "men with humane convictions" was inadequate to "attract an entire society," but might prove a decisive influence if it showed "the method to achieve goals which every man would desire if he had the means."[46] Rather than a novel this was a pedagogical manual in the methods for reshaping the population of an entire country.

He found a sympathetic audience among the student youth. Re-

43. Zasulich, *Vospominaniia,* pp. 58–59.
44. Dobroliubov, *PSS,* II, 348, 360.
45. Chernyshevski, *PSS,* XI, 228.
46. *Ibid.,* IV, 288–89.

ports from school inspectors contained excerpts from student discussions of the book. Notes written by one in 1873 concluded that "it is necessary to renounce traditions," for "under presently existing conditions" it was impossible to "help the people."[47] In a complete exegesis of the work a seminary student found in it a "social-ethical" message for the reshaping of individual behavior and a "social-economic" plan for the reorganization of society. He was impressed by the new style marriage relations between Vera Pavlovna and her men. He also admired greatly the invincible Rakhmetev, whom he compared with "historical world leaders such as Robert Owen, Saint-Simon, Proudhon, etc."[48] Such students found in the novel a program of action which answered their deep need for intellectual guidance. They read it, in the words of one observer, "virtually in a position of worship, with such devotion . . . as the Scriptures are read."[49] Its message transcended ideological divisions among radicals and was an inspiration for decades to come. George Plekhanov, who probably came upon the novel in the mid-1870's, was sure that anyone of intelligence who had read it became "cleaner, better, braver, and bolder under its philanthropic influence" and sought to "imitate the purity of the principal characters."[50]

The ideal new man defended by writers such as Chernyshevski required freedom from constraints of the old moral code. He became the judge of the morality of his own behavior. Reason set strict limits on the actual exercise of egoism, but accepted values were to be defied. Nikolai Sokolov made this attitude a positive virtue in his book *Otshchepentsy* (The rebels), published in 1866. He discussed the alienation of persecuted religious groups, including the early Christians, and implied that the innovative individual was by necessity an outcast struggling to overcome the forces of oppression. This book too joined the library of radical literature and spread illegally, though it was banned shortly after printing. In a report on agitation in 1870, the head of the Third Section remarked that the book "enjoyed great success among youth." His agents found that "it was passed among students in considerable number of copies."[51]

The moral freedom accompanying emancipation made the solitary

47. Quoted in Itenberg, *Dvizhenie*, p. 68.
48. TsGIAL, f. 733, o. 147, d. 785, l. 570.
49. Quoted in Bogdanovich, *Liubov' liudei*, pp. 16–17.
50. Quoted in Mathewson, *Positive Hero*, p. 104.
51. TsGAOR, f. 109, tr. eks., d. 120 (1870), ch. 1, l. 14.

hero an attractive figure. Western literature on this theme served as grist for the mill of radical publicists, who greeted enthusiastically the works of André Léo (pseudonym for Léodile de Champceix) on the right of women to find their own happiness and of the German Friedrich Spielhagen, a prolific writer whose heroes usually proved in defeat their romantic freedom from bourgeois society. Peter Tkachev wrote of their characters in a review in 1868 that they were "ordinary people" whose "good ideas" made them appear much superior to "heroes of the petty bourgeoisie." Since they had found the proper principles on which to base their behavior, old moral restraints were unnecessary. They "should be granted the right to judge *critically,* and *dogmatically* the instructions of moral law in each particular case."[52]

Such glorification of the defiance of traditional (Christian) morality appeared a very dangerous proposition to conservative Russians. Fedor Dostoevski made the premise a motivating force behind Raskolnikov's brutal murder of two women in *Crime and Punishment.* As Raskolnikov explained his theory, humanity was divided into inferior masses, whose duty it was to be docile, and the exceptional men "who possess the gift of the talent to say a *new word.*" These individuals, among whom he counted himself, had the right "in the name of a better future" to violate the established moral code, including the ban on taking human life.[53] Dostoevski thought this arrogation by the individual of final judgment on good and evil so blatantly immoral that it was contrary to human nature.

For the radical publicists, on the other hand, complete personal freedom represented the sole path to happiness for the new people. By this they understood not personal gratification, but the greatest happiness of mankind. They assumed that with abiding individual happiness came concern for the well-being of others. Dobroliubov held out this solution to the "melancholy" of contemporary Russians. Elena, the heroine in Turgenev's *On the Eve,* was eager, he thought, "to create happiness about her, for she cannot understand the possibility for personal happiness or even tranquillity if she is surrounded by grief, unhappiness, poverty, and the humiliation of her fellow

---

52. P. Tkachev, *Izbrannye sochineniia,* I, 195.
53. F. Dostoevski, *Crime and Punishment,* trans. Jessie Coulson (New York, 1964), pp. 276–77 (pt. II, ch. 5).

man."[54] Happiness thus defined depended on the common good, and the new people were the happiest since they alone understood fully what was necessary to bring good to all mankind.

This view rested on the assumption that people were naturally good and could be shown, or made, to bring this goodness into their lives. If the assumption were false the attack on the old beliefs was an act of blind destruction. Dostoevski was by the early 1870's a firm supporter of the latter view. He believed that the happiness promised by freedom from Christian morality was equivalent to death, for man would have lost his purpose in life. Kirillov, a character in *The Possessed,* committed suicide to prove that God did not exist. Seeking ultimate happiness in an insane act of self-destruction, he argued that he was actually helping to usher in the new age. Then, "there will be a new man, happy and proud," who will have achieved full freedom since "it will be the same to live or not to live." He explained to the narrator of the story that under these conditions:

> 'There will be a new life, a new man; everything will be new . . . then they will divide history into two parts: from the gorilla to the annihilation of God, and from the annihilation of God to . . .'
> 'To the gorilla?'
> '. . . To the transformation of the earth, and of man physically.'[55]

It seemed to Dostoevski that this abomination was the logical result of the premises on which the radical writers based their message— the work, not of prophets, but of men possessed by devils. To the radical critics, however, the new man was rational, independent, committed, and constructive. His happiness depended on his ability to work for others and to show the way to real emancipation. The image as drawn by the radical writers was a model for action and an inspiration for the remaking of character.

This search for self-improvement was justified as a means to a greater end. The goal assumed in one form or another service to the people, but the specific ideological content of the program varied from one writer to another and altered as the years passed. The peo-

---

54. Dobroliubov, *PSS,* II, 216.
55. F. Dostoevski, *The Possessed,* trans. Constance Garnett (New York, 1936), p. 114 (pt. 1, ch. 3, section 8).

ple could take the form of mankind, the Russian people, or specifically the Russian peasantry. Most radicals justified their revolt in
terms of the need to serve the people, but the actual lives of the Russian people of the lower classes gave little reason to believe in their
innate goodness. The radicals became interested in the institutions
and way of life of the peasantry from the 1840's, sparked by the
ideological debate between Slavophiles and Westernizers. Interest
grew in later years, but remained a search for virtue, not a study of
actual conditions. Dobroliubov called on Russian literature in the
mid-1850's to emphasize the "fresh, healthy shoots of popular life,
to assist their proper successful growth and blooming, to protect
from rot their marvelous and plentiful fruit."[56]

Like most of his fellow writers, Dobroliubov looked on the imperfections of the people as temporary setbacks caused by the evils of
the existing social and political order. Nikolai Ogarev's solution was
to grant the people "land and liberty." The slogan attracted wide
support, but in 1861 his appeal had no foundation in knowledge of
conditions among the lower classes. The idea of the people was an
abstraction. George Plekhanov, on the verge of withdrawing from the
Mining Institute in 1875 to join the populists, had a "very confused
and undefined understanding, like all of us student revolutionaries,"
of the people. "Though idealizing the 'people,' I knew them very
little, and it would be better to say that I knew them not at all, though
I had grown up in the countryside."[57] It was less important to believe
in the people than to be convinced of the power of men to change
their lives, by themselves or under proper guidance.

These publicists argued that, whatever form the new society might
take and whatever means might be used to reach it, men had the ability to control and remake their environment and, consequently, their
ethical behavior. This article of faith promised that those who rebelled
did not do so in vain. The belief in the upward march of history and
in the perfectibility of man together made the act of revolt appear
constructive. At the beginning of this great revolution, the agents of

56. Dobroliubov, *PSS*, II, 308–9.
57. G. Plekhanov, *Russkii rabochii v revoliutsionnom dvizhenii* (*po lichnym vospominaniiam*) [The Russian worker in the revolutionary movement—my personal memoirs] (Moscow, 1922), p. 3. Some writers lost the faith in the 1870's;
see Richard Wortman, *The Crisis of Russian Populism* (Cambridge, Mass.,
1967).

progress had to be the emancipated intellectuals, by training and understanding ready immediately to begin the struggle. Though not clearly formulated until the late 1860's, this assumption was already implicit in the writings circulating among radical youth.

Peter Lavrov brought out his *Historical Letters* in 1868–1869. A philosopher by choice, he was still sufficiently close to the radicals of those years, young and old, to sympathize with their ideals. His book quickly became a major work in the literature of dissent, for it united a credo of human progress with a reasoned defense of the historical role of the intellectual. Taking inspiration from the discoveries of the natural sciences, he presented human history as a logical extension of the world of nature. Methods of rational analysis made it possible to know the past with the same certainty that scientists could understand nature. The man of reason could therefore discover in the "process of life of mankind" the laws of history, that is, "how the predominance of one or another factor acts on the development of society in general and how it always will act if this predominance repeats itself."[58] He argued that the "critically thinking individual" had the power both to understand and to control the course of history. All who had the ability to comprehend the phenomena of human behavior could influence their own conduct and that of others.

He believed that the most significant law of history was the appearance of ideals, created by these critically thinking individuals, which had the power to move mankind. The striving of men to attain these ideals produced the moral and intellectual progress of humanity. Since men were continually attempting to improve their lives, the history of man was a story of perpetual progress toward greater and greater perfection. There could be no end to the "development of the personality in physical, intellectual, and moral terms as embodied in the social forms of truth and justice." This was for Lavrov the sum and substance of progress.[59] The chief obstacle to the constructive action of individuals was the resistance of society to their ideas and actions. "Societies are threatened by the danger of stagnation if they stifle the critically thinking individuals," for they were solely responsible for "whatever progress humanity has made."[60] His analysis contained a direct appeal to educated people to assume their responsibil-

---

58. P. Lavrov, *Izbrannye sochineniia* (Moscow, 1934), I, 183.
59. *Ibid.*, p. 199.
60. *Ibid.*, pp. 226–27.

ity to lead mankind toward a better life. In the existing situation, contemporary ideals had far outstripped actual social institutions, thus "the contemporary form of society is a pathological form." Lavrov was convinced that his view of historical development provided both a "moral evaluation of history" and a "moral goal toward which the critically thinking individual should strive if he wishes to be a progressive agent."[61] Though he later regarded this argument as overly simplified, Lavrov's book had a continuing effect.

His views spread immediately among student groups. They appeared in a program prepared in 1871 for a meeting of representatives from radical circles. Sparked by the action of the Chaikovtsy circle, these groups had begun an educational campaign to bring the new learning to students in all major cities in the empire. Lavrov's message came through in this program as a pitiless struggle between the "individual development" of the youth in the movement and "a society hostile to us and repressing every progressive action." In political terms, this implied a battle between the "absolute monarchy," defender and organizer of society, and "another force, whose form will be our party."[62] Other radicals thought different modes of action better and attacked the emphasis on individuality, but all agreed on the crucial role of the new people in organizing and conducting the action. To this extent, Lavrov's work assured the doubtful that education was necessary training for the radical cause and could not, if properly used, produce a wasted life. The real loss came from those educated people who did not understand their true role, preferring instead ordinary lives and orderly occupations. The writings of the radicals implied clear options based on fundamental moral principles.

Their picture of the new life was not a mirror of reality. Its ideals were far above the capacities of many people attracted to it and could act as a source of personal emulation and a goal, but only when other conditions were suitable. The Third Section tended to exaggerate the effect of subversive literature as the cause of the radical movement. Books alone were not enough. I. Myshkin tried to explain this fact to his interrogators in 1874. He thought it "absurd" to believe that

61. *Ibid.*, p. 348; see Philip Pomper, *Peter Lavrov and the Russian Revolutionary Movement* (Chicago, 1972), pp. 95–110.

62. "Programma dlia kruzhkov" [A program for circles], *Katorga i ssylka*, No. 67 (1930), 97; the program is discussed in Martin Miller, "Manifestoes of the Chaikovsky Circle," *Slavic Review*, XXIX (March 1970), 7–9.

books, even "the most brilliant and interesting," were "able to trans-form a contented Russian into a wild revolutionary." The bases for revolt came from one's "entire life."[63] This assertion expressed his feeling of disaffection from his past, but does not actually describe the process that led him from lowly soldier's son to leading radical. His frustrated hopes of an educational career had triggered a revolt inspired by the forms of ideology and action of the radical commu-nity. Books formed only a part of his education.

His protest was shaped by specific social and cultural forces which influenced many other Russians of different backgrounds. Radical protest had become by the early 1870's a coherent and regu-larized social process with its own set of values and inducements to new recruits. The literature of dissent justified the rejection of ac-cepted social patterns of behavior and traditional beliefs. It offered the grounds to believe that a new life of freedom and equality was attainable if founded on reason and science, and justified the privi-leges of an intellectual elite fit to lead in remaking a poor and illiterate society. It offered its own rational truth and defined the positive role of the rebel in Russian society. In its own way, it was as unique an educational corpus as the official curriculum of the Russian school system.

The Star in the West

A readiness to borrow and assimilate Western cultural innovations had marked Russian life since Peter's time. The number of Russians attracted by and able to adopt forms and values of European society grew slowly through the eighteenth century, more rapidly in the next. Book imports from Europe tell the story for mid-century Russia. In 1847 more than 826,000 volumes of foreign, that is, Western, litera-ture legally entered the country, and additional thousands undoubtedly came in illegally. Ten years later they totaled over 1.3 million vol-umes.[64] The task of adapting cultural institutions and Western learning to suit Russian conditions required an extraordinary intel-lectual flexibility and receptivity. The rise of Russian literature, sci-ence, art, and higher education by the mid-nineteenth century indi-cated that this process was advancing remarkably well.

63. "Iz zaiavleniia I. N. Myshkina" [From the statement of I. N. Myshkin], *Revoliutsionnoe narodnichestvo*, I, 181–82.

64. Leikina-Svirskaia, *Intelligentsiia*, pp. 212–13.

The disruptive potential of cultural borrowing from and imitation of the West fits the pattern of "acculturation" described by anthropologists on the basis of observation of primitive societies, but valid also for higher cultures. Recognition of the usefulness of foreign ways can lead to the assumption that these imports are of superior moral value and hence that native traditions should give way to them.[65] This model suggests that at the heart of the origins of the Russian radical movement lies the complex relationship between disaffected youth and Western culture. As students they were exposed to a system of education patterned on that of the West and dependent on Western learning for much of its subject matter. As budding intellectuals, they were drawn to the dynamic and creative literary life of countries such as France and Germany. Finally, as men dissatisfied with tradition and searching for examples of constructive innovation, they found in Western historical development the ideals and experience of revolutionary change.

The attractiveness of the West for young radicals appears most clearly in the memoirs of the men who joined the movement in the 1840's. The protest literature of western Europe exerted a tremendous hold over the imaginations of young Russians drawn to intellectual dissent as an expression of their own feelings. George Sand was one of the most popular novelists among such people in the 1840's. Her stories of lower-class oppression and resistance filled the young Dostoevski, while a pupil in the Engineering Institute, with admiration for her "new desires and new ideals." She taught him that "the renewal of mankind must be radical and socialist" and that "a happier future awaited humanity." His first contact with her fiction left him "feverish all night." Thinking thirty-five years later of her influence on his intellectual development, he concluded that "we Russians have two native lands, Russia and Europe."[66] The gloomy climate in the educational institutions and literary world induced an idealization of Western life of which these people knew little but in which they placed all their hopes. Alexander Herzen remembered that as a young man his image of the West was "literary, theoretical." He ad-

---

65. The concept of acculturation is discussed in Ralph Linton, *Acculturation in Seven American Indian Tribes* (New York, 1940), chaps. 9 and 10; also Melville Herskovits, *Acculturation: The Study of Culture Contact* (New York, 1938).

66. F. Dostoevski, *Dnevnik pisatelia* [The diary of a writer] (Moscow, 1929), I, 308, 310–12.

mired those countries so much because he felt such a "hatred for Nicholas I's autocracy and the Petersburg order of things." The fact that Frenchmen "daringly raised the social question" meant to him that they had "at least in part solved that problem."[67] He discovered otherwise on reaching France in 1847, but his earlier illusions gave him hope of something better than the horrible status quo in Russia.

By the early 1860's word that Western life did not coincide with the ideals of justice and equality had begun to filter down among educated Russians, but Europe still exercised the mysterious attraction of an advanced and sophisticated civilization. Nikolai Serno-Solov'evich went directly to Europe upon abandoning his position in the bureaucracy in 1859 to learn what the new life in Russia should be. He expected that the "old structure" of his country would either "collapse by itself" or be destroyed. "But to erect a new structure one must possess knowledge, not superficial, but solid, durable knowledge." He recognized that the "easiest path" to this truth was "borrowing that which has been prepared by other countries." In that time when "everything was changing," he believed that "we Russians need now more than ever before to have a correct understanding of Europe." The country needed "strong, independent men of action" possessing knowledge to remake Russia from its foundations up.[68] Perhaps he thought he might fill that role. He had been trained in the Alexandrovsky Lycée to serve in the bureaucratic elite, but had abandoned that career. His first step in personal emancipation was study of the West.

Most young people attracted in the 1860's to radical change apparently followed the "easiest path." They had little experience with real life and believed religiously the works from the West. German Lopatin, who became active in the radical movement early in the decade, observed that "the largest part" of the "so-called progressive youth" left their provincial surroundings "while still almost children" and "possess hardly any knowledge of the real situation and life of the people." They "judge the questions of our internal life almost exclusively on the basis of theories assimilated from foreign writings."[69] Lopatin may have been drawing his own self-portrait. Immediately

67. Gertsen, *Sobranie sochinenii* [Collected works] (Moscow, 1949), XVIII, 278.
68. "Pis'ma N. A. Serno-Solov'evicha" [Letters of N. A. Serno-Solov'evich], in Koz'min, *Revoliutsionnoe dvizhenie*, pp. 117, 122–23.
69. Quoted in V. Antonov, *German Lopatin* (Moscow, 1962), p. 36.

after graduation from his Siberian *gymnasium,* he had come to study in the university. Only seventeen at the time, he had joined radical circles with little or no knowledge of Western life, but with great faith in the works of Chernyshevski and Dobroliubov.

Travel often strengthened the faith in an ideal Western path of progress. The West provided living proof of the viability of programs of radical change. As disaffected Russians discerned the realities of the West, they selected only those elements which they thought represented the hope of progress and social justice. Zurich was well suited to this special study. In its Russian colony was a community of dissent in which medical studies took second place to the new learning. Vera Figner arrived there, as she later recalled, "without the slightest idea of the social injustice" of Russian life. "Until that time, I accepted human society, its social order and state organization, as a fact, however they appeared at a particular moment, not reflecting on their origins or the possibility of their alteration."[70] She had come looking for a new life for herself and had found the vision of a new life for all mankind. Peter Kropotkin came to Switzerland just a year later, in 1872, with the specific goal of discovering the principles of a social order free of oppression. His first step on reaching Zurich was to contact Russian friends who could give him works on the "great movement." He found in his readings a "completely new world of social relations and completely new methods of thought and action." But reading was not enough. "The more I read, the more I saw that there lay before me a new world, unknown to me and completely unknown to the learned authors of sociological theories." He believed that he could understand this world "by living among the workers of the International and observing their everyday life."[71] His old world of authority had completely disappeared with the death of his father earlier that year and in its place he began to create a new, diametrically opposed life based on anarchist principles.

Even from a distance, the Western visions of social and political progress that played the greatest role in the development of the radical community were those that promised the most sweeping and complete transformation. To Russians even British parliamentarianism represented politically dangerous principles. Such moderate political

70. V. Figner, *Studencheskie gody* (Moscow, 1924), pp. 72–73.
71. Kropotkin, *Zapiski,* pp. 250, 252.

programs won some converts in Russia, where any ideas of reform ran headlong into the rigidity of institutional structures and hostility to innovation among the population. The rebellious youth in and around the centers of learning were drawn to more ambitious solutions. The "enthusiasm" generated by each new philosophy in turn seemed to one observer to come from the "moral and social idealism" of youth, who "search usually for a basic theory which will explain all, the 'last word.' "[72] One of these zealots was Mikhail Saltykov, still a pupil in the Alexandrovsky Lycée, who passed from "learning from the articles of Belinski" to admiration for the utopian socialists and for their birthplace, France. From France "there poured out on us a faith in humanity, . . . the certainty that the 'Golden Age' lay not behind but ahead of us. In a word, everything good, desirable, and beneficial came from there."[73]

The revolutions of 1848 brought the forces of progress into direct confrontation, or so it seemed, with the forces of evil and seemed to be a dramatic enactment of real reforms. Nikolai Chernyshevski, then a young student in Petersburg University, commented regularly in his diary on the course of events in the West and their significance. In August he concluded that "history is faith in progress," a point which Lavrov's *Historical Letters* spelled out in detail twenty years later. He found the proof of this assumption in the dynamic political life of the West. His interest in political reform meant inevitably "respect for the West and the conviction that we can in no way be considered on a level" with the Europeans. It was clear that "they are men, we only children."[74] Two months later he was enthused over the "great truth" being spoken by the socialists in the French Second Republic. "Oh Lord," he prayed, "let victory be on the side of truth!" At one point, he became aware that he was living vicariously the revolutionary events in Europe to the exclusion of real life about him. He thought about a few friends, "about humanity, religion, socialism, etc., and especially about France. I respect Russia very little and hardly ever even think about her."[75]

Though the attraction of Western events had weakened, the Paris Commune of 1871 stirred up similar interest in student circles in Rus-

72. A. Pypin, *Moi zametki* [My comments] (Moscow, 1910), p. 65.
73. Saltykov, *PSS*, XIV, 160.
74. Chernyshevski, *PSS*, I, 66.
75. *Ibid.*, pp. 111, 121.

sia. According to one student in the Technological Institute, his comrades were not well informed about the struggle, but "practically everyone was instinctively on the side of the communards."[76] By then the works of Russian radical literature provided inspiration by themselves and suggested that perhaps Russia could achieve that radical change denied the West.

That the impact of the West was becoming a complex process of attraction and reaction was apparent in the attitudes of some of the men who joined the radical movement in the 1850's. Nikolai Shelgunov returned from a trip to the West in 1857, just after having abandoned his career as an officer, convinced of the possibility of "complete renewal of Russia on humanitarian and just principles." He explained that his conviction rested on the evidence of the growing ranks of radicals in Russia and "also because in Europe the work of renovation and emancipation is proceeding."[77] In the pamphlet he and Mikhailov wrote in 1861, "To the Young Generation," he played on the more satisfying note of bettering the Europeans. "We studied the economic and political structure of Europe," he wrote, "and saw what was poor and understood the definite possibility to escape the pitiful fate of present-day Europe."[78] The hope appeared in many places in the same period. Herzen had already suggested this possibility. Dobroliubov expressed a similar thought in a review of a book by a Russian author blinded by the perfection of the West and the squalor of Russia. He admitted that "we entered the field of historical development later than other peoples." He was "certain" that Russia "must follow that same path," an eventuality "in no way regrettable for us." Possibly "our path will be better," since "our civic [*grazhdanskoe*] development can pass somewhat more quickly through those phases which were traversed so slowly in western Europe."[79] This reevaluation of the model of Western progress introduced into the radical literature of Russia an ideal of perfection that has endured for a century. But the comparison with the West remained a source of creative inspiration offering real hope that the future could reward those who sacrificed their own past and all the comforts and security of ordinary, orderly lives.

76. Quoted in B. Itenberg, "Parizhskaia kommuna" [The Paris Commune], *Istoriia SSSR,* March-April 1961, p. 160.

77. Shelgunov, *Vospominaniia,* pp. 83–84.

78. *Ibid.,* pp. 293–94.

79. Dobroliubov, *PSS,* IV, 402.

Continual evaluation of Russia's life in terms of the West was capable of eating away attachment to Russian institutions. Alexander Herzen felt keenly the resulting sense of rootlessness. Speaking of men like himself, he declared that they shared Europe's "doubts" and "hatreds" without experiencing the restraining influences of its "half-freedoms," its *"arrière-pensées"* and "scruples." The "thinking Russian" had no respect for his country's past, since the "starting point of Russian history" was Peter's "negation of nationality and tradition" for the sake of Westernization. The Petersburg period was so repulsive that "it releases us definitively" from traditional loyalties. The special breed of Russian possessing a "clear view and incorruptible logic" and understanding Russia's past as Herzen did could "free himself quickly from the faith and ways of his father."[80] The Western model of revolutionary change and socialist renewal had thus a magnetic force in the radical community, attracting people and creating the extremist ideological attitude that so deeply marked the radicals, yet repelling them by its complexity and its failure to accomplish fundamental reforms. This left the Russian dissenters with strong ties neither to their own country nor to the West, only to themselves and their cause.

Intellectual Schism

Over the years, the books and essays of the school of dissent piled up into an impressive corpus of knowledge. Its volume was a stiff intellectual test of a young Russian's powers of reason, but it promised a great deal. It possessed the special ability to convince its readers of the reality of an imaginary world of social justice, equality, and progress more attractive than the actual life around them. The popularity of the radical publicists spread beyond the centers of learning into the provinces, where the Slavophile Ivan Aksakov sadly discovered that "the name of Belinski is known to every half-educated youth, to everyone eager for a breath of fresh air in the fetid swamp of provincial life." It seemed to him that "there was not a single *gymnasium* teacher in a provincial city who does not know by heart Belinski's 'Letter to Gogol.' "[81] This learning sparked discussion on forbidden subjects, crystallized discontent into conscious protest, and

80. Gertsen, *PSS*, (1916), VI, 455–56.
81. *I. Aksakov v ego pis'makh* [I. Aksakov in his letters] (Moscow, 1892), III, pt. I, 290.

brought together individuals who otherwise would have remained isolated.

Formal schooling offered by comparison the wrong information on the wrong subjects. It was vocational training plus ethical instruction in leadership qualities. It might provide bits and pieces of relevant information, but lacked clarity and comprehensiveness for training in libertarian ideology. One student of those years dismissed "university knowledge" because it "did not give the answer to many contemporary, vital questions."[82] By the late 1850's it was being replaced by an active and forceful school of dissent. An increasing number of student youth found the curriculum of the latter both challenging and illicit, more attractive than courses in the schools. One participant recalled that "Saint-Simon, Büchner, Feuerbach provided the favorite readings which reached among the students in secret editions." He found in the student body of Petersburg University a great deal of reading, "especially of forbidden books," much discussion and debate, "but little studying. We had no good advisers, and did not trust the administration and many of the professors."[83] The new sources of authoritative knowledge were not extensive, the illegal books were difficult to obtain, and the radical journals subject to arbitrary control by the government. When one young student learned in 1862 of the closing of *The Contemporary* and *The Russian Word,* he was angered and distressed. He wrote to his sister: "No joking, this hurt me very much. With whom can I now pour out my feelings? What's the meaning of all this, anyway? Such terrible anguish—oppressive, numbing, deadly! At times I found peace of mind thanks only to *The Contemporary,* and now what?!"[84] In the highly intellectual environment of the school of dissent, personal gratification came in special forms.

The attraction exerted by the new learning resembled in many cases a fad of short duration. "In spite of the brilliant success of *The Contemporary,*" one university student of those years admitted, "the progressive social-political ideas had a relatively limited circle of followers." In fact, "many later dropped" these ideas "very easily."[85] The "drop-outs" of the school of dissent were far more numerous than

82. F. Ustrialov, "Universitetskie vospominaniia" [University memories], *Istoricheskii vestnik,* July 1884, p. 132.
83. L. Modzalevski, "Iz pedagogicheskoi avtobiografii," pp. 22–25.
84. Quoted in Antonov, *Lopatin,* p. 20.
85. Panteleev, *Vospominaniia,* p. 164.

those who moved from intellectual curiosity, perhaps under the impetus of student agitation, to a commitment to radical action.

The abstruse language of this literature was hard to understand. The formal education of the secondary schools gave a very poor preparation for critical analysis and debate. A young woman who frequented the student circles of the early 1860's felt that their participants had little capacity for abstract discussions of philosophical and social problems. They had "received a pitiful education in their families, military schools, institutes, and seminaries." As a result, the "great majority were not used to independent thinking, analysis, and criticism."[86] Without the support and encouragement of more experienced intellectuals, these novices might understand nothing at all and abandon the effort. The cause was lost if the message could not get through to its audience.

The forcefulness of the critical thought and analysis depended on the reader's frame of mind. Many issues fundamental to the new learning supposed a prior awareness of the significance of the problem discussed. A subject such as social reform had little appeal for someone whose mind was not attuned to the problem of social change. Vera Zasulich first tried to read Chernyshevski's translation of and commentaries on J. S. Mill's *Principles of Political Economy* while a pupil in a private girls' school. "But the affair proceeded very poorly; the book seemed to me at the time understandable, but not interesting enough." She made a second attempt after having rebelled at the prospect of life as a governess and gone to St. Petersburg to try to make a new life. This time, the meaning of the essay was so clear that she could "read a chapter and then repeat to myself its contents" and could guess Chernyshevski's opinion of various topics in the essay without reading his notes.[87] The conditions of her life were then such that this knowledge appeared meaningful and significant. Even a book as explicit as *What's to Be Done?* did not automatically win converts. Lenin himself recalled how he had attempted unsuccessfully to grasp the novel's message at the age of fourteen. He returned to the book after his brother's execution, for it was "one of his favorite books. . . . I sat over it not for several days, but for several weeks. Only then did I understand its depth."[88] At that moment it could offer

86. Vodovozova, *Na zare zhizni,* II, 99.
87. Zasulich, *Vospominaniia,* p. 59.
88. N. Valentinov [N. Volski], *The Early Years of Lenin,* trans. R. Theen (Ann Arbor, Mich., 1969), p. 136.

him, as countless young Russians earlier, the intellectual basis on which to remake his life. The young readers needed intellectual assistance and encouragement to help them assimilate radical literature. Such aid was hard to find in the 1840's, but within two decades the new learning had literally its own schools and instructors. Men who had come upon the new truth naturally wished to convert others.

The arrival of two former Petersburg students at Kazan University in 1848 was the beginning of Wilhelm Bervi's interest in Fourierism. The Kazan students had, in Bervi's words, "no understanding of how a student should properly involve himself in the pursuit of knowledge," for they simply "memorized lectures." The newcomers were men of a different intellectual caliber. They taught the truth of utopian socialism. Bervi began "under their influence the independent pursuit of learning, that is, socialist ideology." His studies elevated him above the "crude, bestial life of the students" and introduced him to "the ideal of brotherly love and universal equality."[89] The two Petersburg students found a sympathetic and understanding pupil in Bervi. All spoke a common language, for they were formed in the same educational system and had the same passionate concern for rational learning in the service of mankind.

The new style of teaching required new talents. The diffusion of learning took place among equals, both in age and status. Authority came from mastery of the new learning and ability to make this knowledge understandable to the uninitiated. In his last year in the Pedagogical Institute, Nikolai Dobroliubov noted with pleasure in his diary that he had met a young university student who showed real promise. The young man suffered still from some "dogmatic forms . . . in his mind, but respect for rational convictions is already strongly embedded in his soul." Dobroliubov helped him along by discussing "the inequality of conditions, wealth, and marriage." His recruit was "not at all repelled by the radical explanations which I gave him on these matters. Deep in his soul he has long since sympathized with them and vaguely sensed them, but was simply afraid until now to speak them out directly."[90] The truth of one convert became thus the source of learning for the next. As a result, the process of cultural diffusion of the radical ideals could accelerate and bring an even larger number of recruits to the movement.

89. N. Flerovskii [V. Bervi], *Tri politicheskie sistemy,* pp. 11–12.
90. Dobroliubov, *Dnevnik,* p. 183.

In the 1860's and early 1870's the methods of spreading the new learning became much more sophisticated. The formation of numerous student circles provided an ideal setting for this type of instruction. The circles of "self-education" which appeared among students in secondary and higher educational institutions in the early 1870's offered a comprehensive education in intellectual dissent. Their model and inspiration was the Chaikovtsy circle. It appeared originally in 1869 and by early 1870 was functioning as a parallel school. Its organization and development are discussed in detail in the next chapter. Its immediate goal of formulating and distributing knowledge of the new life and ideals put it in the midst of the countereducation. The commitment to learning by all the members led them to develop the equivalent of a graduate program in social and philosophical problems. In the summer of 1871 the group rented a cottage near the capital where all fifteen members could live and study together. Their topics included logic, psychology "to the extent it is necessary for the solution of every kind of ethical problem," political economy "to the extent it is required for a clear understanding of the working-class and land questions," and the history of the revolutionary movement. The readings were drawn from Russian and Western books. The first volume of Marx's *Capital* (in German since no Russian translation had yet appeared) provided their text on political economy. The previous year the circle had begun providing literature suitable for student youth in the self-education circles. The books distributed included Marx, Louis Blanc (on the French revolution), Mill, Spencer, and Voltaire, in all sixteen Western authors, among them six whose works discussed the French revolution. Ten Russian authors appeared on their list, including Chernyshevski, Lavrov, and Bervi-Flerovski (on the Russian working class).[91]

The work of collecting, printing, and distributing these books was difficult, but was accepted as a sacred duty. Nikolai Chaikovski recalled many years later that he and his comrades constituted a new intellectual elite. They felt that "history itself" had given them "the mission to reveal to the people *some sort of truth* which we alone knew and to produce a social miracle thanks to our education and our culture."[92] The "people" to whom their message first appealed were student youth in centers of higher education and secondary schools.

91. [Morozov], "Ocherk," pp. 214, 220–21, 226–27.
92. Titov, ed., *N. V. Chaikovskii*, p. 279.

This was a receptive audience, already possessing the intellectual training (however meager) transmitted by the school system and searching for rational inspiration and a model of behavior suitable to a new life of social justice.

The circles spread rapidly. The motto of self-education (*samoobrazovanie*) set the tone for the activities of the participants. Like the educational institutions in which these young people studied, the alternative schools assumed that reason was the sole guide to proper action and could provide moral truth as well as verifiable knowledge. But they threw out the normal curriculum and dethroned the professors. Some of their participants may have looked upon the officially sanctioned teachers, as one young woman in the mid-1860's, as "paid bureaucrats who on the orders of higher authorities intentionally distorted the truth."[93] They did not need professorial guidance since they believed that the truth for which they were searching was accessible to any "critically thinking individual." They could very well teach themselves.

The dissemination of these circles among the country's student youth brought about a rapid diffusion of the radical literature. Due to the relatively easy availability of reading material, the circles could provide in their discussions a comprehensive survey of all the propositions on which the community of dissent justified its existence. They discussed the qualities and activities of the new people. One circle active in 1872 made this topic a central theme. Its members repeated Chernyshevski's argument that the new man represented the fulfillment of the potential of the "normal person," who possessed "all the possibilities for the fully harmonious development of both his physical and mental personality."[94] The dream was to discover, as a participant in one of these circles declared later to the police, "the root of all ills and suffering of mankind." He and his comrades looked on the work of their circle as the "acquisition of general, truthful [*nauchnogo*] education." They were primarily interested in the study of political economy and socialist writings, which gave them knowledge of "ideal systems of social reorganization" to solve social injustice.[95]

93. A. Komarova, *Odna iz mnogikh: iz zapisok nigilistki* [One of many: From the notes of a nigilistka] (St. Petersburg, 1881), p. 64.
94. O. Aptekman, "Bervi-Flerovskii i kruzhok Dolgushina" [Bervi-Flerovskii and the Dolgushin circle], *Byloe*, No. 18 (1923), 57.
95. "Avtobiograficheskoe zaiavlenia A. A. Kviatkovskogo" [The autobiographical statement of A. A. Kviatkovskii], *Krasnyi arkhiv*, No. 14 (1926), 160–61.

The extraordinary popularity of this new learning gave vivid proof of the existence of a reservoir of potential recruits for the radical cause predisposed to listen to the message of dissent. From this larger group came the crusaders of the "to the people" movement.

The Third Section was aware of the increased power and attractiveness of this school of dissent. Until the late 1860's, it had focused primarily on the negative qualities of "that young generation which made itself known several years ago under the name of nihilists." It characterized the group in a report for the tsar in 1867 as made up of people who "deny the bases of Christian religion and monarchical rule" and consider "the criminal Chernyshevski the ideal of human wisdom."[96] Though these attitudes were highly regrettable, only a madman like Karakozov could leap to the conclusion that the monarch must be assassinated to make way for a new order. The report for 1869 sounded a more ominous note. There had occurred, it stated, a significant "modification" of the nihilist movement, which "already not only refutes, but asserts. It acts in the name of an idea, and this gives its followers the characteristics of sectarians, that is, the desire to propagandize their teachings and the readiness to suffer for them."[97] This was a dangerous development. For two centuries the Russian state had struggled with the religious sectarians without being able to suppress them. This new sect was more serious, for it recruited its members from the educated elite of the empire and was dedicated to a profound transformation of the social and political order.

The first institutions to feel the disruptive force of the new learning were the schools. Their students provided the largest group of radical recruits, who were abandoning academic learning. Both new and traditional approaches to knowledge emphasized the great value of the pursuit of learning. Thus the clash between the two created a personal dilemma for some students. The appeal of the radical cause to the highly motivated students was great because it played on their desire for real knowledge. The secret police became conscious of the clash between school and revolutionary activism first from the reports of its agents, then from the statistics it collected on the background of individuals arrested on suspicion of political crimes. The data covering the middle and late 1870's included a total of 520 people

96. TsGAOR, f. 109, o. 85, d. 32 (1867), ll. 14–15.
97. "Revoliutsionnoe i studencheskoe dvizhenie," p. 119.

with higher education. Of these almost 40 percent (197) had not finished their studies.[98] This figure provided vivid evidence of the power of the radical cause to disrupt the normal path of social promotion of the country's educated elite. Count Valuev, member of a committee in 1874 to analyze the causes of the student agitation, attacked bitterly that "moral disease" which was transforming higher education into an "instrument for hatred against the established order."[99] Studying seemed to be only an excuse for such moral perversion; the path to revolt led straight through higher education. This was true of the women in St. Petersburg, as the secret police noticed. Among the young women whom they arrested in the 1870's, a sizable proportion sought to study at the Medical-Surgical Academy. Graduates from other women's schools and women who had abandoned studies at other institutions to come to St. Petersburg, "mostly without any stated occupation, always explain that, living in Petersburg, they are preparing to enter the Academy." In addition, they frequented "circles of women medical students."[100]

Converts to the new learning saw their future in a new light. Their voices began to be heard widely in the late 1860's, at the very time when the corpus of radical literature had assumed impressive proportions and enrollment in the institutions of higher education had reached unprecedented levels. The student ferment of the winter 1868–1869, which led to the disturbances of the spring of 1869, raised the issue of studies versus agitation. One student activist recalled that the question was: "Work or knowledge, that is, should one devote oneself to scholarship" to obtain a diploma "in order later to lead a life of a privileged educated professional?" Or, "remembering one's debt to the people, [should one] abandon the institutions of higher education to take up a trade" and work with the people?[101] There could be only one answer. The Chaikovtsy stated the new moral imperative in unambiguous terms. They argued that the "honest individual has no choice but to abandon all privileges of birth and of education and to go to the people to teach justice, equality, and liberty." The rightfulness of this decision followed obviously from "the unequal distribution of the products of labor, . . . the inequal-

98. Itenberg, *Dvizhenie,* p. 376, table 2.
99. TsGIAL, f. 908, o. 1, d. 125, l. 75.
100. Sidorov, "Statisticheskie," p. 33.
101. Chudnovski, "Iz davnykh let," p. 284.

ity of political rights, . . . the inequality and injustice in the family, falsehood in religion, the monopoly of knowledge and its venality."[102] As this message increased in volume and force, the call to complete their formal studies became fainter and fainter among the rebellious students.

The issue often presented itself as a choice between two moral obligations, one to pure learning and the other to radical reform. George Plekhanov had abandoned his studies in military school to devote himself to science in the Mining Institute. He was an outstanding student and dreamed of pursuing graduate studies in chemistry abroad in order to prepare for a career as a teacher. In the fall of 1875 a close friend lectured him on the frivolity of his scholarly ambitions. "If you are going to train for such a long time in chemistry," he asked, "when will you begin to work for the revolution?" Such dreams of specialization in science were a "luxury."[103] The dilemma had probably already occurred to Plekhanov, but conversations such as this increased the pressure to abandon the normal path of scholarship. By the fall of 1876 he had made up his mind. That December he was one of the principal organizers of the demonstration at the Kazan Cathedral; the next spring he was dropped from the student rolls of the institute for failure to keep up his studies. He had cut his ties permanently with formal learning. The Russian educational system offered wealth and prestige to its intellectual elite, who were expected to accept their privilege as part of the natural order. The literature of dissent denied this view. As one student declared at a meeting of his circle in 1872 (attended by a police informer), "it is dishonest for a minority to enjoy higher education at the expense of the majority who do not have enough bread."[104]

The school of dissent posed a real challenge to the operation of the country's system of educational promotion. Its appeal mystified and outraged those who did not feel the call of revolt. Communication between those entering the radical movement and their former circle of family and friends was not easy. One first-year student in the Medical-Surgical Academy tried to explain to his mother in a letter written in 1873 why he had decided to abandon his studies. "The question is

102. [Morozov], "Ocherk," p. 226.
103. Quoted in L. Deutsch, "Gorniak G. V. Plekhanov" [Plekhanov as a mining student], in *Na puti k pobede* (Leningrad, 1925), pp. 24–25.
104. TsGAOR, f. 109, tr. eks., d. 63 (1872), ch. 1, 1. 162.

not whether my studies in the Academy satisfy me," he explained. If he were "searching at present for this type of activity," he would certainly choose the natural sciences. "But the real question, you see, is whether there is any use at all to be obtained from pure learning." The only valid criterion of utility he recognized was service to the "laboring people" rather than to "bourgeois society." It seemed clear to him that "any person who does not devote all his activity and does not give himself completely to service to the people is necessarily a parasite and a thief."[105] For him the only true morality lay in defying traditional standards of behavior. He had accepted liberation as his ideal. His education could go no further.

The existence of large groups of young people whose thoughts were turned in the same direction allowed the radical community to expand and organize spontaneously and seemingly at will. Revolt appeared by the early 1870's a perfectly natural action. One young populist explained to the police that he had abandoned his studies shortly after having come to St. Petersburg in the fall of 1873 because "during meetings and conversations with friends and comrades . . . , we determined that the presently existing social order is founded on principles of injustice and therefore should undergo a change." Having reached this apparently obvious conclusion, the group "proposed to busy ourselves immediately with the preparation of the people for an uprising against the established order." He and his comrades therefore abandoned scholarly activities to go to the people to work as teachers or in some other profession.[106]

Nothing in his formal education had prepared him for this decision. Yet without his years as part of the Russian student elite, he would never have reached this turning point in his life. The educational atmosphere in the schools nurtured and encouraged the special learning in radical dissent and contributed its own intellectual rigor and rationalism to the radical frame of mind. The school of dissent flourished in this environment. By the 1860's it was sufficiently developed to offer a complete course on progress, reason, the new man in the new society, and the social obligation to participate in this great work. The success of the circles of self-education in the early 1870's was vivid evidence of the vitality and success of this informal cur-

105. "Iz pisem S. S. Golousheva" [From the letters of S. S. GLoushev], *Revoliutsionnoe narodnichestvo*, I, 161.
106. Cited in *ibid.*, p. 252.

riculum of revolt. In substance, the literature of dissent represented the adaptation of European radical thought to the conditions of a non-Western society. It existed in close and constant contact with Europe and reflected the great intellectual debates of European radicals, but it had acquired a dynamism and creativity of its own by the mid-century sufficient to inspire a unique community of dissent in Russia.

6 | A New Society

The radical community embodied in its organized life the ideals of egalitarianism and spontaneity by which its members hoped all of society would ultimately be guided. Its capacity to accommodate as equals young people from all ranks of the Russian social order stood as living proof of the possibility of eliminating class differences. Its independence from external authority freed it from the social constraints under which the student community operated. These characteristics made it the best vehicle to distribute the literature of dissent. Thus, the intense and unimpeded communication it offered to groups scattered throughout the country disseminated the models for the meager experiments in socialist living and action possible under Russian conditions. It was a unique creation.

Yet the actual substance of this life did not add up to a great deal. Circles gathered together small but disorganized groups of individuals for free but undirected discussion and debate. They could act as school, family, social gathering, or even radical cell, depending on the degree of commitment and preparedness of their members. At times, informal popular schools provided an immediate opportunity to disseminate the new learning, in a very watered-down form, among the poor. A few workshops run on egalitarian principles, called "artels," introduced young Russians to the socialist principles of production of such nonessential items as dresses and bookbindings. Communal living groups arose, which conducted their affairs with total disregard for personal property and often without any regular income. It was all a meager effort at providing a life of freedom and equality in an authoritarian, hierarchical society, yet it represented the only visible evidence that radical reform could possibly occur in Russia.

Without the students, the radical community would not have existed. The students provided large numbers of recruits who transformed the radical movement from a feeble collection of small, isolated groups into a significant social phenomenon. Just as important, the new forms of organization and action devised by the student corporation passed over directly into the radical community, such as assemblies, libraries, treasuries, and communes. Young radicals found in them a new meaning. Some of these activities had the appearance of apprenticeship in socialist living, acting as a further refinement of the recruitment process for the radical movement. They appeared only with the development of the student corporation in the 1850's and 1860's. Prior to that time, the student community could provide little but a few martyrs to the cause. It was thus no coincidence that the student and radical movements burst into prominence at approximately the same time. The latter lived in a state of close dependency on the former until by the 1870's it had shaped these habits and institutions into a tradition of its own and could exist somewhat independently. Yet the ties were never completely broken.

This dependency weakened the radical movement, for it was competing directly with the state for student recruits. The regime could offer regular income, security, and the respect of society. A political dissenter could find comradeship and idealism, but these provided weak protection in the face of the state's system of rewards for the obedient and stern punishments for the wayward. Many tempted by the new life failed ultimately to sustain the faith. Few of them left records, but their story is as important in understanding the rise of the community of dissent as that of the herculean figures so prominent in the radical martyrology. These failures established the extreme limits of possible recruitment and illustrate the dilemma of the radical community, hopeful of becoming the model for all society yet condemned to exist as an esoteric cult in mid-century Russia.

The School of Dissent

The years of greatest trial for the radical movement were during the reign of Nicholas I. Radical literature from the West penetrated only a few educational institutions and intellectual groups. It found little resonance in Russian publications—the censors saw to that—and only a limited audience. Those few individuals attracted by the vision of radical change tended naturally to seek protection and comfort among themselves. Their gatherings possessed neither organiza-

tion nor legal status, and their very existence was precarious. Like
the meetings of writers and other intellectuals, they were dignified
with the title of "circle" (in Russian, *kruzhok*). In using this term its
members could underline their special role in Russian society.

Several politically oriented circles existed in Moscow University
in the 1830's and a few appeared in St. Petersburg in the 1840's.
They were the only manifestation of the radical movement in the
reign of Nicholas I. In them, as in the circle Alexander Herzen
helped create in Moscow University, the disaffected could find refuge.
Herzen recalled that the "major characteristic" of the members of
the circle he knew as a student was a "deep feeling of alienation from
official Russia, from their surroundings, and at the same time a long-
ing to escape."[1]

The circles initiated and protected those entering the radical movement, though their *"rites de passage"* had no particular form until the
1860's. Their activities consisted primarily of the pursuit of learning
in a group of sympathetic and loyal comrades. The circle in Moscow
University which formed in the early 1830's around Nicholas Stankevich, Belinski, and Mikhail Bakunin resembled the others in that
it provided "the intellectual stimulation that could not be found elsewhere." In addition, it gave "comradeship, community of interest, and
collective support in all one's affairs."[2] The circle members represented a special elite of the discontented and offered a select audience
for preachers of the new word.

Belinski used his circle in St. Petersburg in the 1840's to diffuse his
own views on social and political injustice and utopian socialism.
Fedor Dostoevski joined the circle in the mid-decade without advanced formal education but with a great capacity for self-education.
He had retired from his position as draftsman in the Naval Ministry
to make a career as a writer, but his intellectual interests had been
shaped by his attraction to the Western social critics such as George
Sand. Belinski recognized a kindred spirit. As the young writer remembered it, "In the first days of our acquaintance, Belinski received me with open arms and immediately set out to convert me to
his faith. I found him a passionate socialist . . . and all his teaching

---

1. Gertsen, *Byloe i dumy*, I, 364; Herzen's circle is described in Malia,
Alexander Herzen, pp. 65–67.
2. Edward Brown, *Stankevich and His Moscow Circle* (Stanford, 1966),
pp. 12–13.

came with passion."[3] His eagerness to teach was matched by the readiness of his listeners to learn. All had received a similar intellectual formation and shared a common isolation and disaffection within society.

These similarities created an atmosphere of comradeship. The circle formed by Mikhail Petrashevski was large by contemporary standards. It welcomed newcomers with an openness not shared by other radical circles. Petrashevski's proselytizing zeal led him to welcome any and all acquaintances interested in progress and a better life through radical social and moral improvement. His meetings nevertheless attracted only a handful of dilettantes and curiosity-seekers. The radical reputation of the circle made it different from the usual run of weekly circles of Petersburg society. Its members gathered not for cards and gossip, but for learning. One member described the circle as "one family, whose ties were not blood but moral and social affinity, a family by bonds of learning and common experiences,"[4] despite wide divergences of outlook and conviction. Petrashevski's efforts to give the meetings a systematic program of instruction and discussion met with little success as most members had already completed formal schooling and had begun regular careers. The circle operated primarily as a place of intensive and chaotic social interaction among educated men united primarily by their alienation. Dostoevski recreated the atmosphere with cruel precision in his description of Peter Verkhovenski's circle in *The Possessed*. This circle had little to offer besides comradeship and common intellectual interests. It was a family in the sense of providing security and reassurance to its members isolated in a hostile society. It did not have the base of recruitment or the body of learning that permitted later circles to function as active training grounds for rebels.

The circles developed in the early years of the reign of Alexander II, the most innovative period in the elaboration of an organized process of recruitment for the radical community. All the functions of the circles apparent in the earlier years expanded and became far more systematic, due in large part to their close connections with the student movement. An organized social life unique to this subculture

3. Quoted in V. Komarovich, "Iunost' Dostoevskogo" [The youth of Dostoevski], *Byloe*, XXIII (1924), 4.
4. *Delo petrashevtsev* [The Petrashevtsy affair], 3 vols. (Moscow, 1937–1951), II, 93–94.

developed rapidly under the pressure of the growing interest in and systematization of radical learning and the increased readiness of youth already trained in student corporate life.

A new world appeared to open up before these activists. Their intense desire to exchange ideas and to work on a collective enterprise for the sake of the new cause is apparent in a letter written in 1858 by a young medical student to a friend in his circle. "There is so much we still have to do in the future," he wrote, "and so much we must tell one another, that our strength is hardly sufficient."[5] They needed some focus for their new aspirations. The circle offered paltry rewards, but there was nothing else. The circle formed around Nikolai Dobroliubov in the Pedagogical Institute was a petty affair, but assured its members that, as one participant recalled, they were developing the capacities of new men on a level "with the demands of the century." Their task was "to understand the contemporary currents of thought and to assimilate the acquired knowledge by learning its application to their own lives."[6] Another member believed that they would speed the "rational development of society" when they were able to "inform the world of the many new truths prepared by us in our little institute circle."[7] Considerable faith was required to believe that their modest efforts could have such tremendous consequences, that reason really would sweep the world on to a new age of freedom and equality, and that their collective efforts would aid in their own improvement and soon that of all society. It was much easier to hold to these ideals in company than alone.

As this faith strengthened and spread, the circles became to interested youth both family and teacher. They were places of real comradeship created by a concern for true learning of use to mankind, not just to one's career. One young "proletarian student," as he described himself, in his first year in Petersburg University in the late 1850's led a life of "wild, romantic daydreams and isolation." Simple physical survival was his main goal. He joined a circle the next year, which provided him with friends, reading in radical literature, and a new model for behavior. The circle subscribed to journals such as *The Contemporary,* whose articles taught him for the first time how

5. TsGIAL, f. 1282, o. 1, d. 71 (1862), l. 191.
6. Quoted in V. Polianski, *N. A. Dobroliubov* (Moscow, 1935), p. 31.
7. B. Stsiborski, "Vospominaniia" [Memoirs], *Literaturnoe nasledstvo, XXV/XXVI* (1936), 300.

"to group individual phenomena of life in general categories" and to "compare our life with the life of developed Europe." The discussion among members touched also on standards for personal behavior. The circle became "for us a real school of social and moral guidance [*kontrol'*] over our actions."[8] They provided a center for the student youth for independent activity outside of their school life. Though inherently no more subversive than the student corporation, they existed beyond official control and focused on subjects judged dangerous by the authorities. Their organized activities existed on the uneasy boundary between the new life and the old, from which individuals could easily move into actual opposition.

The major concern of the student circles centered on the interests of the students. Rising enrollments stimulated the formation of circles of young people from the same region or even school. These so-called *"zemliachestva"* (from *"zemliak,"* a person from the same region) came the closest of any Russian student organization to the model of the German students' *Landsmannschaften,* also based on regional loyalty. They first became common in the early 1860's, after the new student regulations of 1861 forbade corporate activity by the student body of the universities, and became more numerous later in the decade as enrollments in the professional schools climbed. Their growth reflected primarily the desire of students far from home to find comrades with whom they shared a common background. The secondary school from which one came provided an easy pole of attraction. As a result, the greatest number of student circles "generally were formed of people well acquainted with one another," as one student testified to the police after his arrest, such as "comrades from a *gymnasium.*"[9] There were circles in St. Petersburg by the end of the 1860's from the Don region, from Saratov, from Vologda, from the Tula seminary, and so on. They took on some of the activities of the student corporation, organizing student-aid funds and setting up their own libraries. The university administration had apparently acquiesced in their existence as a tolerable substitute for the forbidden corporate life of the student body. The governor-general of Moscow noted in 1866, in a report on the Karakozov affair, that the school authorities "had not foreseen their aim of hostility against the gov-

8. Ostrogorski, *Iz istorii,* pp. 52–55, 59.
9. "Iz pokazanii L. M. Shchigoleva" [From the testimony of L. M. Shchigolev], *Revoliutsionnoe narodnichestvo,* I, 252–53.

ernment."[10] He condemned the entire institution because a few members of one Moscow circle had appeared in the group around Kara-kozov.

The regional circles appeared far less subversive to youth already committed to revolutionary action. The "majority" of them, in the opinion of one young radical, were only marginally involved in political agitation. The "reading of an essay" was for most "an affair of great importance."[11] Their members dabbled in forbidden literature and discussed dangerous subjects, but most had no stomach for open resistance or even collaboration in revolutionary activities.

An incident later in the 1870's, when the populist movement appeared at its peak, underlined the narrow base of support for the radical movement among these groups. In 1879 the members of one regional circle tried to form a union of several such circles in St. Petersburg to aid the revolutionaries. A majority of the forty students who came to the meeting refused even to give financial support to the movement. "The revolution is not our business," they argued, "our concern is learning. We did not come here for the revolution and do not see why we should sit quietly and contribute our last kopek for people whom we do not know and perhaps do not want to know."[12] Their decision represented a victory for the organized and orderly system of social promotion set up and defended by the government.

It was often hard to distinguish where partying ended and subversive activities began in the life of the informal student groups in the capital. Their chief characteristic seems to have been lack of rigid organization. What they lost in methodical work they gained in spontaneity. Like the student corporation from which they had sprung, they were anarchistic in their operations. The police agent who followed the activities of the student assemblies in the Agronomy Institute in 1870–1871 meticulously noted their confused evolution. He reported that their "entire conversation turns on revolutionary themes" interrupted often with "revolutionary songs." Individuals offered toasts "to the French republic, to the success of the red flag, and to revolution in general," which were "triumphantly received" by the participants. They were living the drama two thousand miles

10. Quoted in Vilenskaia, *Revoliutsionnoe podpol'e*, pp. 190–91.
11. [Morozov], "Ocherk," pp. 207–8.
12. V. Dmitrieva, "Teni proshlogo" [Shades of the past], *Katorga i ssylka*, No. 11 (1924), 118.

to the west of the fall of Napoleon III's empire and the rise of the Paris Commune. But fun came with serious discussion. One meeting began with a talk on the work of the German socialist Ferdinand Lassalle, followed by a social hour of dancing and drinking. When the participants returned to their political problems, "everyone was shouting, making noise, and arguing almost to the point of fighting."[13] These meetings in the institute were large affairs, at times bringing together over one hundred students from all over the city. Their tone and activities were in substance no different from the smaller student groups. Circles came and went, members appeared and moved away. There was no structure to this new society.

Consequently, the circles depended primarily on the mood and interests of the youth moving through the institutions of higher education. They were an expression of the concern for learning as the tool for radical change and the desire for comradeship. They reinforced the readiness of some to move further on the path of political revolt, but never became exclusively training schools in dissent. One student of the mid-1870's found among his comrades in the capital a large mass of "searchers for a new path, for revolutionary activity," who were completely unorganized and lacking any fixed plan of action. They "went to meetings and discussions, convulsively seizing on anything which carried the slightest trace of the struggle for truth, for liberty, for the people."[14] Some of the women's circles firmly resisted the call of the radical movement, preferring to pursue their own special interests. In St. Petersburg in the early 1870's there were "meetings of women, to which men were not admitted and in which discussion centered for the most part on women's emancipation." One such circle, which kept "to itself" and had a "very conspiratorial appearance," took a dim view of radical involvement. One of its members who defected to the Chaikovtsy circle was accused of "treason to the women's circle."[15] The instability of membership, the weak organization, and the variety of interests of the circles made them shaky foundations on which to build a real radical movement.

Lenin got to know their atmosphere well as a student in the 1880's and raged later against the slipshod habits they tolerated when he

13. TsGAOR, f. 109, tr. eks., d. 120 (1870), ch. 1, ll. 41–42.
14. Timofeev, "Perezhitoe," pp. 98–99.
15. E. Koval'skaia, "Iz moikh vospominanii" [From my memoirs], *Katorga i ssylka*, No. 22 (1926), 83.

tried to cement a solid revolutionary party. He accused them of "Oblomovism," of "capriciousness," and of "impulsiveness, called the 'free process of intellectual struggle.' "[16] Their activities in pursuit of the new learning appeared very much like an academic exercise, undertaken with the same seriousness and attitude of remoteness from real life as formal education. Like movements in defense of student corporate privileges and honor, they could attract the attention temporarily of a sizable number of students, but they were too formless to hold most of their members for long. It is remarkable that, under these chaotic conditions, they did succeed so well.

The circles, like the educational system, provided their own form of moral upbringing. Youth looking for inspiration and guidance sought others like themselves. The literature of dissent, defining an ideal of personal conduct and principles for political and social liberation, offered a basis for the formation of friendships. Student agitation stimulated the rapid growth of a large network of circles during and after the disorders of 1869. In the atmosphere of resistance and activism following the repression of the student movement that spring, students came together in small groups. These circles were "very ill-defined." Their participants "often met without knowing why or what they would talk about." They were interested in "social issues," had the "determination to act somehow in a manner harmful to the regime," and felt the magic of the word "revolution."[17] Contact with the circles, disorganized though they were, provided precious experience in resistance to authority.

By the early 1870's the circles offered a wide variety of options in collective living. One young populist, arrested during the "to the people" movement, described in his testimony the new life that began following his arrival in St. Petersburg in 1873. He came ostensibly to study in the Technological Institute, but he had already begun his own study of radical literature in a small *gymnasium* circle. He arrived in the capital hoping to meet "people sharing my outlook, that is, discontentment with the existing order of things, since I had heard that such people were in St. Petersburg." He was first exposed to this new society at a student assembly held in a private apartment. The organizer greeted his guests, most of whom he did not know, by ex-

16. V. Lenin, *PSS* (Moscow, 1959), VIII, 381.
17. [Morozov], "Ocherk," pp. 206–7.

plaining that "it is desirable generally for us to come together." The young neophyte recalled that the meeting produced "much noise" but no concrete knowledge. Within a few months, he found what he was looking for in an anarchist circle.[18] Out of this chaotic ferment, most intense in the late 1860's and 1870's, came the hard core of radicals whose close-knit community could withstand persecution and massive arrests.

No rules governed the selection of these special kinship groups of the radical community. Like the Petrashevtsy circle of the 1840's, they resembled extended families whose ties were based primarily on personal affinities created by attitudes of social alienation and interest in radical change. The formation of circles depended, as another arrested populist youth testified, "not on a previously determined program." It came "simply by itself," on the basis of "the intimacy of individuals." He distinguished between the ordinary student youth around him and the "decent individuals" with whom he sought to associate after he came to study in the capital. He finally found kindred souls. He revealed to them his "social convictions, they did the same and it turned out that we were absolutely in agreement on our fundamental beliefs."[19]

The circles presented a range of personal and intellectual experiences far richer than anything these youth had previously known. Alexander Mikhailov, who passed through this parallel school in the mid-1870's on his way to becoming a leader of the People's Will party, felt the circles absolutely indispensable to make Russian students take "their first step toward an autonomous life," by which he meant a commitment to resistance and dissent. He believed that "in the vast majority of cases . . . neither the families of privileged classes nor the schools" provided this training.[20] The circles filled this unusual role after a long period of preparation and experimentation. In the 1840's they showed a tendency in this direction, but neither the circumstances nor their own procedures made it possible for them to recruit large numbers of young Russians. By the late 1860's the situation had changed dramatically. The student agitation

---

18. "Iz pokazanii Gorodetskogo" [From the testimony of Gorodetski], *Revoliutsionnoe narodnichestvo*, I, 298, 300–1.

19. *Ibid.*, pp. 254–56.

20. Quoted in A. P. Pribyleva-Korba, *Narodovolets A. D. Mikhailov* (Moscow, 1925), p. 93.

of 1868–1869 seemed to generate interest for radical activity within the educational institutions. The circles of "self-education" were an indirect product of these events. The special type of circle that was vital to radical recruitment resembled closely the student circles from which it had sprung, but was adapted to a unique purpose.

The young men and women who gathered in these groups were the elite of the radical community. Their own moral rigor and commitment assumed impressive proportions when concentrated within narrow limits. The authority they acquired allowed them to reject potential recruits who could not meet their standards. The Chaikovtsy circle set a model for ruthlessness in selecting new members, who were admitted only by unanimous agreement. Any candidate who showed "morbid, vain pride" or the "absence of sufficient rigorousness in [his] personal life," had no chance of admission. Even minor questions of appearance and taste were important. An individual was unacceptable who "could not do without a tie or starched shirt, who liked to drink or who treated women disparagingly."[21] The older generation of radicals were amazed (some pleasantly, others unpleasantly) with the example set by the young radical elite. Wilhelm Bervi, whose own path to revolt had been long and solitary, admired tremendously the capacity of the circles associated with the Chaikovtsy to "cultivate those stern and reliable personalities which subsequently gave the government so much trouble." The group was like a company of saints, to which "people entrusted their money, their honor, their future, without the slightest apprehension of being betrayed."[22]

Entry into this inner group came in stages, according to the memoirs of those who were accepted. The circles of students did not usually figure in the radical movement, but they provided an introduction to the activities and ideals of the new people and thus opened the door to radical circles. Nikolai Chaikovski himself had come into the movement in this manner. He noted in an outline of his memoirs that he had passed from a university "circle of comrades, former *gymnasium* classmates," to a circle "for public activities," whose members later appeared in the group which bore his name. He thought the "acquaintances" he made in this manner were responsible

21. L. Shishko, *Sergei Mikhailovich Kravchinskii i kruzhok chaikovtsev (iz vospominanii i zametok starogo narodnika)* [S. M. Kravchinski and the Chaikovtsy circle—the memoirs and notes of an old populist] (St. Petersburg, 1906), p. 13.
22. N. Flerovski [V. Bervi], *Tri politicheskie sistemy*, pp. 268–69.

for providing the "solid foundations" for his intellectual revolt. The process worked in the other direction, too, since without the approval of these new friends he could never have been admitted. His own suitability was never in doubt. In fact, the "Chaikovtsy" circle acquired its name largely because he enjoyed an unquestioned reputation for moral rectitude and purity.[23] This process of recruitment was multiplied many times over. The only restrictions were the size of the student community and the strength of the conviction among the country's educated elite that they should provide the phalanx of the new order.

By the 1870's the bonds of trust and the eagerness to recruit new members resulted in special expeditions to rescue young people in peril. The problem was most acute for young women unable to leave home without parental permission. Word reached the Chaikovtsy circle in late 1871 of the plight of a sixteen-year-old priest's daughter in the distant provinces. The story was the familiar one of a stern father unwilling to allow his young daughter to go to St. Petersburg to pursue her studies. Her reliability was vouched for by her school-teacher, already an active proselytizer with close friends among the Chaikovtsy. The group decided to organize her "escape." One of its members, Sergei Sinegub, volunteered for this mission of mercy. Twenty years old, he had just arrived in the capital to begin studies at the Technological Institute. Through a secret exchange of letters, he and the girl whom he had never met arranged an elaborate hoax to convince her father that Sergei was her secret fiancé, whose love was so great that it could wait no longer. In mid-winter, Sinegub arrived in a state of considerable anxiety to meet his bride-to-be and her family in the small village where her father had his parish. The girl who rushed to embrace him when he entered the house was— as he later recalled—stunningly beautiful. Her father, won over by their story, organized an elaborate religious wedding. After a very awkward wedding night spent locked up in the bridal chamber, the two left for St. Petersburg. Sinegub congratulated his wife on her hard-won freedom, and she headed immediately for a women's commune.[24] The mock love affair was a remarkable demonstration of talent by two absolute strangers and proof of the crucial work the

23. D. Odinets, "V kruzhke Chaikovtsev" [In the Chaikovtsy circle], Titov, ed., *N. V. Chaikovskii*, p. 45.

24. S. S. Sinegub, *Zapiski chaikovtsa* (Moscow, 1929), pp. 38–45; see also Jaakoff Prelooker, *Heroes and Heroines of Russia: Builders of a New Commonwealth* (London, 1908), pp. 51–77.

circles could perform to assist in the process of radical recruitment.

The educational activities of the circles lacked the romantic interest of this incident, but were much more influential in attracting converts. The most systematic effort at turning circles into schools of dissent came with the spread of "self-education" circles in the early 1870's. This moderate approach to radical agitation found ideological justification in Peter Lavrov's philosophy of progress through intellectual and moral development. The program struck a sensitive chord among those students attracted by unorthodox learning and eager for constructive activity. The circles provided an excellent means for young radicals to proselytize among the unconverted. They put into action the basic tenets of the radical community.

The number of circles concerned with the reading and discussion of radical literature seems to have grown rapidly through the 1860's. The student unrest of 1869 helped crystallize the forms and action of the student movement outside of the institutions of higher education. By this time, the radical movement as a whole possessed more structure, more clearly defined goals, and a much more exhaustive corpus of social criticism than before. Student and radical forms of action met in the self-education circles, emancipated from academic life and from direct involvement in student affairs and committed to a type of learning far more ambitious than that of formal education. They had become parallel schools in revolution.

The circle that left the most extensive records was the Chaikovtsy. Its evolution reflected the basic forces that developed the radical community; its members consciously sought to spread their model of active study among the students all over Russia. Its origins can be traced back to the student life of the capital at the end of the 1860's. Its organizers, Mark Natanson and Vasili Alexandrov, both entered the Medical-Surgical Academy in the fall of 1868, both became delegates to the student library, and both were briefly held by the police as a result of the disturbances in the academy in the spring of 1869. They learned how to buy literature at cheap rates from Petersburg book dealers while involved in the medical students' library. Sometime after their release, they and other comrades formed a circle and a commune. The principal goal of the circle was to acquire knowledge, but they sought the key to transforming man and society, not irrelevant abstractions or vocational skills. To make this information more easily accessible, Natanson and Alexandrov contacted book dealers from whom they could expect discounts and could hope to obtain illegal publications. Ultimately they organized the publication of manuscripts. By 1871 the circle had acquired a strong sense of mission to aid others as they were aiding themselves.

Like earlier circles, it sought both learning and moral improvement, but with remarkable zeal. The history of the circle written a decade later, based on personal reminiscences of participants, describes a life as severe as in an ascetic religious order, though without segregation of the sexes. In the summer of 1871 it moved to a cottage near the capital to pursue its advanced course of learning. Acquisition of knowledge about psychology, political economy, logic, and the other disciplines studied that summer was only part of the work. Self-perfection was as important. The fifteen participants began a sort of group therapy through "the criticism of each by all, that is, the objective analysis of the characteristics and peculiarities of a given individual at a general meeting of everyone who wished [to attend]." They believed they had discovered "completely by accident the exact method for the regulation of relations between individuals and society."[25]

The circle set out to encourage other groups to imitate their activity, acting as a cultural nucleus radiating inspiration and innovation for the receptive student community in the capital and the provinces of Russia. Self-education was its message. Alexandrov appeared at a meeting in the Agronomy Institute to defend the cause of learning. "We wish to save the people," he argued, "but know nothing ourselves." He believed that "we should begin by studying" and indicated "a few circles" in which work had already begun.[26] He and Natanson had been eager from the beginning to share the literature they acquired for their circle with other groups. They sold some books and gave others away to those too poor to pay even their cheap prices. The losses were recovered by "donations and contributions."[27] In this manner, they could circulate the corpus of the literature of dissent among a far wider audience than would otherwise have existed. The Third Section became quite interested in the activities of this self-appointed ministry of popular enlightenment. Its agents tracked down

25. [Morozov], "Ocherk," p. 221.
26. I. Deniker, "Vospominaniia" [Memoirs], *Katorga i ssylka*, No. 11 (1924), 23.
27. Tikhomirov, *Nachala*, pp. 54–55.

the distribution network for one of the books circulated, Wilhelm Bervi's *ABC of the Social Sciences,* published in 1871 in a printing of 2,500 copies. Of these, 800 went to bookstores and Nikolai Chaikovski purchased the rest. He sold copies to his friends, including 300 to a medical student who acted as one of the many distributors in this volunteer "book affair."[28]

The Chaikovtsy believed that their own circle was transformed by these activities and that "in the course of time, the distribution of books . . . created ties between the circle and a mass of people who would otherwise have remained completely outside the movement." Their organizational activity made them both teacher and model for political activism. The isolation of the first circles of the 1840's had disappeared. The Chaikovtsy and similar circles offered protection and encouragement to student youth interested in dissident action but fearful of abandoning the security of their old life. The ground was prepared, and the Chaikovtsy gave the inspiration sought by many. Its members believed that its "plans, activities, and ideals . . . met the demands of its time" and made it the "true spokesman" of the self-education movement.[29]

The action of these self-education circles spread throughout the country under the protective cover of the student community. In early 1871 the Chaikovtsy circle organized a meeting of delegates from circles from every university city to attempt to define a common program of action and to establish basic goals. Representatives from Moscow presented a draft of a program that summed up their ideals and procedures. It cited Lavrov on the need for "critically thinking individuals" but focused almost entirely on students as the source of new recruits. It urged the formation of circles, libraries and reading rooms, student cafeterias, and artels. It also called for close collaboration with the working classes to develop the base of agitation. It was both a revolutionary document and a proposal for winning new supporters away from the traditional path of education and social promotion.[30]

---

28. TsGAOR, f. 109, tr. eks., d. 185 (1871), ll. 30–32.
29. [Morozov], "Ocherk," pp. 214–15.
30. This document was published in *Katorga i ssylka,* No. 67 (1930), 95–106; its place in the ideological development of the Chaikovtsy is discussed in Martin Miller, "Ideological Conflicts in Russian Populism," *Slavic Review,* XXIX (March 1970), 5–9.

The identity of basic outlook and style of life shared by the student elite made it possible for the activities and interests of one circle to be copied easily and quickly by others in other cities. The Third Section was aware of this development. It did not appear to appreciate immediately the implications of the growing organizational unity provided by the circles, both as a framework for assimilating new members into the radical movement and as a preparation for revolutionary action. The circles had an innocuous appearance; student "self-education" was no crime. Among the letters intercepted by the police was one sent in February 1871 by a Kharkov student describing his new circle. It had been formed at the initiative of another Kharkov student who had gone to St. Petersburg to learn about the operations of such circles. The letter stressed the strictly educational character of his circle. The young man was convinced that "in the future, each of us will have to work in the quality of social leaders," so one must acquire a "basic and varied knowledge of Russia." His circle wished to understand Russian life by studying the economic distribution of wealth, the class hierarchy, education, industry, and more still.[31] Other groups were more ambitious, including constructive work to implement their ideals. When a circle was formed in November 1871 in one of the technical institutes of the capital, its goals included "self-education, the collection of funds for the formation of a commercial enterprise on socialist principles [usually called an artel], and the opening of a literacy school."[32] This was to be the beginning of a new life, on the model first outlined in Chernyshevski's novel *What's to Be Done?* and codified in the action of circles like the Chaikovtsy.

By late 1871 the circles were quite numerous, well organized, and closely united. A police report in November called attention to the existence of a "network of 'self-education' circles" maintaining "relations with all the universities and with our emigrants living abroad." It noted the similarity of activities, in which the members were "obligated to distribute books, to collect money for the treasury, to attempt to obtain as large a supply of books as possible, and to set up new circles." St. Petersburg and Moscow were the main centers of activity and had "constant dealings with one another by means of agents, and act in complete harmony."[33]

31. TsGAOR, f. 109, tr. eks., d. 65 (1871), l. 139.
32. *Ibid.,* d. 63 (1872), ch. 2, l. 56.
33. *Ibid.,* d. 51 (1870), ch. 1, ll. 101–2.

The organizational ferment extended down into some of the country's *gymnasia*. There, too, learning could bring together small groups out of which came new recruits for the radical movement. The account by one activist *gymnasium* pupil provides a good picture of the gradual evolution of his group from simple intellectual exploration and fraternization into a real underground organization. It began meeting around 1870, when he was about sixteen years old. The members, all "materialists, atheists, by prevalent standards nihilists of the Bazarov type," organized a "self-education circle," with a library including the works of such major Russian radicals as Pisarev and Chernyshevski. By 1873 the circle was "fully formed," with a secret apartment for lodging radicals coming through town, a library, and a small mimeographing machine for the distribution of leaflets. It was an active avocation for the members, but apparently did not interrupt their educational life. The author of these memoirs admitted that the circle went into a decline by the mid-1870's, when he had to prepare his final examinations for graduation in anticipation of entering an advanced educational institution.[34] That was where real life began for him, as for most of the radicals.

The evolution of the circles into living embodiments of the new life was a major step forward in the process of recruitment for the community of dissent. Previously there had been no such organized activity which could envelope and protect the neophytes. Now they found activities promising meaningful action as well as learning and comradeship. The Third Section kept increasingly close watch on these circles, finally sending out in March 1872 a secret circular describing their peculiar and dangerous characteristics. Their "external signs" included "the formation . . . of any sort of society which . . . is kept a secret by its members," the development of "a definite organization with written rules," a "periodical publication," a treasury, an "artel or cooperative with some external, frequently false aim as, for example, the translation of foreign books into Russian . . . or the assistance of poor students," and "the systematic distribution and the secret reading among student youth of books and essays."[35] The activities of the circles made them a little world to themselves, partially hidden and protected by the large student community.

34. Timofeev, "Perezhitoe," pp. 94–95.
35. TsGIAL, f. 1282, o. 1, d. 292 (1869), l. 248.

The transformation of radical recruitment since the 1840's was re-markable. Then a few isolated circles had found members in a small number of schools and among a tiny group of bureaucrats and officers to read and discuss literature, mostly Western, on ideal social and political conditions far removed from Russian reality. By the early 1870's a large body of available recruits in the expanded educational system could be offered an extensive set of readings and practical sug-gestions for bringing to life the communal and egalitarian vision of the ideal future in their own surroundings. The works distributed through the self-education circles offered knowledge of the mysteries of the new order. The Chaikovtsy felt themselves real teachers in choosing works for the "book affair." The readings were intended to provide the basis for discussion of "those questions particularly im-portant for the elaboration of meaningful and solid convictions."[36] The ranks of the faithful swelled as the secret, organized life of the circles initiated more and more members into the moral code and ideology of the radical movement.

Young women occupied a small but important place among the new recruits. They moved as equals within the radical community, more fully emancipated than anywhere else in Russian society. They, in turn, contributed their special outlook and commitment to the men. They struck the Third Section as one of the most remarkable elements in the radical community. One report noted that the women medical students among the radicals were "extremely fanatical in many ways, more extreme than men, . . . on whom they have an electri-fying influence."[37] Their presence symbolized the ability of the radical movement to recruit members at will and to protect them despite all obstacles.

The number of radicals was not great in comparison with the mass of students in the educational system, but the chances by the early 1870's of finding and recruiting potential rebels were much greater than three decades earlier. The process had integrated itself into stu-dent life to the point where it appeared an inevitable part of the educational experience. Dimitri Klements left this impression in dis-cussing in his memoirs his path from quiet *gymnasium* graduate to member of the Chaikovtsy in the short space of three years. After

36. [Morozov], "Ocherk," p. 214.
37. Sidorov, "Statisticheskie," p. 33.

leaving his provincial town in 1867 to begin university studies, he recalled later that "I fell into new surroundings, returning home only during the summer vacation. I met new people, as they were called, and under their influence gradually began to alter my understanding and view on life assimilated in childhood in the midst of serfdom."[38]

As the organization and size of this new society expanded, its members could feel confident in its potential for real action. One of the renegades of the 1880's, Lev Tikhomirov, spoke warmly of his life with the Chaikovtsy. Referring to his years in self-education circles, he wrote later that "we saw and understood that people like us were everywhere, we felt ourselves unified rather than isolated, we had leaders everywhere in whom we had faith."[39] The atmosphere and conditions created in and around the radical community made possible the "to the people" movement of 1874. A youth active in the circles remembered how in 1873–1874 "the movement among youth grew and increased. New circles appeared in large numbers. Parallel with this student assemblies multiplied." Out of this ferment developed the collective feeling that "the moment for talk, debate, and analysis had passed, the time had come for practical activity."[40] The result was a "youth crusade" of a sort which had never appeared before in Russia or any other country. Thousands of student youth— perhaps two to three thousand—set out to bring word of the new faith to an illiterate and suspicious peasantry. The story of this extraordinary event belongs with the history of the revolutionary movement of Russia. The desire it expressed for "practical activity" points to a crucial problem in the formation of the radical community.

Apprenticeship in the New Life

Dreams of a new life required visible proof if they were to convince large numbers of recruits. How could Russian student youth bring to life institutions of social equality and personal freedom? The political and social conditions of the country made such efforts extremely difficult. The students were isolated by their academic world and by their intellectual and social background. The government watched for uncontrolled activity that could threaten the established

38. D. Klements, "Iz proshlogo: Vospominaniia" [From the past: Memoirs] (Leningrad, 1925), p. 79.
39. Tikhomirov, *Nachala,* p. 59.
40. Aptekman, *Obshchestvo,* p. 128.

order, closing down even the most innocuous institutions when they appeared to become subversive. The circles offered a form of organized, directed activity, but the only reward was familiarity with the literature of dissent and new friends. This was not the same as creating an egalitarian society.

The radical community was able by the 1860's to define a style of personal life suitable to student rebels. It possessed a body of literature to support the contention that the new people were a model for mankind. It was much less successful in creating institutions to provide an actual apprenticeship in the life of brotherhood and justice. The most coherent and highly developed attempts at collective activity were the communes, the artels, and the literacy schools. None was original with the radical movement, but all flourished as practical training in socialism.

Faith in the power of learning was a natural product of the forces shaping the radicals. They expanded its potential for change far beyond the modest limits set by pedagogues and most writers. They hoped that the dissemination of knowledge about social equality, progress, and reason would somehow hasten the time when all mankind would realize its potential for reason and goodness. The desire to teach came easily to the Russian radicals. Throughout the years of the mid-century, some sought to make their message known to the unenlightened. Mikhail Petrashevski dreamed of a teaching career and turned his circle into an informal classroom. Many of the populists in the 1870's went out to the peasants as schoolteachers. For a few years in the late 1850's and early 1860's joining groups of volunteer teachers in literacy schools for the illiterate urban classes was an outlet for the desire for social involvement. To the new recruits in the community of dissent, the literacy schools represented much more than a chance to spread reading and writing or to improve the job qualifications of Russian artisans. They were trying themselves as apprentices in the reconstruction of Russian society.

The movement for literacy schools was a product of the unusual social atmosphere of the early years of Alexander II's reign. Learning was widely admired; for its sake new forms of public activity were tolerated. The government itself was willing to raise the cultural level of the masses, among whom literacy was still a rarity. The campaign to spread literacy appeared spontaneously in several cities in the late 1850's, partly as a serious economic effort to raise the level of training of urban artisans. In June 1858 the industrial board of the Petersburg city duma appealed for the creation of a special set of schools to teach literacy to Russian artisans in order to overcome the "very unsatisfactory development of artisanry, part of which is in the hands of foreigners." Even earlier, in late 1857, a circle of Kharkov University students, among them Sergei Rymarenko, had begun on their own to teach reading and writing to working people in the city. A few of these students transferred to Kiev University the next year, where their efforts received the support of a professor of history, P. A. Pavlov.

In the same year a group of young officers and students opened the first real literacy school in St. Petersburg. Held every Sunday, the workers' only free day, they came to be known in Russian as "Sunday schools." Pavlov moved to the capital in late 1859 and a few months later founded the Society for the Diffusion of Popular Literacy to organize public support for the schools.[41] The government gave its formal approval to the movement in May 1860. A circular from the Ministry of the Interior noted the "establishment in cities of literacy schools" which "should bring considerable benefits to the urban population." It approved the participation of volunteer teachers since this made "the organization of such schools" possible at "very limited expense."[42] Government approval also signified government controls. That year the educational council of the Petersburg educational district laid out the basic plan of studies for the schools. The courses included reading and writing, arithmetic, drawing, and the Orthodox catechism. The schools were put under the supervision of the educational authorities of the Ministry of Education. They represented nonetheless a very unusual innovation in the Russian educational experience.

The schools spread rapidly, carried on a wave of enthusiasm to disburse by private initiative the benefits of learning among the lower urban classes. By 1862 there were 274 schools, at least one in every province of European Russia and a few in Siberia. For a year the

41. The development of the schools is traced in an official report prepared in 1862, found in TsGIAL, f. 1282, o. 1, d. 73 (1862). See also Reginald Zelnick, "The Sunday-School Movement in Russia, 1859–1862," *Journal of Modern History*, XXVII (June 1965), 151–70; R. Taubin, "Revoliutsionnaia propaganda" [Revolutionary propaganda], *Voprosy istorii*, Aug. 1956, pp. 80–90.

42. TsGIAL, f. 1282, o. 1, d. 72 (1862), l. 100.

young Leo Tol'stoi had his own literacy school on his estate of Iasnaia Poliana. But it was primarily an urban movement.

The institutions of higher education had a major role in organizing the schools. St. Petersburg, chief educational center of the empire, had twenty-eight, the largest number of literacy schools; Moscow province had eight. Most had appeared before or during 1860, when the government first required that they be registered with the Ministry of Education. Only eight opened the next year, and one in the early months of 1862. They varied widely in size. One had in the first months of its existence taught up to seven hundred pupils. Most oscillated between fifty and one hundred.[43] The number of teachers fluctuated widely as well, since the work was entirely voluntary, and many came from the student body. In St. Petersburg in 1862, there were 407 teachers in the literacy schools, of whom 174 were students. Another 78 were bureaucrats; 85 were women, among whom only a few had a regular occupation.

This campaign provided an opportunity for all committed to learning to contribute, regardless of social position or qualifications. One of the schools was organized and run entirely by society women, headed by a leading crusader in the women's movement, Nadezhda Stasova. University students formed a school, students from the Medical-Surgical Academy another, the Orthodox Academy a third, and a fourth was entirely in the hands of bureaucrats from the State Bank.[44] The equality among all participants in the cause of learning resembled that which reigned among the students. Even the organizational ties between the student community and the schools were close. The school run by university students came out of discussions in a student circle, whose members were united by an interest in social progress and a desire for some constructive activity. They found financial support from a wealthy merchant and set out to become educators with a zeal sufficient to overcome any pedagogical difficulties.[45]

The leaders of the Petersburg literacy schools included Nikolai Serno-Solov'evich, recently returned from his trip abroad after retiring from the bureaucracy. In May 1860 they formed a Council of

43. *Ibid.*, d. 73 (1862), ll. 234–49.
44. *Ibid.*, d. 72, ll. 345–58.
45. V. Sorokin, "Vospominaniia" [Memoirs], *Russkaia starina*, IX (1888), 634–36,

Representatives of Literacy Schools, to which each school sent a delegate. It helped to solicit funds, to organize the schools, to distribute books, and generally to provide a center for the discussion of problems raised by this unprecedented popular crusade. It sponsored the efforts of Sergei Rymarenko, now a student in the Medical-Surgical Academy, and others to write a spelling book under the editorship of Serno-Solov'evich. The latter put together in his house a library of over two thousand volumes for the use of the pupils in the schools. Other libraries, less well furnished, also appeared.[46] This activity in support of the schools lasted as long as the schools themselves were allowed to function.

The instruction provided by the literacy schools was restricted to the rudimentary skills of reading, writing, and arithmetic. The pupils were for the most part artisans and workers, for whom literacy represented the opportunity to improve their own professional skills. The organization of the schools was informal, since the numbers of pupils and teachers varied from week to week. One volunteer inspector, regularly employed as a primary-school principal, described his literacy school in the capital. It was held in several rooms of one building; in each room were several "classes" made up of a teacher and some pupils. There were "as many groups as there were available teachers. Each group studies specially with its own teacher: in one, reading is taught with the aid of movable letters; in another, they are discussing pictures of animals . . . ; in a third, they are doing addition with figures on a blackboard, and so on." The inspector was impressed by the "conscientiousness" of the teachers, but still considered that the classes "will lead absolutely nowhere."[47] He was certainly less concerned with ideals and enthusiasm than with rigor of teaching methods and regularity of instruction. To him, the spontaneity of the movement was its greatest weakness.

This very spontaneity made the schools rewarding for anyone who saw learning as a tool necessary to overcome, by moderate or radical means, the hardships and oppression of the lower classes. The practical goal of the industrial board of the duma was to improve the quality of the city's Russian artisans. For others, the goal was moral improvement as well. Progress lay in the diffusion of knowledge;

46. Taubin, "Revoliutsionnaia propaganda," pp. 84–87.
47. TsGIAL, f. 1282, o. 1, d. 73, l. 290.

through education the people would raise themselves to a higher level. People like Nadezhda Stasova interpreted the schools in purely humanitarian terms. Those women who gathered in her circle found volunteer teaching to the lower classes "the very first outlet for our aspiration for work, for the public good, for contacts with the people."[48] The idealism of these volunteers was based on their belief that learning would transform individuals and society as a whole without conflict. A young bureaucrat from the State Bank who prepared a survey of the activities of the Petersburg schools ended his brief account with a sort of hymn in praise of the "beneficial light" which these newly educated Russians would spread. "This light is not yet strong, it is still hidden, but the time will come when, thanks to it, our thoughts will stand out brightly and life will be joyful [*otradno*] in mother Russia."[49] It required great faith in the active force of learning to see the germs of such a marvelous future in the modest efforts of the literacy schools. The perspective the bureaucrat adopted blurred reality close around him in St. Petersburg in 1862 to focus on the vision of an enlightened Russia.

Only a short distance separated this view from that of alienated young Russians searching for the means to achieve a rapid and profound transformation of Russian life. The schools were a sort of crucible in which the commitment to a new life could be tested without outright illegal activity. In this sense, the literacy school campaign differed strongly from the "to the people" movement a decade later. Participation in the latter required a readiness for martyrdom; the former did not. The idealism built up around the movement expressed a faith in knowledge, not in any specific political program or ideology. The participants in the literacy schools were a mixture of political persuasions as well as of social classes. The spontaneity of organizing the schools offered individuals a chance to take part in their own creation, to aid the people, and to overcome class barriers. It was for Alexander Sleptsov the expression of "the craving for altruistic activity." In 1860 he was a graduate of the Alexandrovsky Lycée serving in the imperial chancellery. He recalled later that he threw himself that year into the campaign for literacy schools with "absolutely no conception of the cost of things, of the amount of work demanded

48. Z. Bazileva, "Arkhiv semei Stasovykh" [The archives of the Stasov family], *Revoliutsionnaia situatsiia* (Moscow, 1965), p. 439.
49. TsGIAL, f. 1282, o. 1, d. 74 (1862), ll. 190–91.

by one or another task." But he had the "conviction that any affair could be managed provided it be sincere, profound, and desirable."[50] He worked energetically for the literacy schools, founding two in 1860. A year later he became one of the founders of the secret Land and Liberty organization. Work in the schools was his first step toward oppositional activity. His "altruism" expressed a growing disaffection with Russian life and expanded his circle of friends. His schools brought together student teachers attracted to the radical cause, including Sergei Rymarenko who served as a teacher and inspector.

The campaign for the literacy schools provided action and comradeship for the disaffected, strengthening the ties within this subculture of protest. A young army officer, Ivan Averkiev, left in his papers personal impressions of this movement. The schools represented for him "action, not lifeless talk and tales." He saw the leaders of the movement as a separate group of people, not a part of ordinary society. His own role as inspector put him in touch with people like Peter Tkachev, who worked in the same school. Averkiev was among the new people and far from his army life. He believed that such people needed "to unite" in order to "form a separate, strong society, standing on the side of the people and in opposition to the government, from which we are now independent." Their task was to defend "the right of development of the people," who had to be protected from the influence of the "evil enemy and the priests." In awkward and frequently incorrect Russian he tried to express his enthusiasm for the life his work in the literacy schools had opened before him, which he wished to share with others. Those "who look with indifference on the work" in the schools should feel "shame." They stood in the way of men like himself who were "socialists of the deed."[51] The schools by themselves were no seedbed of socialism, no matter how radical the teachers. Averkiev was only twenty years old when he volunteered as inspector in 1860 and apparently had had no previous contacts with radicals. He was becoming aware of himself as a member of a "separate society" opposed to the established order and with its own great vision of a new life. His work in the schools facilitated his contacts with others who felt like himself and made the radical

---

50. "Tetrad' A. A. Sleptsova" [The notebook of A. A. Sleptsov], *Literaturnoe nasledstvo*, LXVII (1959), 679–80.
51. TsGIAL, f. 1282, o. 1, d. 73, l. 54.

cause a reality in his personal life. This was real apprenticeship in the radical community.

There were probably only a few teachers as rebellious as he, but by June 1862 the government had become suspicious of the movement. In June a worker attending one literacy school reported that his teacher had handed out two revolutionary tracts, "What Do the People Need?" and "What's to Be Done to the Army?" It was a minor incident, but sufficient for the War Ministry on June 8 to close all schools located in its buildings. The authorities declared that "under the pretext of spreading literacy among the people, individuals with evil thoughts plotted in these schools to develop harmful teachings, disturbing ideas, distorted concepts of property rights, and godlessness."[52] The next week the Ministry of the Interior ordered all literacy schools closed.

The crusade had ended, but had already been declining. Reports appeared in 1861 of the lack of teachers and smaller number of pupils than before. Late in that year Alexander Sleptsov had to ask former volunteers to return and to hire replacements to fill the gaps in the teaching staff of his schools. A writer for *The Contemporary* saw the root of the trouble in the state-imposed curriculum and regulations which were replacing "living ideas" by "scholasticism." Since teachers could no longer teach what they wished, they were less willing to volunteer.[53]

Lack of spontaneity in curriculum was a small part of the problem. The schools never had an extensive program, but taught the basic skills of reading and writing, not a glamorous occupation. This required commitment and patience, which by then were in short supply. A supervisor of the Petersburg schools reported that "by the end of the winter of 1861 a strong cooling toward the literacy schools was already evident among some teachers. They attended irregularly, sometimes for an hour or a half an hour, often not at all." The result was that "one teacher had not infrequently between 20 and 30 pupils." This was a great change from the early months when "each teacher was able to teach groups of five or six pupils."[54] The school supported by the Medical-Surgical Academy had 35 teachers in 1860;

52. Quoted in Bazilevski, ed., *Gosudarstvennye prestupniki*, I, 112–13.
53. "O napravlenii shkol gramotnosti" [On the conduct of the literacy schools], *Sovremennik*, No. 89 (1861), 8–9.
54. TsGIAL, f. 1282, o. 1, d. 72, l. 317.

by early 1862 it had only 10. Too few student youth were really committed to popular education. People like Sleptsov, Rymarenko, and Tkachev hung on, but they were exceptional. The opportunity to put into practice hopes for social liberation was thwarted by its very precociousness. Only after a decade more of organization, discussion, and crystallization of views would it be possible to create a real "to the people" movement. But then the campaign represented an obvious threat to political order and brought immediate repressive action from the government. There was no easy middle ground in the search for action.

The yearning for such proselytizing remained. In later years, free schools appeared that sought to carry on the educational crusade. One small circle of students in the new Petrovsky Agronomy Academy near Moscow in the fall of 1869 taught reading and writing to peasants in surrounding villages and planned to create an "agricultural cooperative" upon graduating the next year.[55] The members' modest dreams and small deeds were upset forever by the arrival of Sergei Nechaev, who turned to them as promising recruits for his revolutionary party. When one member balked, Nechaev convinced the circle that he was a spy and murdered him. The "Nechaev affair" had begun. These guileless searchers for a new life were not "possessed by the devil" as Dostoevski portrayed them in *The Possessed*. They had prepared themselves to respond sympathetically to Nechaev's dream of a European revolutionary movement, but their learning turned out a dangerous thing.

While the literacy school movement was still under way, a new form of apprenticeship appeared based on the principle of association. The "artel" was a traditional labor institution in which workers banded together for a particular job and shared the income equally. The leader was elected by the group. The crews of peasants who every summer hauled the barges along the Volga and other Russian rivers organized themselves in this manner, as did peasant workers who came to the cities seeking temporary employment. From a distance, the artel appeared a natural solution to the problem of the exploitation of labor and inequalities of wealth. Educated Russians idealized it as a free association of individuals equal among themselves. Working as a group, its members shared whatever income the artel earned. Pov-

55. Zasulich, *Vospominaniia,* pp. 30–31.

erty was a constant problem among students and all those not drawn to ordinary work. The artel satisfied both communitarian ideals and practical needs. It seemed to offer training in socialist life and a real test of commitment.

Originally, it appeared as part of the movement to help the poor, lower-class urban population. The initiative came from circles active in the literacy schools, especially those around Nadezhda Stasova. Her efforts to aid the people had made her a leader in the organization of schools, and she sought other ways to aid the "needy classes" of the capital. She believed, that "it is the duty of society to aid the people." She worked to improve the housing conditions of the poor through the Society for Low-Cost Housing, which she helped found in 1861. She was particularly anxious to help poor women who frequented her literacy school to find dignified and honorable employment. The artel seemed the perfect answer. It was the "most just, most real, most natural and simple" of worker associations. If people worked together, "one [person] will help, stimulate and urge on the others"; all would benefit equally by their labor. Her brother, who aided her in this affair, recalled that the ideals of "association" and "equality" were "on the lips of everyone" involved in the movement to help the people.[56] The result was an artel for seamstresses, founded in early 1861.

From the early 1860's, the capital was attracting a steady stream of young women in search of freedom, some looking for an education at institutions like the Medical-Surgical Academy. Most had little or no means and few skills. Like the students, they frequently banded together in communes to share living quarters and money. They needed help, and the artel suited their new style of life. In 1862, Nikolai Serno-Solov'evich and Alexander Engel'gardt founded a "printing artel" for the translation and publication of foreign books. This was perfect work for emancipated women.[57] They were far more responsive than the illiterate poor to the ideal of cooperation. By 1862 many people were finding work in artels, but most of the members were not lower-class Russians. They were from the upper and middle classes escaping the old constraints and seeking support and

56. V. Stasov, *N. V. Stasova: Vospominaniia i ocherki* [N. V. Stasova: Memoirs and notes] (St. Petersburg, 1899), pp. 122–23.

57. Z. Bazileva, *"K istorii pervykh artelei"* [Concerning the history of the first artels], in *Voprosy istorii sel'skogo khoziaistva* (Moscow, 1961), p. 208.

aid from others with similar aspirations in St. Petersburg. The young women felt with special harshness the barriers to an independent life and thus provided the most numerous recruits. From a means to aid the poor, the artels had become a device to strengthen the new society.

The movement received its greatest stimulus with the publication in the spring of 1863 of Chernyshevski's novel *What's to Be Done?* Part of the book was devoted to a detailed description of an artel for working-class seamstresses founded and run by the emancipated heroine, Vera Pavlovna. Its organization and goals were a close reproduction of Stasova's artel, with which Chernyshevski was well acquainted. The innovation had entered the corpus of the new learning. By the fall of that year, artels were spreading in large numbers wherever the novel found a sympathetic audience.

Problems appeared immediately. The amateur seamstresses often had no more perseverance than the volunteer teachers, and the experienced, working-class seamstresses cared mostly about wages. Vera Zasulich, a student in Moscow in the mid-1860's, came across some of these real-life Vera Pavlovnas at their apprenticeship in association. The artels she found were organized by women "sufficiently well-off to purchase the sewing machines, rent quarters, and hire seamstresses" in the hope that the latter would, like Vera Pavlovna's workers, learn the "principle of association." A sizable part of the company consisted of *nigilistki,* "unable to sew but eagerly searching for some cause," whose enthusiasm tended to wane after a month or two of sewing eight to ten hours a day. As members pulled out, the affair fell apart. Some of the artels even ended in courts of arbitration to decide who should receive the collective property. The seamstresses claimed the sewing machines for themselves, but the idealistic founders "insisted" that property belonged only "to work." Zasulich had no sympathy for these dilettantes. "What work did they do?! They just talked among themselves," she declared.[58] Like the literacy schools, this training proved to many that the new life was not for them.

There was a place for the artels in the radical community. Those youth who had broken with their past still needed economic assistance. Zasulich herself turned to a bookbinding artel for support after

58. Zasulich, *Vospominaniia,* pp. 18–19.

fleeing in 1868 to St. Petersburg "in order to escape the fate of eventually becoming a governess."[59] The artel she joined provided both a means to live and companionship. Ten years earlier she would have been alone, but now a community existed with its own institutions, style of life, and consciousness of unity.

One of those who helped organize the support for the new recruits was a young officer, Pavel Mikhailov. He founded a literacy school in 1863 and soon afterward an artel for seamstresses, headed by the sister of Peter Tkachev. His explanation to the Third Section of his concern to assist the needy was purely in terms of the problems of the radical community: to "give work and funds to educated people without regular means of existence" as the only way "to protect young people from the despair which can have the most terrible consequences."[60] He did not add that most of these people had accepted such hardships for the sake of freedom, first for themselves and ultimately for all Russia.

By the end of the 1860's the artel had become a part of the new life, one of the standard activities of the "self-education" circles and frequently associated with the communes. It no longer inspired a public campaign of aid to the poor, but had found a proper setting within the radical community.

Artels too were closely associated with the student community. The Third Section discovered one in 1870 that a Technological Institute student had organized for the production of chemical products. It was run according to traditional guidelines, operating with the "common funds of the participants," and distributing its income in equal shares, but the members did not expect "great material profits." They knew that the technical careers for which their education was training them would "bring much greater benefits" and were not attracted by wealth and honor. The organizer was planning to start another artel for people without technical training but with a "similar outlook" and a commitment "not to enter any regular occupation." The members would have been apprentices in radical living. The Third Section agent believed that the aim of this activity was to "bring

59. Quoted in L. Deutsch, "V. I. Zasulich," *Golos minuvshego*, Nos. 5–12 (May-Dec. 1919), 201.
60. TsGAOR, f. 95, o. 1, d. 220, l. 59; his activities are described in Vilenskaia, *Revoliutsionnoe podpol'e*, pp. 341–43.

to life extreme socialist teachings."[61] A large part of the attraction of the artels was that they made tangible one aspect of the society for which the radicals were working. They were a sort of group experiment that tested the fitness of the new recruits while it reinforced faith in the reality of socialist living.

The most comprehensive effort at providing this life of equality and brotherhood came in the communes. These institutions appeared in the reign of Alexander II, like the literacy schools and the artels. A few very tentative attempts had been made to organize communal living earlier, but with no enduring results. Fedor Dostoevski became involved for a few months in the winter of 1846–1847 in what he and his comrades called an "association." The socialist teachings of Fourier inspired this small group to set up a protophalanstery as a personal act of defiance against "oppression and injustice." They shared a large apartment and conducted all their housekeeping affairs in common. Living was not harsh, for each member had to contribute 35 rubles a month, a considerable sum in those days. But money was no guarantee of success. Interest in communal life soon fell, and the members drifted off. Dostoevski and a few others moved on to the Petrashevtsy circle.[62] Despite the widespread interest in Fourier, efforts such as this to bring to life socialist ideals were rare.

The student community furnished the real social base for the spread of the communes. The institution flourished there despite the vagaries of individual experiences and the frequent disintegration of separate communes. From the 1850's a few were active in cities like St. Petersburg and Moscow where the ideals of equality and brotherhood were being applied in day-to-day student affairs. They provided a more thorough training than the circles in the new style of life and social relations, while also serving an educational function.

The communes appeared first as a practical response to the acute financial need of poor students arriving in ever larger numbers in the capital in the late 1850's. Like the student assemblies, which developed at the same time, they existed on the basis of absolute equality among the members and recognized no formal organization or rules. They made the principle of mutual aid an active tradition in student life. Lev Modzalevski, a student leader in those years, had received

61. TsGAOR, f. 109, tr. eks., d. 120 (1870), ch. 1, ll. 1–2, 15.
62. Sarukhanian, *Dostoevskii,* pp. 64–65.

in 1857 a small stipend for his second year in the university, but still was unable to cover even minimal living expenses. He and some friends had "to roam continually from apartment to apartment," carrying their few possessions. To Modzalevski, this meant only his books. They shared what they had, including lodgings and whatever funds they acquired. "Money came in irregularly, and we therefore had to live on mutual aid. . . . We regarded clothes and money as our collective property. A poor comrade could stay with us for weeks or months on end." They were, in his words, "applying communism in our affairs without any theory."[63] Though these communes appeared by Western standards highly developed examples of ideological action, in Russian circumstances they were a natural and easily assimilated method of collective living.

They frequently had no connection with the radical community. The future writer Vladimir Korolenko came to St. Petersburg in the early 1870's to join the crowds of poor students in the Technological Institute. With four other comrades from his *gymnasium,* he formed a small commune. As was customary, they shared property completely and spent their money as the group decided. A few rubles would pay some of the back rent and for a "dinner" of sausage— usually made of horsemeat—cheap black bread, tea of the cheapest variety, and a few lumps of sugar. Or they might just go off to the neighborhood tavern. Korolenko recalled that he and his friends were a "good-natured group" in which "it was always easier to play cards and drink beer than eat a real dinner or attend lectures. . . . Nobody kept any accounts; the person with a little money treated the others. . . . This was true communism of happy idleness."[64] It was also a sure route to expulsion from school, perhaps with tuberculosis added for good measure.

The communes were most useful in assisting the rebels of the time. They suited perfectly the tastes and aspirations of young Russians in revolt against family and class and searching for new libertarian principles on which to lead their lives. Thus they were important in the women's emancipation movement. The women who fled to the capital seeking freedom from family, father, or husband had great

63. L. Modzalevski, "Iz pedagogicheskoi avtobiografii," pp. 17–20.
64. V. Korolenko, *Istoriia moego sovremennika* [The history of my contemporary] (Moscow, 1948), pp. 327–29.

need of help. One of the emancipated women of those years recalled that others, less fortunate than she, were "drawn to the capital from the provinces by the craving for knowledge and the desire for independence. Often they arrived without any means of subsistence, having broken all ties with their rich and even distinguished relatives."[65] With few friends and little chance of finding work, these women depended largely on the aid of others, particularly in their first months in the capital.

One of their most prominent benefactors was the writer Vasili Sleptsov, who put his wealth and energy to finding employment and lodging for them. He founded a commune in 1863 exclusively for women, renting a very comfortable apartment with several servants to provide quarters at low cost for six women. A circle of men and women formed around the commune. This activity impressed an agent of the Third Section as the work of "young people of immoral and harmful character" who "repudiate all the laws of public order, do not recognize parental relations or marriage, which they replace by the equal rights of both sexes to intimate relations among themselves and share the idea of the community of property and work."[66] He gave the members more credit than they deserved. Actually, the commune never developed as Sleptsov had hoped into a model for communal living in the spirit of Fourier's utopian socialism. One of the members tried to keep it free of "capitalist parasites," but most had deplorably bourgeois materialistic tastes and enjoyed fully its luxurious comforts.[67]

These communes easily lent themselves to the new style of life, however. Many mixed sexes in open defiance of social custom, giving visible proof of the revolt of the members against the moral code in which they had been raised and cultivating the sense of a new community. A young woman who joined a mixed commune in the mid-1860's wrote in her memoirs that, at that time, she imagined "everybody divided into two unequal groups: the commune and all the rest of the world. I considered only the members of the commune to be decent and honorable, while all the rest were idiots or scum."[68] Out-

---

65. A. Kornilova-Moroz, *Perovskaia i kruzhok chaikovtsev* [Perovskaia and the Chaikovtsy circle] (Moscow, 1929), pp. 22–23.
66. TsGAOR, f. 109, o. 85, d. 29, ll. 52–53.
67. K. Chukovski, *Liudi i knigi* [People and books], pp. 288–90.
68. Komarova, *Odna iz mnogikh,* p. 65.

siders saw these communes as centers of sexual depravity. She played on this theme herself, though her memoirs are somewhat suspect since they were written as a public confession of youthful sins. Free love did represent one of the facets of liberation among radicals, but it probably did not include promiscuity. Those worthy of the cause had to adhere to a moral code as strict as the old one. Freedom supposed responsible behavior based on honor and mutual respect.

Severity and self-sacrifice were the hallmark of the commune around which the Chaikovtsy circle formed. It was, as members recalled later, the "mother" of communes associated with the self-education circles. At its origin in 1869, it consisted primarily of medical students, but included women. In the two-story wooden house the students had rented, the women had their quarters in the upper floor, the men downstairs. Every member had to contribute his entire income and received what money he needed from the treasurer. For food a live horse might be purchased and the help of a veterinary student obtained to butcher the animal. If times were very hard, one of the men might go out in the evening to look for an alley cat or a stray dog, whose days ended in the commune's kitchen. The rule for living was "great severity: tobacco and tea was the cheapest available, breakfast consisted of black bread and tea." Some needy students were usually fed free. Survival was important for its own sake, but as important was the proof the commune provided of the practicality and relevance of the principles of mutual aid and equality. The old utopian dreams of the Western socialists could not find roots in Russian society, but the communes lived and prospered—or failed—in the midst of the student community. They provided "a very powerful means for the development of communitarian inclinations in youth and were a sort of school of practical socialism."[69]

When conditions were right, the communes offered a complete experience in the life and aspirations of the new people. They were an excellent test to determine the commitment of a young Russian to the radical movement. One of the participants in the Chaikovtsy commune praised its advantages for any person "attracted by socialism." He could "apply its principles in his personal life, actually disowning all the blessings of the 'old world' by living in surroundings not better or worse than those of a factory worker, by not distinguishing be-

69. [Morozov], "Ocherk," pp. 208, 235 n. 4.

tween 'mine' and 'thine' and by refusing personal use of property."
The communes encouraged the development of the radical movement,
since they became "the center for encounters between youth and increased the influence of the more developed and mature on new ar-
rivals."[70]

Word of the style of life and ideals of the new people spread out
to a large audience, among whom ambitions frequently far exceeded
the capacity to perform. The records of failures are hard to find, for
memoirs came from those who succeeded. The others preferred si-
lence. The Third Section came across one abortive attempt at communal living, traced it back to its origins, and gave the documents
to the St. Petersburg judicial procurator. His report on the affair, complete with ample citations from the records, constitutes a precious
account of how the new life could turn sour.

In the early 1870's a young *gymnasium* teacher in a provincial
town had preached the new learning to a small group of his students
bound for higher education in the capital. He had just arrived with
his common-law wife from Moscow University where he had almost
completed his advanced degree in mathematics. The couple gathered
around them a group of admirers from the town's secondary schools
who regarded both as "intellectually far superior" to themselves. As
an emancipated woman who had earlier contracted a "fictitious marriage," the teacher's wife defended such marriages for young women
as a "good means to free oneself from the guardianship of parents"
and achieve "an independent position and the possibility to act" according to one's beliefs. Her companion praised the new collective life,
with which he was obviously familiar from his Moscow years. He
advised his young followers "to live in common, join communes,
share everything," and to do without "material wealth." His message
fell on eager ears.

When these students reached St. Petersburg in the fall of 1871,
they set out to follow the instructions of their mentor. Ten of them
founded a commune. All went marvelously during the first months.
The leader of the group wrote back that "our development on the new
path [of life] is going very swiftly." All their property was communal,
with a collective fund to cover their expenses. As their teacher had
recommended, they were spending considerable time on their own

70. Kornilova-Moroz, *Perovskaia*, p. 17.

education, reading in social theory the works of John Stuart Mill, Dimitri Pisarev, Ferdinand Lassalle, and Nikolai Dobroliubov. The student leader admired the personal qualities of the hero of a German novel recommended by his teacher. He wrote that this individual embodied admirable courage and dedication in defending his comrades and his ideals. The young Russian was apparently trying to bring into his own life the vision of a new man in a new society.

He and his comrades did everything "by the book." The model for the socialist community they sought to reproduce was collective living and work. They therefore set up a bookbinding artel to provide income and to train themselves in cooperative labor. Unfortunately, they still lacked one essential feature of the complete commune—a woman— or, as the leader put it, the "female element in the activities and life of the commune." He found one soon, but his *nigilistka*-in-residence did not meet with expectations. In another letter, he complained that "she lives by herself, completely occupied with her own activities," and did not seem to care about real collective living. She was "not at all the sort of woman whom the commune needs." It turned out that these young apprentice nihilists were themselves unable to become new men. The other members accused their leader of being a "vain person who thought a great deal of himself while doing little." He reciprocated their dislike. By the following spring, the commune had collapsed, each member going his own way.[71] They had failed the crucial test in their efforts to join the new people. All would have disappeared completely from view had the Third Section not found their trail.

Their brief flirtation with radical living reproduced in miniature every significant element of the process of recruitment into the radical community. They had passed successfully through the elitist secondary schools and joined the ranks of the students. Along the way, they had learned about the new life from others whom they respected as true authorities and on whom they could model their own behavior. They had set out to absorb the values of the radical movement through their own program of reading, which had probably begun in the *gymnasium* circle. Their life in St. Petersburg had followed the example of many other students who, like them, dreamed of a future, not of careers and academic excellence, but of commitment to

71. TsGAOR, f. 109, tr. eks., d. 76 (1871), ch. 2, ll. 107–16, 126.

socialism and radical reform in Russia. They had attempted to bring to life these ideals in their own group by constituting themselves as commune, circle, and artel. They hoped to establish relations based on equality and mutual trust, with no special recognition of class, wealth, or sex. Their unhappy contact with a representative from the women's emancipation movement only proved that some people did not understand revolt in collective terms. Nothing they did was unusual for the time. They had attempted to reproduce the style of life of the radical community. Even their failure to maintain its rigorous standards was probably not unusual.

Cases such as this suggest the limited attraction which the radical movement exerted among the students. Secondary and higher education remained a fragile base in which to recruit rebels. The class hierarchy of society accommodated most youth at the end of their studies. The universities, institutes, and academies continued producing large numbers of trained and loyal members of the state and professional elite. The actual differentiation between rebel and loyal subject came in most cases during the years of schooling through the action of disorganized institutions and unsystematic reading. By the 1860's circles had formed to serve the needs of the student community. They also provided a channel by which information on radical ideals could reach these youth and a social framework within which the ties of friendship and dedication could bind together new members of the radical community. No formal rules defined the conditions of membership. No regular activity offered the immediate satisfaction of putting ideals into practice. The communes stood out as the best the movement could offer, and even they appeared frivolous in the hands of happy-go-lucky students. To defy social tradition and confront the forces of order was deadly serious. The school of dissent, despite its originality, had a very low percentage of "graduates" by comparison with the total number of students in higher education.

This fact offered little consolation to the authorities. They knew that a part of the select group of educated Russian youth destined for prominence and power were not following the indicated path. These young people came primarily from the socially privileged classes of society, as shown in the statistics collected by the Third Section in the 1870's. The data I compiled on the Petersburg radicals add a few refinements. The landowning and bureaucratic nobility of Russia had good reason to be receptive to the call of higher education for their offspring, since a degree was a good guarantee of professional success. Some of these men had done remarkably well in rising out of lower classes into the elite. Social mobility, however, cannot be considered a special force determining the spread of radical revolt. The soundest conclusion to be drawn from the material on social origins is that the radical youth were probably no different in class composition than the student group from which they came.

This situation only worsened the problem for the government. Certain social classes could have been excluded from the schools to preserve public order, and this policy was occasionally applied. But if the schools themselves were at fault, was it necessary to shut them down? The formal system of education, borrowed largely from Europe, offered a difficult program of studies to a few youth, whose numbers progressively declined as the years of schooling went by. An elitist type of learning was intended to incorporate its graduates into a rigidly stratified society by assuring that they would possess a high degree of intellectual skill and moral backbone. The German ideal of "'cultivation" (*Bildung*) represented the ideal of learning offered by the universities, pinnacle of the educational system. It signified the moral virtue granted by the command of true knowledge as understood by men of reason. Though the professional schools had a somewhat less lofty mission, their educational style was deeply marked by admiration for learning. Even such a system was not immune to corruption. Somehow, among the successful survivors of this rigorous educational program, a few youth were reinterpreting the pursuit of knowledge to produce a totally different form of "cultivation." Reason and intellectual excellence lay at the core of this new, radical form of education. Yet it served to undermine, not strengthen, the political authority it was intended to serve.

The disruption of the pattern of education came most obviously in the rise of student unrest. The 1860's set a new model for Russian higher education—the independent and occasionally rebellious student. The community life which began to develop spontaneously, first in the universities then in the professional schools, owed nothing to Western models. Its combination of egalitarianism and elitism was uniquely Russian. The assemblies, libraries, cafeterias, and other forms of association symbolized while they encouraged the feeling of corporate solidarity uniting students within and among schools. In St. Petersburg by the end of the 1860's a city-wide student body defended its honor and privileges and ignored official efforts at control. It provided the volunteers for the student agitation of 1869; from it came the men and women who initiated the movement for "self-education" circles. With historical hindsight, one can say that it was the first indication of the trend which would build into the youth crusade of the "to the people" movement. Then, as earlier, the educational system continued to turn out its yearly small contingent of graduates and its large group of "drop-outs," almost none of whom ever joined the radical movement.

The disruptive effect of student community organization was enhanced by the diffusion of a literature of dissent capable of rivaling the official curriculum of the educational institutions. This new learning owed its inspiration to Western philosophical and socialist thought, assimilated and adapted to Russian conditions by a highly talented and dedicated group of radical writers. It emphasized the role of learning to provide the instructions for the creation of a new, free society of benefit to all the people, to be attained in part through the efforts of new people trained in the tools of rational analysis and criticism to show the way, somehow and at some slow or rapid pace, to the others. The premises of the literature of dissent sanctioned the resistance of Russian radicals to the established order and gave them hope that their efforts would actually bear fruit. The channels for communicating this knowledge came from a few radical journals and other printed literature—legal and illegal. It also came through the active efforts of proselytizers of the new word working singly or, most often, in circles of students and other groups. The promise of liberation attracted others besides the students. Its message reached some Russian women, excluded from higher education. They joined ranks with the other recruits in a subculture clearly distinguished on both social and intellectual grounds from the society that had engendered it.

This radical community traced its origins to the 1840's. The Petrashevtsy circle was an embryonic version of its structure and operations. It did not really appear fully developed until the 1860's, when it had direct ties with the dissension spreading within the schools and in the intellectual world and had assimilated the organizational structure and activities which would make dissent a constant part of the educational life of the country. The circles and communes provided the classrooms for the school of dissent, without which no massive movement of social protest would have been possible. They reflected a unique style of life, yet were close enough to the student community to retain the indispensable ties for continual recruitment of radicals.

By the 1860's the process of radical recruitment had become regularized and institutionalized through the informal working of the school of dissent. The circles, artels, and communes provided centers of activity, albeit of a very modest level, where learning could fuse with dissent, emancipation with socialism. They represented the last stage in the preparation of radical recruits. Not many youth proceeded this far. A far greater number only dabbled in revolt, and even more ignored this special extracurricular schooling. The school of dissent served only a minority; it was remarkable still by its ability to attract and train a steady stream of neophytes.

The argument presented in these six chapters can be summarized schematically. The "flow chart" presented on this page is a simplified

Chart 1. The process of radical recruitment in Tsarist Russia: A conceptual model

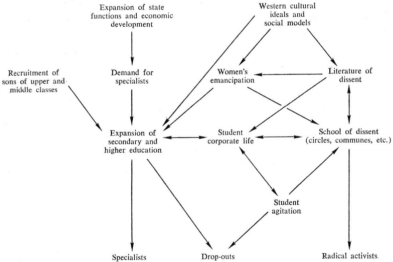

conceptual model of the social dynamics of Russian education, both the system sanctioned by the state and the derivative, informal system of training for the radical movement. The arrows indicate the direction of "inputs," in the form of manpower, institutions, or ideals. Some of the arrows show movement back and forth, or "feedback."

Most students moved into and out of the student community without interrupting or altering their career goals. Some even participated in student agitation, only to return subsequently to an orderly life. A somewhat different process took place in diffusion of the literature of dissent. Radical publicists owed much to Western writings, but also drew on the experience of Russian radicals to formulate models of "new people" and an egalitarian style of life (the best example being the novel *What's to Be Done?*). Their books in turn provided inspiration to succeeding generations of student youth.

Both systems of schooling found their recruits in the same source, since the radicals appear undifferentiated by estate origins from the student community. But the people leaving the educational institutions no longer shared the same traits. A few had acquired the skills and diplomas of "specialists" and were incorporated into the upper occupational strata of society. Many others had failed to survive, most because they had been unable to pass the required courses; some had suffered the stern penalties for participation in student disorders. Both of these groups fitted into the official conception of the output of an elitist educational system. But there was still another type of graduate. The school of dissent produced its own elite, the radical activist, who by the 1870's was as much a part of the world of higher education as the other groups.

Efforts to suppress the school of dissent invariably failed. Enrollments were cut back. Repression hit suspected centers of sedition and swept up the hapless young radicals who attempted, as in the "to the people" movement, to create a massive revolutionary movement. By that time the radical community was firmly established, and it lasted until the revolution. The process of radical recruitment was well rooted in the educational life of the country. Radical revolt had become an inescapable part of the transformation of Russia.

Selected Bibliography

This bibliography includes only those sources that were of use in my research. It does not cover all the works I examined, nor does it provide a comprehensive survey of the voluminous literature on the Russian radical movement.

I. Archival Collections

Central State Historical Archives of Leningrad (TsGIAL)

ff. 733, 744. Ministry of Education, with numerous reports on academic affairs in institutions of secondary and higher education.

f. 908. Archives of Count Valuev, including a series of reports on student unrest (d. 125).

ff. 1280, 1282. Ministry of Justice, containing police reports on radicals.

f. 1343. Genealogies of noble families, kept by the Department of Heraldry, State Senate.

f. 1349. Service records (*formuliarnye spiski*) of the state bureaucracy.

Central State Archives of the October Revolution, Moscow (TsGAOR)

f. 95. Commission of Inquiry of 1862, active in the pursuit of subversives until 1871.

f. 109. Third Section of His Majesty's Chancellery, including secret police reports, investigations, and the yearly reports to the tsar through 1869.

Central State Military-Historical Archives, Moscow

f. 9. Investigative Department of the War Ministry, charged with the Petrashevtsy affair (d. 55).

II. Memoirs and Other Published Sources

Akhsharumov, D. D. *Iz moikh vospominanii (1849–1851)*. St. Petersburg, 1905.

Aksakov, K. S. *Vospominaniia studenchestva*. St. Petersburg, 1911.

Aptekman, O. V. *Obshchestvo 'Zemlia i Volia' 70-kh godov po lichnym vospominaniiam.* Moscow, 1924.

Arsen'ev, K. K. "Vospominaniia ob Uchilishche pravovedeniia," *Russkaia starina,* LVI (April 1886), 199–220.

Balin, N. P. "Petrashevtsy i ikh vremia," *Katorga i ssylka,* No. 63 (1930), 80–89.

Bekkarevich, N. "Orenburgskaia gimnasiia starogo vremeni," *Russkaia starina,* CXVI (Nov. 1903), 401–17.

Bel'chikov, N. "S. G. Nechaev v sele Ivanove v 60-e gody," *Katorga i ssylka,* No. 14 (1925), 134–56.

Belinski, V. G. *Polnoe sobranie sochinenii.* 13 vols. Moscow, 1953–1959.

Bibergal', A. N. "Vospominaniia o demonstratsii na Kazanskoi ploshchadi," *Katorga i ssylka,* No. 29 (1926), 21–29.

Biriukov, A. A. "Vospominaniia 60-kh godov," *Katorga i ssylka,* No. 95 (1932), 226–46.

Boborykin, P. D. *Za polveka (moi vospominaniia).* Moscow, 1929.

Bukh, N. K. *Vospominaniia.* Moscow, 1928.

Bulanova-Trubnikova, O. K. *Tri pokoleniia.* Moscow, 1928.

Charushin, N. A. *O dalekom proshlom.* Moscow, 1923.

Chernavski, M. M. "Demonstratsiia 6 dekabria 1876 goda," *Katorga i ssylka,* No. 28 (1926), 7–20.

Chernyshevski, N. G. *Polnoe sobranie sochinenii.* 16 vols. Moscow, 1939–1953.

Chudnovski, S. L. "Iz davnykh let," *Byloe,* Sept. 1907, pp. 278–95. (Book edition: Moscow, 1934.)

Debogori-Mokrievich, V. *Vospominaniia.* Paris, 1894.

Deich [Deutsch], L. G. *Za polveka.* Moscow, 1922.

Delo petrashevtsev. 3 vols. Moscow, 1937–1951.

Deniker, I. E. "Vospominaniia," *Katorga i ssylka,* No. 11 (1924), 23–43.

Dmitrieva, V. I. "Teni proshlogo," *Katorga i ssylka,* No. 9 (1924), 28–45; No. 11 (1924), 111–23.

Dobroliubov, N. A. *Dnevnik, 1851–59.* Moscow, 1932.

———. *Polnoe sobranie sochinenii.* 6 vols. Moscow, 1934–1939.

Drago, N. I. "Zapiski starogo narodnika," *Katorga i ssylka,* No. 6 (1923), 10–22.

Entsiklopedicheskii slovar' Russkogo bibliograficheskogo instituta Granata. Vol. XL: "Avtobiografii revoliutsionnykh deiatelei russkogo sotsialisticheskogo dvizheniia 70-kh godov i pervoi poloviny 80-kh godov." Moscow, 1927.

Figner, V. I. *Memoirs of a Revolutionist.* New York, 1927.

———. "Studencheskie gody," *Golos minuvshego,* March-April, 1922, pp. 165–81; Jan.-Feb., 1923, pp. 27–45; March-April, 1923, pp. 125–45 (book edition: Moscow, 1924).

Filosofskie i obshchestvenno-politicheskie proizvedeniia petrashevtsev. Moscow, 1953.

Flerovski, N. [V. V. Bervi]. *Tri politicheskie sistemy: Nikolai I, Aleksandr II i Aleksandr III.* London, 1897.

Frolenko, M. P. *Zapiski semidesiatnika.* Moscow, 1927.

Gertsen, A. I. *Byloe i dumy.* 2 vols. Moscow, 1962.

———. *Sobranie sochinenii.* 30 vols. Moscow, 1954–1965.

Gol'denberg, L. B. "Vospominaniia," *Katorga i ssylka,* No. 10 (1924), 89–105; No. 11 (1924), 44–56.

Golitsyn, N. C. "Ocherki i vospominaniia," *Russkaia starina,* LXVIII (1890), 365–81.

Golovina-Iurgenson, N. A. "Moi vospominaniia," *Katorga i ssylka,* No. 6 (1923), 23–38; No. 8 (1924), 101–8.

Goncharov, Ivan. *Oblomov.* Trans. Natalie Duddington. New York, 1960.

Iakhontov, A. I. *Istoricheskii ocherk Imperatorskogo Aleksandrovskogo Litseia.* Paris, 1936.

———. "Vospominaniia tsarskosel'skogo litseista v 1832–1838 godakh," *Russkaia starina,* LX (Oct. 1888), 101–24.

Jelavich, Barbara, and Jelavich, Charles, eds., *The Education of a Russian Statesman: The Memoirs of Nicholas Karlovich Giers.* Berkeley, 1962.

Kavelin, K. D. "Zapiska o bezporiadkakh v Sanktpeterburgskom universitete, osen'iu 1861 goda," in *Sobranie sochinenii.* Vol. II. St. Petersburg, 1900.

———. "Zapiska o nigilizme," *Istoricheskii arkhiv,* V (1950), 323–41.

Kelsiev, V. I. *Ispoved'.* Moscow, 1941.

Khronika sotsialisticheskogo dvizheniia v Rossii, 1878–87; Ofitsial'nyi otchet. Moscow, 1907.

Khudiakov, I. A. *Zapiski karakozovtsa.* Moscow, 1930.

Klements, D. A. *Iz proshlogo: Vospominaniia.* Leningrad, 1925.

Komarova, A. A. *Odna iz mnogikh: Iz zapisok nigilistki.* St. Petersburg, 1881.

Kornilova-Moroz, A. I. *Perovskaia i kruzhok chaikovtsev.* Moscow, 1929.

Korolenko, V. G. *Istoriia moego sovremennika.* Moscow, 1948.

Kostenetski, Ia. I. "Vospominaniia o moei studencheskoi zhizni," *Russkii arkhiv,* XXV (1887), 99–117, 229–42, 321–49, 383–88.

Kostomarov, N. I. *Avtobiografiia.* Moscow, 1922.

Kropotkin, P. A. *Zapiski revoliutsionnera.* Moscow, 1966.

Kuliabko-Koretski, N. G. *Iz davnykh let: Vospominaniia lavrista.* Moscow, 1931.

Kuzmin, P. A. "Zapiski general-leitenanta," *Russkaia starina,* LXXXIII (1895), 154–73.

Kviatkovski, A. A. "Avtobiograficheskoe zaiavlenie," *Krasnyi arkhiv,* No. 14 (1926), 159–75.

Lamanski, E. I. "Vospominaniia," *Russkaia starina,* CLXI (1915), 73–87, 367–75, 576–89.

Lavrov, P. L. *Izbrannye sochineniia po sotsial'no-politicheskie temy.* Vol. I: 1857–1871. Moscow, 1934.

"Mezhdu strokami odnogo formuliarnogo spiska," *Russkaia starina,* XXXII (Dec. 1881), 817–80.

Mikhailov, A. D. "Avtobiograficheskie zametki," *Byloe,* Feb. 1906, pp. 158–67.

Mikhailov, M. I. *Zapiski (1861–62).* Petrograd, 1922.

Ministerstvo vnutrennykh del, Tsentral'nyi statisticheskii komitet. *Istoriko-statisticheskii ocherk obshchego i spetsial'nogo obrazovaniia v Rossii.* St. Petersburg, 1883.

———. *Sanktpeterburg po perepisi 15 Dekabria 1881 goda.* 2 vols. St. Petersburg, 1883.

———. *Sanktpeterburg po perepisi 10 Dekabria 1869 goda.* 3 vols. St. Petersburg, 1872.

———. *Universitety i srednye uchebnye zavedeniia 50-ti gubernii Evropeiskoi Rossii po perepisi 20-ogo Marta 1880 goda.* St. Petersburg, 1888.

Modzalevski, B. A. "Iz istorii peterburgskogo universiteta 1857–1859 godov (Iz bumag L. N. Modzalevskogo)," *Golos minuvshego,* Jan. 1917, pp. 135–70.

Modzalevski, L. N. "Iz pedagogicheskoi avtobiografii," *Russkaia shkola,* March 1897, pp. 15–29.

[Morozov, N. A.] "Ocherk istorii kruzhka chaikovtsev," in *Revoliutsionnoe narodnichestvo.* Vol. I, pp. 202–40. Moscow, 1964.

"N. A. Speshnev o samom sebe," *Katorga i ssylka,* No. 62 (1930), 93–97.

Nikitenko, A. V. *Dnevnik.* 3 vols. Moscow, 1955.

Nikoladze, N. "Vospominaniia o 60-kh godakh," *Katorga i ssylka,* No. 33 (1927), 29–52; No. 34 (1927), 28–46.

Oksman, Iu. G., ed. *N. G. Chernyshevskii v vospominaniiakh sovremennikov.* Saratov, 1958.

Ostrogorski, V. P. *Iz istorii moego uchitel'stva.* St. Petersburg, 1914.

Palen, K. *Uspekhi revoliutsionnoi propagandy v Rossii (Zapiska Ministra Iustitsii).* Geneva, 1899.

Pal'm, A. I. *Aleksei Slobodin: Semeinaia istoriia.* Leningrad, 1931.

Panteleev, L. F. *Vospominaniia.* Moscow, 1958.

Perovski, V. *Vospominaniia o sestre.* Leningrad, 1928.

Pisarev, D. I. *Izbrannye pedagogicheskie sochineniia.* Moscow, 1951.

———. *Izbrannye sochineniia.* 2 vols. Moscow, 1934–1935.

Plekhanov, G. V. *Russkii rabochii v revoliutsionnom dvizhenii (po lichnym vospominaniiam).* Moscow, 1922.

Pokushenie Karakozova: stenograficheskii otchet po delu D. Karakozova i drugikh. Moscow, 1928.

Pomialovski, N. G. *Ocherki bursy.* Moscow, 1914.

Popov, I. I. *Minuvshee i perezhitoe: Vospominaniia za 50 let.* Moscow, 1933.

Pravitel'stvuiushchii Senat. Departament Geral'dii. *Adres-Kalendar.* An official yearly publication giving the name, rank, and position of Russian bureaucrats, brought out with a variety of subtitles, including: *Obshchii shtat rossiiskoi imperii; Obshchaia rospis' vsekh chinovnykh osob v gosudarstve; Obshchaia rospis' nachal'stvuiushchikh i prochikh dolzhnostnykh lits po vsem upravleniiam v imperii.*

"Programma dlia kruzhkov samoobrazovaniia i prakticheskoi deiatel'-nosti," *Katorga i ssylka,* No. 67 (1930), 89–106.

Protokoly zasedanii soveta Sanktpeterburgskogo universiteta. Published yearly in St. Petersburg and including between 1870 and 1883 the yearly report on the university's activities.

Protsess 50-ti. Moscow, 1906.

Protsess 193-kh. Moscow, 1906.

Pypin, A. N. *Moi zametki.* Moscow, 1910.

Ralli-Arbore, Z. "Iz moikh vospominanii," *Byloe,* July 1906, pp. 136–46.

"Revoliutsionnoe i studencheskoe dvizhenie 1869 goda v otsenke tret'ego otdeleniia," *Katorga i ssylka,* No. 10 (1924), 106–21.

Revoliutsionnoe narodnichestvo 70-kh godov XIX veka: sbornik dokumentov i materialov. 2 vols. Moscow, 1964–1965.

Rozanov, V. "Iz studencheskikh vospominanii," *Katorga i ssylka,* No. 51 (1929), 75–83.

Saltykov, M. E. *Polnoe sobranie sochinenii.* 20 vols. Moscow, 1933–1941.

Semenov-Tian'-Shanski, P. P. *Memuary.* Vol. I: *Detstvo i iunost'.* Petrograd, 1917.

Shchegolev, P. E., ed. *Petrashevtsy: Sbornik materialov.* 3 vols. Leningrad, 1926–1928.

Shelgunov, N. V. *Vospominaniia.* Moscow, 1923.

Shemanovski, M. I. "Vospominaniia o zhizni v Glavnom Pedagogicheskom Institute 1853–1857 godov," *Literaturnoe nasledstvo,* XXV–XXVI (1936), 271–99.

Shestakov, P. D. "Studencheskie volneniia v Moskve v 1861 goda: Vospominaniia," *Russkaia starina,* LX (1888), 203–23.

Shishko, L. *Sergei Mikhailovich Kravchinskii i kruzhok chaikovtsev (iz vospominanii i zametok starogo narodnika).* St. Petersburg, 1906.

Sidorov, N. I. "Statisticheskie svedeniia o propagandistakh 70-kh godov v obrabotke III otdeleniia (zapiska M. M. Merkulova o propagandistakh)," *Katorga i ssylka,* No. 38 (1928), 27–56.

Sinegub, S. S. *Zapiski chaikovtsa.* Moscow, 1929.

Skabichevski, A. *Literaturnye vospominaniia.* Moscow, 1928.

Smirnov, I. "G. V. Plekhanov v Voronezhskoi gimnazii," *Katorga i ssylka,* No. 61 (1929), 140–44.

Sokolov, P. P. *Vospominaniia.* Moscow, 1930.

Sorokin, V. "Vospominaniia starogo studenta," *Russkaia starina,* LX (1888), 617–47; CXXVIII (1906), 443–72.

Stasov, V. *Nadezhda Vasil'evna Stasova: Vospominaniia i ocherki.* St. Petersburg, 1899.

Statisticheskie materialy dlia opredeleniia obshchestvennogo polozheniia lits, poluchivshikh obrazovanie v Imperatorskom Derptskom Universitete (1802–52). St. Petersburg, 1862.

Tikhomirov, L. N. *Nachala i kontsy: "Liberaly" i terroristy.* Moscow, 1890.

———. *Vospominaniia.* Moscow, 1927.

Timofeev, M. A. "Perezhitoe: Otryvok iz vospominanii o 70-kh godakh," *Katorga i ssylka,* No. 56 (1929), 94–117.

Tkachev, P. N. *Izbrannye sochineniia no sotsial'no-politicheskie temy.* 4 vols. Moscow, 1932–1933.

Turgenev, Ivan. *Fathers and Sons.* Trans. Rosemary Edmonds. Baltimore, 1965.

"Universitet i korporatsiia: Otryvok iz vospominanii," *Istoricheskii vestnik,* April 1880, pp. 779–804.

Uspenskaia, A. "Vospominaniia shestidesiatnitsa," *Byloe,* No. 18 (1922), 19–45.

Ustrialov, F. N. "Universitetskie vospominaniia," *Istoricheskii vestnik,* June 1884, pp. 578–604.

Vasil'ev, N. V. "V 70-y gody: Iz moikh vospominanii," *Mir Bozhii,* June 1906, pp. 215–48.

Vereshchagin, A. *Doma i na voine: Vospominaniia i rasskazy (1853–81).* St. Petersburg, 1886.

Veselovski, K. S. "Vospominaniia o Tsarskosel'skom litsee, 1832–38," *Russkaia starina,* CIII (1900), 449–56; CIV (1900), 3–29.

Vodovozova, E. N. *Na zare zhizni i drugikh vospominaniia.* 2 vols. Moscow, 1934.

Vrutsevich, M. "Dukhovnoe uchilishche starykh vremen," *Russkaia starina,* CXXI (March 1905), 693–704.

Zasulich, V. I. *Vospominaniia.* Moscow, 1931.

III. Secondary Literature

Abramov, Ia. V. *Nashi voskresnye shkoly: Ikh proshloe i nastoiashchoe.* St. Petersburg, 1900.

Aleshintsev, I. *Istoriia gimnazicheskogo obrazovaniia v Rossii (XVIII i XIX vek).* St. Petersburg, 1912.

——. "Soslovyi vopros i politika," *Russkaia shkola*, Jan. 1908, pp. 5–50.

Alston, Patrick. *Education and the State in Tsarist Russia*. Stanford, 1969.

Anderson, Robert. "Secondary Education in Mid-Nineteenth Century France: Some Social Aspects," *Past and Present*, No. 53 (Nov. 1971), 121–46.

Antonov, V. I. *Myshkin*. Moscow, 1959.

——. "K voprosu o sotsial'nom sostave i chislennosti revoliutsionerov 70-kh godov," in *Obshchestvennoe dvizhenie v poreformennoi Rossii*. Moscow, 1965.

Bazileva, Z. P. "K istorii pervykh artelei raznochintsev," in *Voprosy istorii sel'skogo khoziaistva, krest'ianstva i revoliutsionnogo dvizheniia v Rossii*. Moscow, 1961.

Bazilevski, V., ed. *Gosudarstvennye prestupniki v Rossii v XIX veke*. 3 vols. Paris, 1903–1905.

Becker, Christopher. "Raznochintsy: The Development of the Word and of the Concept," *American Slavic and East European Review*, XVIII (Feb. 1959), 63–74.

Berman, Ia. "Vliianie sotsial'no-pravovogo i ekonomicheskogo faktorov na gosudarstvennuiu prestupnost'," *Pravo*, No. 33 (Aug. 18, 1913), 1912–24.

Billington, James. *Mikhailovsky and Russian Populism*. London, 1958.

Bogdanovich, T. A. *Liubov' liudei shestidesiatykh godov*. Leningrad, 1929.

Chukovski, K. I. "Istoriia sleptsovskoi kommuny," in *Liudi i knigi (sbornik)*. Moscow, 1958.

Coquart, Armand. *Dimitri Pisarev et l'idéologie du nihilisme russe*. Paris, 1946.

——. "Le nihiliste Pisarev," *Revue des études slaves*, XXII (1946), 128–61.

Deiateli revoliutsionnogo dvizheniia v Rossii: Bio-bibliograficheskii slovar'. Vols. I, II, III, V. Moscow, 1927–1934.

Deich [Deutsch], L. G. *Dmitrii Aleksandrovich Klements*. Petrograd, 1921.

——. *S. M. Kravchinskii*. Petrograd, 1919.

——. "Vera Ivanovna Zasulich," *Golos minuvshego*, Nos. 5–12 (1919), 199–210.

Dement'ev, A. *Ocherki po istorii russkoi zhurnalistiki 1840–1850 godov*. Moscow, 1951.

Dobrovol'ski, L. M. *Zapreshchennaia kniga v Rossii, 1825–1904*. Moscow, 1962.

Egorov, Iu. N. "Russkie universitety i studencheskoe dvizhenie vo vtoroi polovine 1830 do 1850 godov." Candidate's dissertation. Leningrad State University, 1958.

Eidel'man, N. "Pavel Aleksandrovich Bakhmetov," in *Voprosy istorii sel'-skogo khoziaistva, krest'ianstva i revoliutsionnogo dvizheniia v Rossii.* Moscow, 1961.

Eisenstadt, Schmuel. *From Generation to Generation: Age Groups and Social Structure.* Glencoe, Illinois, 1956.

Evgen'ev-Maksimov, V. *Sovremennik v 40-50 godakh ot Belinskogo do Chernyshevskogo.* Leningrad, 1934.

———. *Zhizn' i deiatel'nost' N. A. Nekrasova.* Vol. I. Moscow, 1947.

Fedosov, I. A. *Revoliutsionnoe dvizhenie v Rossii vo vtoroi chetverti XIX veka.* Moscow, 1958.

Feuer, Lewis. *The Conflict of Generations: The Character and Significance of Student Movements.* New York, 1969.

Flynn, James. "The Universities, the Gentry, and the Russian Imperial Services, 1815–1825," *Canadian Slavic Studies,* II (Winter 1968), 486–503.

Ganelin, Sh. I. *Ocherki po istorii srednei shkoly v Rossii.* Moscow, 1954.

Georgievski, A. I. *Kratkii ocherk pravitel'stvennykh mer i prednachertanii protiv studencheskikh bezporiadkov.* (Also listed under title *Materialy po universitetskomu voprosu.*) Stuttgart, 1902.

Gershenzon, M. O. *Istoriia molodoi Rossii.* St. Petersburg, 1908.

Grigor'ev, V. V. *Imperatorskii Sanktpeterburgskii Universitet v techenie pervykh 50 let ego sushchestvovaniia.* St. Petersburg, 1870.

Grossman, L. *Dostoevski.* Moscow, 1965.

Gutman, D. S. "Studencheskoe dvizhenie v Kazanskom universitete 1859–61." Candidate's dissertation. Kazan State University, 1955.

Hegarty, Thomas. "Student Movements in Russian Universities 1855–61." Ph.D. dissertation. Harvard University, 1965.

Istoriia imperatorskoi voenno-meditsinskoi (byvshei mediko-khirurgicheskoi) akademii za sto let (1798–1898). St. Petersburg, 1898.

Istoriia Moskovskogo Universiteta. Vol. I. Moscow, 1955.

Istoriia Rossii v XIX veke. 9 vols. St. Petersburg, 1909.

Itenberg, B. S. *Dmitrii Rogachev, revoliutsioner-narodnik.* Moscow, 1960.

———. *Dvizhenie revoliutsionnogo narodnichestva.* Moscow, 1965.

Ivanov-Razumnik, R. V. *Istoriia russkoi obshchestvennoi mysli: Individualizm i meshchanstvo.* 2 vols. St. Petersburg, 1908.

Johnson, William. *Russia's Educational Heritage.* New York, 1969.

Kamosko, L. V. "Izmeneniia soslovnogo sostava uchashchikhsia srednei i vysshei shkoly Rossii (30-80-e gody XIX veka)," *Voprosy istorii,* Oct. 1970, pp. 203–7.

Kazanovich, E. D. *I. Pisarev (1840–56).* Petrograd, 1922.

Kimball, Alan. "The Russian Past and the Socialist Future in the Thought of Peter Lavrov," *Slavic Review,* XXX (March 1971), 28–44.

Klevenski, M. M. *I. A. Khudiakov, revoliutsioner i uchenyi.* Moscow, 1929.

Kobeko, D. F. *Imperatorskii Tsarskosel'skii Litsei: Nastavniki i pitomtsy, 1811–43.* St. Petersburg, 1911.

Komarovich, V. L. "Iunost' Dostoevskogo," *Byloe,* XXIII (1924), 3–43.

Koz'min, B. P. *Nechaev i nechaevtsy: Sbornik materialov.* Moscow, 1931.

———. *P. N. Tkachev i revoliutsionnoe dvizhenie.* Moscow, 1922.

——— and Gor'ev, B. I., eds. *Revoliutsionnoe dvizhenie 1860-kh godov.* Moscow, 1932.

Kunkl', A. *Kruzhok dolgushintsev.* Moscow, 1927.

Lampert, Evgenii. *Sons against Fathers: Studies in Russian Radicalism and Revolution.* London, 1965.

Leikina-Svirskaia, V. R. "Formirovanie raznochinskoi intelligentsii v Rossii v 40-kh godakh XIX veka," *Istoriia SSSR,* Jan.-Feb. 1958, pp. 83–104.

———. *Intelligentsiia v Rossii vo vtoroi polovine XIX veka.* Moscow, 1971.

———. "N. A. Mombelli," *Byloe,* No. 26 (1924), 61–70.

———. "N. A. Speshnev," *Byloe,* No. 25 (1924), 12–31.

———. "O kharaktere kruzhkov petrashevtsev," *Voprosy istorii,* April 1956, pp. 96–106.

———. *Petrashevtsy.* Moscow, 1924.

Lemke, M. *Ocherki osvoboditel'nogo dvizheniia shestigesiatikh godov.* St. Petersburg, 1908.

Levin, Sh. M. *D. A. Klements: Ocherki revoliutsionnoi deiatel'nosti.* Moscow, 1929.

———. *Obshchestvennoe dvizhenie v Rossii v 60–70 gody XIX veka.* Moscow, 1958.

Likhacheva, E. *Materialy dlia istorii zhenskogo obrazovaniia v Rossii, 1856–1880.* St. Petersburg, 1901.

Makashin, S. *Saltykov-Shchedrin: Biografiia.* 2 vols. Moscow, 1949–1951.

Malia, Martin. *Alexander Herzen and the Birth of Russian Socialism.* New York, 1961.

Mathes, William. "The Origins of Confrontation Politics in Russian Universities: Student Activism, 1855–1861," *Canadian Slavic Studies,* II (Spring 1968), 28–45.

Meijer, J. M. *Knowledge and Revolution: The Russian Colony in Zurich.* Assen, 1955.

Mel'gunov, S. *Iz istorii studencheskikh obshchestv v russkikh universitetakh.* Moscow, 1904.

Miller, Martin A. "The Formative Years of P. A. Kropotkin, 1842–1876: A Study of the Origins and Development of Populist Attitudes in Russia." Ph.D. dissertation. University of Chicago, 1967.

Moser, Charles A. *Antinihilism in the Russian Novel of the 1860's.* The Hague, 1964.

Nahirny, Vladimir C. "The Russian Intelligentsia: From Men of Ideas to Men of Convictions," *Comparative Studies in Society and History,* IV (July 1962), 403–35.

Nasonkina, L. "Moskovskii universitet i ego studenty v obshchestvennom dvizhenii Rossii 1821–31 godov." Candidate's dissertation. Moscow State University, 1958. Published as *Moskovskii universitet posle vosstaniia dekabristov.* Moscow, 1972.

Nifontov, A. S. "Formirovanie burzhuaznogo obshchestva v russkom gorode vtoroi poloviny XIX veka," *Istoricheskie zapiski,* LIV (1955), 239–50.

Novikova, N. N. *Revoliutsionery 1861 goda ("Velikoruss" i ego komitet).* Moscow, 1968.

O'Boyle, Lenore. "The Problem of an Excess of Educated Men in Western Europe, 1800–1850," *Journal of Modern History,* XLII (Dec. 1970), 471–95.

Okun', S. B. *Ocherki istorii SSSR: Vtoraia chetvert' XIX veka.* Leningrad, 1957.

Orlov, V. I. *Studencheskoe dvizhenie Moskovskogo universiteta XIX stoletii.* Moscow, 1934.

Ovsianiko-Kulikovskii, D. N. *Istoriia russkoi intelligentsii.* 2 vols. St. Petersburg, 1911.

Pollard, Alan. "Consciousness and Crisis: The Self-Image of the Russian Intelligentsia, 1855–1882." Ph.D. dissertation. University of California, Berkeley, 1968.

Pomper, Philip. *Peter Lavrov and the Russian Revolutionary Movement.* Chicago, 1972.

Pozner, S. V. *Evrei v obshchei shkole.* St. Petersburg, 1914.

Rashin, A. G. "Gramotnost' i narodnoe obrazovanie v Rossii v XIX i nachale XX vekakh," *Istoricheskie zapiski,* XXXVII (1951), 28–80.

Revoliutsionnaia situatsiia v Rossii v 1859–61 godakh. 5 vols. Moscow, 1960–1970.

Riasanovsky, Nicholas. *Nicholas I and Official Nationality in Russia, 1825–55.* Los Angeles, 1959.

Rieff, Philip, ed. *On Intellectuals.* New York, 1969.

Ringer, Fritz. *The Decline of the German Mandarins: The German Academic Community, 1890–1933.* Cambridge, Mass., 1969.

Rogers, James. "Darwinism, Scientism, and Nihilism," *Russian Review,* XIX (Jan. 1960), 10–23.

Rozhdestvenski, S. V. *Istoricheskii obzor deiatel'nosti Ministerstva Narodnogo Prosveshcheniia, 1802–1902.* St. Petersburg, 1902.

———. "Soslovnyi vopros v russkikh universitetakh v pervoi chetverti XIX veka," *Zhurnal Ministerstva Narodnogo Prosveshcheniia,* May 1907, pp. 83–108.

Sarukhanian, E. P. *Dostoevskii v Peterburge.* Leningrad, 1970.

Semevski, V. I. M. V. *Butashevich-Petrashevskii i petrashevtsy.* Moscow, 1922.

———. "Petrashevtsy A. P. Beklemyshev i K. I. Timkovskii," *Vestnik Evropy,* Nov. 1916, pp. 57–103.

———. "Petrashevtsy Durov, Pal'm, Dostoevskii i Pleshcheev," *Golos minuvshego,* Nov. 1915, pp. 5–43; Dec. 1915, pp. 35–76.

———. "Petrashevtsy: Kruzhok N. S. Kashkin," *Golos minuvshego,* Feb. 1916, pp. 41–61; March 1916, pp. 48–68; April 1916, pp. 174–92.

———. "Petrashevtsy: Studenty Tolstov i T. P. Danilevskii," *Golos minuvshego,* Nov. 1916, pp. 5–28; Dec. 1916, pp. 98–118.

———. "Propaganda petrashevtsev v uchebnykh zavedeniiakh," *Golos minuvshego,* Feb. 1917, pp. 138–69.

Shetinina, G. I. "Intelligentsiia, revoliutsiia i samoderzhaviia," *Istoriia SSSR,* Nov.–Dec. 1970, pp. 154–72.

Shilov, A. A., ed. *German Aleksandrovich Lopatin (1845–1918).* Petrograd, 1922.

Sinel, Allen. *The Classroom and the Chancellery: State Educational Reform in Russia under Count Dmitry Tolstoi.* Cambridge, Mass., 1973.

Snytko, T. "Studencheskoe dvizhenie v russkikh universitetakh v nachale 1860-kh godov i vosstanie 1863 goda," in V. D. Koroliuk and I. S. Miller, eds., *Vosstanie 1863 goda i russko-pol'skie revoliutsionnye sviazi.* Moscow, 1960.

Steklov, Iu. M. *N. G. Chernyshevskii: Ego zhizn' i deiatel'nost'.* 2 vols. Moscow, 1928.

Strelsky, Nikander. *Saltykov and the Russian Squire.* New York, 1940.

Svatikov, S. G. "Studencheskoe dvizhenie 1869 goda (Bakunin i Nechaev)," *Nasha strana,* Jan. 1907, pp. 165–249.

Taubin, R. A. "Obshchestvennoe dvizhenie v Rossii v 50-e gody XIX veka." Doctoral dissertation. Institute of History, Academy of Sciences of the USSR, 1965.

———. "Revoliutsioner-demokrat S. S. Rymarenko," *Istoriia SSSR,* Jan.–Feb. 1959, pp. 136–54.

———. "Revoliutsionnaia propaganda v voskresnykh shkolakh Rossii v 1860–1862 godakh," *Voprosy istorii,* Aug. 1956, pp. 80–90.

Tekhnologicheskii Institut: Sto let, 1828–1928. Leningrad, 1928.

Titlinov, B. V. *Mologezh' i revoliutsiia: Iz istorii revoliutsionnogo dvizheniia sredi uchashcheisia molodezha dukhovnykh i srednykh uchebnykh zavedenii, 1860–1905.* Leningrad, 1925.

Titov, A. A., ed. *Nikolai Vasil'evich Chaikovskii: Religioznye i obshchest-vennye iskaniia.* Paris, 1929.

Tkachenko, P. S. *Moskovskoe studenchestvo v obshchestvenno-politi-cheskoi zhizni Rossii vtoroi poloviny XIX veka.* Moscow, 1958.

Torke, Hans-Joachim. *Das russische Beamtentum in der ersten Hälfte des 19 Jahrhunderts (Forschungen zur Osteuropäischen Geschichte,* Vol. XIII). Berlin, 1967.

Venturi, Franco. *Roots of Revolution: A History of the Populist and Socialist Movements in Nineteenth-Century Russia.* Trans. Francis Haskell. New York, 1960.

Vilenskaia, E. S. *M. Khudiakov.* Moscow, 1969.

——. *Revoliutsionnoe podpol'e v Rossii v seredine 60-kh godov XIX veka.* Moscow, 1965.

Walicki, A. *The Controversy over Capitalism.* Oxford, 1969.

Zelnik, Reginald. "The Sunday-School Movement," *Journal of Modern History,* XXVII (June 1965), 151–70.

Index

Training the Nihilists

Designed by R. E. Rosenbaum.
Composed by Joe Mann Associates,
in 10 point linotype Times Roman, 2 points leaded,
with display lines in monotype Deepdene.
Printed letterpress from type
on Warren's No. 66 Text, 50 lb. basis
with the Cornell University Press watermark.